Virg

Virginia Woolf

Ambivalent Activist

Clara Jones

EDINBURGH
University Press

Edinburgh University Press is one of the leading university presses in the UK. We publish academic books and journals in our selected subject areas across the humanities and social sciences, combining cutting-edge scholarship with high editorial and production values to produce academic works of lasting importance. For more information visit our website: www.edinburghuniversitypress.com

© Clara Jones, 2016, 2017

Edinburgh University Press Ltd
The Tun – Holyrood Road
12 (2f) Jackson's Entry
Edinburgh EH8 8PJ
www.euppublishing.com

First published in hardback by Edinburgh University Press 2016

Typeset in 11/13 Adobe Sabon by
IDSUK (DataConnection) Ltd
Printed and bound in Great Britain by
CPI Group (UK) Ltd, Croydon CR0 4YY

A CIP record for this book is available from the British Library

ISBN 978 1 4744 0192 0 (hardback)
ISBN 978 1 4744 2316 8 (paperback)
ISBN 978 1 4744 0193 7 (webready PDF)
ISBN 978 1 4744 1029 8 (epub)

The right of Clara Jones to be identified as the author of this work has been asserted in accordance with the Copyright, Designs and Patents Act 1988, and the Copyright and Related Rights Regulations 2003 (SI No. 2498).

Contents

Acknowledgements	vi
Abbreviations	viii
Introduction	1
1 Virginia Stephen and Morley College, 1905–7	17
2 Virginia Stephen and the People's Suffrage Federation, 1910	65
3 Virginia Woolf and the Women's Co-operative Guild, 1913–31	108
4 Virginia Woolf and the Rodmell Women's Institute, 1940–1	154
Conclusion	207
Appendix 1 The 'Morley Sketch'	210
Appendix 2 The 'Cook Sketch'	216
Bibliography	222
Index	238

Acknowledgements

First I must thank Michèle Barrett who supervised the doctoral research on which this book is based with patience and generosity. My thinking in this book owes much to Michèle's work on Virginia Woolf's political agency and I am more grateful than I can say for all her wit, wisdom and encouragement. I also owe special thanks to Suzanne Hobson for her advice throughout the development of this project and her incisive feedback on a number of drafts. Anna Snaith's and Brenda Silver's constructive criticism and advice has been invaluable and I am extremely grateful for their continued support. It has been a pleasure to work with Jackie Jones, Dhara Patel and Adela Rauchova at Edinburgh University Press and I am grateful to EUP's readers for their thoughtful responses to my book proposal and manuscript.

I visited a number of literary and institutional archives during the course of my research for this book and I would like to thank the archivists and librarians at the following libraries and collections for their help: the Hull History Centre, the British Library Manuscripts Department, the East Sussex County Records Office, King's College London Archives, the Lambeth Archives at the Minet Library, the London School of Economics Archive Collection, the Morley College Library, the Trades Union Congress Library, the Women's Library and the J. P. Morgan Library. I am especially grateful to Rose Lock at the University of Sussex Library Special Collections for her unfailing helpfulness on my frequent visits.

I am grateful to the Society of Authors as the Literary Representative of the Estate of Virginia Woolf for their permission to quote from unpublished material by Virginia Woolf and to include my transcriptions of the 'Morley Sketch' and the 'Cook Sketch' as appendices to this book. Thanks to Caitlin Adams for allowing me to quote from her fascinating unpublished work on inter-war village drama. I am also grateful to Laura Ponsonby for her kind permission to quote from her grandmother, Dorothea Ponsonby's, diary, and to Jane Wynne Willson for allowing me to quote from her great-aunt, Margaret Llewelyn Davies's, letters. Thanks to Sybil Oldfield for generously sharing her knowledge about the lives of Llewelyn Davies and Mary Sheepshanks and for our enjoyable conversations about these women in the early days of this project.

Funding from the Arts and Humanities Research Council allowed me to undertake the doctoral research upon which this book is based. Queen Mary University of London funded my research trip to the Morgan Library during the course of my PhD and I am indebted to the English Department at Queen Mary for their generous financial support, which made possible the inclusion of the Morgan facsimile in this book.

My family and friends have supplied support and delightful distractions during the writing of this book. I am especially grateful to Amanda Eve, Joanna Przygoda, Emrys Jones, Julia Hine, Andy Hine and my wonderful mother Victoria Hine Jones. Loving thanks to my grandmother, Sesyle Joslin, for her sustaining and unfailing enthusiasm for this project. To Ciaran Bermingham I owe boundless thanks. Our conversations about the relationship between literature and politics over the last ten years have been invigorating and illuminating – thank you for these.

Abbreviations

All references to the following texts by Virginia Woolf in this book are to these editions unless otherwise stated and are given after quotations in the text.

AROO	*A Room of One's Own and Three Guineas*, with introduction and notes by Michèle Barrett (London: Penguin, 2000)
BTA	*Between the Acts*, with introduction and notes by Gillian Beer (London: Penguin, 2000)
CSF	*The Complete Shorter Fiction of Virginia Woolf*, ed. Susan Dick (San Diego: Harcourt, 1989)
D 1–5	*The Diaries of Virginia Woolf*, 5 vols, ed. Anne Olivier Bell with Andrew McNeillie (Harmondsworth: Penguin, 1979–85)
E 1–6	*The Essays of Virginia Woolf*, 6 vols, ed. Andrew McNeillie and Stuart N. Clarke (London: Hogarth Press, 1986–2012)
L 1-6	*The Letters of Virginia Woolf*, 6 vols, ed. Nigel Nicolson and Joanne Trautmann Banks (London: Hogarth Press, 1975–80)
IL	'Introductory Letter', in Margaret Llewelyn Davies (ed.), *Life As We Have Known It* (London: Virago, 1977)
M	*Melymbrosia*, ed. Louise DeSalvo (San Francisco: Cleis Press, 1982)
MB	*Moments of Being*, ed. Jeanne Schulkind (New York: Harcourt Brace Jovanovich, 2002)
ND	*Night and Day*, with introduction and notes by Julia Briggs (London: Penguin, 1992)

OBI	*On Being Ill,* introduced by Hermione Lee (Ashfield, MA: Paris Press, 2002)
P	*The Pargiters: The Novel-Essay Portion of The Years*, ed. Mitchell A. Leaska (London: Hogarth Press, 1978)
PA	*A Passionate Apprentice: The Early Journals,* 1897–1909, ed. Mitchell A. Leaska and introduced by David Bradshaw (London: Pimlico, 2004)
TG	*A Room of One's Own and Three Guineas*, with introduction and notes by Michèle Barrett (London: Penguin, 2000)
TTL	*To the Lighthouse*, with introduction and notes by Hermione Lee (London: Penguin, 2000)
TY	*The Years*, with introduction and notes by Jeri Johnson (London: Penguin, 2002)
VO	*The Voyage Out*, with introduction and notes by Jane Wheare (London: Penguin, 1992)

Introduction

> Would it be any use if I spent an afternoon or two weekly in addressing envelopes for the Adult Suffragists?
> I dont know anything about the question. Perhaps you could send me a pamphlet, or give me the address of the office. I could neither do sums or argue, or speak, but I could do the humbler work if that is any good. You impressed me so much the other night with the wrongness of the present state of affairs that I feel that action is necessary. Your position seemed to me intolerable. The only way to better it is to do some thing I suppose. How melancholy it is that conversation isn't enough! (*L1* 421)

As this 1910 letter shows, Virginia Stephen understood that certain circumstances demanded action. This letter to Janet Case, offering help to the beleaguered adult suffrage cause, clarifies Virginia Stephen's familiarity with the mechanics of activism and shows that she understood the need for political action, not just that of others but specifically her own. This book is about Virginia Stephen's, and later Woolf's, political and social involvement and the nature of her attitudes towards this action. That this letter was written on 1 January 1910 makes Virginia Stephen's commitment to act – her modest desire to 'do the humbler work' – all the more compelling, as if it were part of a carefully considered new year's resolution.

Over the last thirty years a number of Woolf scholars have emphasised Woolf's politics by tracing the political engagements of her fiction and non-fiction texts. Berenice Carroll's 1978 essay on Woolf's political thought argued that her writing demonstrates a 'consistent and intense concern with the political foundations of the social order'.[1] In 1986, Alex Zwerdling challenged prevailing, aestheticist approaches to Woolf's work by taking the social vision of her writing as his point of departure.[2] Hermione Lee's 1996 biography of Woolf placed new emphasis on Woolf's social and political awareness.[3]

Woolf scholars continue to investigate the politics of Virginia Woolf's writing. Jane Goldman has explored Woolf's feminist aesthetics,[4] while Melba Cuddy-Keane focuses on the pedagogic 'social project' and democratic aspirations of Woolf's essays.[5] Anna Snaith provides contextualised accounts of Woolf's writing in her book on Woolf's 'engagement with concepts of public and private' and in essays on Virginia Stephen's period of study at King's College London, with Christine Kenyon-Jones, and the letters written to Woolf in response to *Three Guineas*.[6] In her recent study, Alice Wood explores the development of Woolf's 'late feminist-pacifist politics'.[7]

Thanks to the sustained work of these scholars and others, to posit a politically and socially engaged version of Virginia Woolf in 2015 is nothing new, in fact, it has arguably become something of a scholarly commonplace. The preoccupation with the political engagements of Woolf's writing we find in much Woolf scholarship, however, is rarely accompanied by a sustained focus on Woolf's personal involvement in political and social organisations.[8]

Scholars, especially those who see *Three Guineas* as the ultimate expression of Woolf's political principles, have accepted Virginia Woolf's account of herself as an outsider to conventional forms of political and social activism. Carroll states that Woolf felt 'an intense revulsion against the world of "politics as usual"' and believed all political parties to be equally implicated in a 'system that crushed people's lives'.[9] Pamela Transue has a similar take on Woolf's practical politics: 'Woolf was persistently sceptical of organized political movements in any form'.[10] For these scholars Woolf's perceived antipathy towards organised and party politics is what renders her feminist politics all the more radical.

This tacit acceptance of Woolf as an 'outsider' to organised politics and social organisations often leads to the suggestion that in the absence of a political practice rooted in participation or activism, Virginia Woolf's writing practice stood in for this. This book queries the image of Woolf as consummate non-juror, someone at constant odds with organised politics, and rescues the particularities of Woolf's political and social activism, re-asserting the distinction between her textual and practical politics. Chapter 1 focuses on Virginia Stephen's period of teaching at Morley College between 1905 and 1907, while Chapter 2 revisits Virginia Stephen's involvement in the suffrage campaign in 1910. Chapter 3 considers Woolf's life-long affiliation with the Women's Co-operative Guild and Chapter 4 focuses on Virginia Woolf's fractious relationship with the Rodmell Women's Institute from April 1940 until the end of her life in 1941. Collectively these chapters trace her career as an activist across forty-five years, establishing the details of her involvement with these four political movements and social organisations and re-reading her fiction and non-fiction in light of this. Drawing on research in the archives of these organisations, each of the following four chapters begins with an account of Virginia Woolf's involvement set within the context of the institutional moment in which she worked. This work builds on what Woolf scholarship has taught us about Woolf's political awareness in her writing. It constructs a Woolf who was not simply attuned to inequality and injustice in society or committed to ideas of democracy, but also a highly critical but nonetheless committed participant. Woolf was sensitive to the internal politics and conflicts of the bodies she was associated with and interrogated her ambivalent attitudes towards this activism in her writing.

Activism and ambivalence

Existing critical accounts have mobilised a range of discourses and motifs when addressing the question of Woolf's ambivalent activism. In the first published study of Woolf in 1932, Winifred Holtby, herself a committed feminist and Labour activist, wrangles with what she calls Woolf's 'indirect connection with the world of action'.[11] Holtby's 'world of action' is formulated in opposition to an aesthetic realm of beauty and she convincingly casts Woolf as often torn between them. The 'real world' of the title of Alex Zwerdling's study performs a not dissimilar function from Holtby's early model, standing as it does for 'the whole range of external forces that may be said to influence our behaviour: familial ideals, societal expectations, institutional demands, significant historical events or movements'.[12] More recently, Anna Snaith's focus on Woolf's engagement with ideas of public and private has facilitated a discussion of Woolf's participation in the public realm of political and social activism.

Given my emphasis on the details of Woolf's activity it has been necessary to establish a more immediate language for describing this work. Virginia Stephen's 1910 letter to Janet Case is instructive in this regard: she uses the word 'action' to identify herself with the adult suffrage body she is offering to help. The People's Suffrage Federation (PSF) refer throughout a March 1910 newsletter to the need to find 'openings for action in every direction', to establish 'agitations'.[13] The Women's Co-operative Guild (WCG), with whom Virginia Woolf had her most long-standing affiliation, make use of the same vocabulary in their internal literature, characterising their campaigning work as 'action'.[14] This use of action to refer to the kind of work undertaken by the PSF and the WCG, ranging from letter-writing to setting up a local bread shop to combat wartime food shortages, suggest that 'activism' is the best way to describe Woolf's work with these organisations. Just as her references to mundane office tasks in this letter reveal her understanding of administration, Virginia Stephen's use of the word action hints at an investment in a language of political and social involvement that would develop into our contemporary understanding of activism as the membership of and campaigning for (frequently grassroots) organisations.[15] Action continues to bear this political inflection wherever it appears in Woolf's fiction and non-fiction, revealing her sustained awareness of its necessity. Even when she appears to be making the case for non-participation, calling for women to 'maintain an attitude of complete indifference' in *Three Guineas*, it is clear that this is a political strategy still based on action: 'Such then will be the nature of her "indifference" and from this indifference certain actions must follow' (*TG* 234).

As Jessica Berman has noted,[16] Leonard Woolf provides an alternative account of Woolf's political activity stressing its activist character: 'she took part in the pedestrian operations of the Labour Party and Co-operative Movement. And by "pedestrian" I mean the grass roots of Labour politics'.[17] Leonard Woolf's emphasis on the 'pedestrian' and grassroots quality of Woolf's activities supports my characterisation of this work as activism, and also hits precisely on what makes this activism so compelling – its being so ordinary and yet so crucial.

While Woolf's work with the PSF and the WCG can be aptly described as activism, given their identities as campaigning bodies and their links with the Labour and Trade Union Movements, her voluntary teaching at Morley College between 1905 and 1907 and her later work with the WI need to be described a little differently. Neither of these organisations can be characterised as pressure groups and both explicitly stipulated their non-political character – although we will see that in practice neither organisation was free from either internal politics or political loyalties. Both Morley College and the Rodmell WI did, however, possess social programmes and interact significantly with public questions and, as such, I believe the most accurate way to describe Woolf's work with them is as social participation or involvement. This new language of activism and social participation supports this book's recuperative project and its desire to take seriously Woolf's involvement with these organisations. While wanting to challenge a view of this activity as a begrudged duty performed under duress – which goes something like 'She wasn't really interested and only did it as a favour to Mary Sheepshanks/ Janet Case/ Margaret Llewelyn Davies/ Leonard Woolf/ Diana Gardner ...' – I am equally wary of suggesting that Woolf's work with these various organisations was characterised by unproblematic commitment.

Despite the obvious practical and political distinctions between Woolf's work with these different organisations, she approached these activities with a similar reticence and remained ambivalent about the value of her political and social action throughout her career. Ambivalence, the other of this study's twinned key terms, is one that Woolf herself found both interesting and useful. In 1939, under the influence of Freud, Woolf writes of a busy two-day trip to London: 'I dislike this excitement. Yet enjoy it. Ambivalence as Freud calls it' (*D5* 249). Writing later in 1941 of her complicated feelings towards her father in which 'rage alternated with love', Woolf comments: 'It was only the other day when I read Freud for the first time, that I discovered that this violently disturbing conflict of love and hate is a common feeling; and is called ambivalence' (*MB* 116). This passage is significant in terms of Woolf's engagement with Freud, in particular her misleading suggestion that she was reading Freud in 1941 'for the first time'. But it also demonstrates in a more general way the kind of purchase this term held for her. Woolf's relief in finding such mixed feelings 'common' is palpable here, perhaps because she encountered them often, not just when remembering her father.

Such feelings characterise Woolf's personal records of her political and social participation. They are clear in a 1905 letter describing her work at Morley: 'It is so odd to plunge into philanthropic society, living on the other side of the river of a sudden' (*L1* 198). And again in her pleading letter of 1941: 'I spoke to the Women's Institute yesterday about the Dreadnought hoax. And it made them laugh. Dont you think this proves, beyond a doubt, that I have a heart?' (*L6* 407). Whether it is Virginia Stephen's anxiety that her teaching at Morley College is tainted by philanthropy or Virginia Woolf's cautious and self-critical delight at her reception from her local WI, ambivalence accompanies all of Virginia Woolf's activist enterprises.

The question of Woolf's ambivalence has been drawn out by a number of scholars. Gillian Beer's *Virginia Woolf: The Common Ground* describes Woolf's ambivalent engagement with ideas of community and communality in her writing.[18] Writing in a similar vein but regarding Woolf's activism, Michèle Barrett describes how in the late 1930s Woolf might condemn the 'idiotic societies' supporting anti-fascism one day and offer a rousing defence of the political credentials of Bloomsbury the next, so capturing what she describes as the 'contradictions of Woolf's own political activity and reflections on it' (*TG* xlviii). Hermione Lee's references to Woolf's political activity in her biography place a similar onus on Woolf's paradoxical attitude towards this engagement. Writing of Woolf's bitter response to the downfall of the Labour Government in 1924 – 'we are now condemned to a dose of lies every morning: the usual yearly schoolboys wrangle. If I were still a feminist, I should make capital out of the wrangle' – Lee notes '[t]his is a very political way of disowning politics'.[19] By arguing for the significance of her actual political and social engagements while also recognising the powerful and, crucially, political implications of Virginia Woolf's scepticism towards this activity, my book contributes to this discussion of Woolf's ambivalence.

I am not concerned with projecting onto Woolf's political activism and social involvement any hard-and-fast theory of political practice or with tying these activities to a logic of progressive commitment. The very heterodox character of Woolf's activism would make this problematic and I am less concerned with arriving at an understanding of what motivated Woolf's activism than with establishing the diversity and longevity of this work and the complicated processes by which she engaged with and reacted against this activity in her writing. This book considers trends that might link these activities together and Woolf's ambivalence about the value of her political and social activities represents one such trend. We also repeatedly encounter Woolf's commitment to these organisations evidenced by her unerring willingness to call upon family, friends and sometimes even mere acquaintances to offer their support. Throughout these activities we also glimpse an organisational verve rarely associated with Woolf, for instance in her co-ordination of speakers for the WCG and later in her quest for an 'Epi-dia-scope' to show slides for WI talks.

Woolf studies and Woolf's politics

This book is inspired both by a fascination with the details of Woolf's political activism and by a parallel preoccupation with what Woolf studies has made of Woolf's politics. The following discussion explores the crucial and contested role of Woolf's politics in Woolf studies and positions the current study as a critical inheritor to these debates.

The Virginia Woolf most in currency in Woolf studies today is a slippery one that resists compartmentalising and 'doesn't easily stay put'.[20] Thanks to the pioneering work of scholars such as Rachel Bowlby and Brenda Silver we have a deeper understanding of the various ways in which meaning is projected onto Woolf by different schools and groups. Both scholars have written, in particular, on the subject of Woolf's iconisation by the feminist movement and how, as Bowlby puts it, 'the question of identifying the real nature of Woolf gets bound up with identifying the real nature of woman, or literature, or feminism, or feminist literature'.[21]

That the acceptance of this indeterminate Woolf has been so enthusiastic is in part because it offers contemporary Woolf scholars the opportunity to draw a line under the protracted and partisan intellectual battle over Woolf's political identity that raged throughout the 1970s and 1980s. This subject receives attention in Silver's study of the 'shifting reception of *Three Guineas*', which includes a discussion of the feminist rediscovery and rehabilitation of this text in the 1970s,[22] and more recently in a perceptive essay by Laura Marcus concerning the 'symbiotic' relationship between Woolf and feminism.[23] The following discussion looks at one particular and influential critical debate between Jane Marcus and Quentin Bell, which revolved around the questions of Woolf's feminism and her Marxism.[24] It is important to recognise how much is owed to both sides of this debate and how much we can learn about the development of feminist critical practice and the emergence of a political Woolf through these disputes. This survey also makes clear the ways in which the particularities of Woolf's real world political involvement were neglected in these arguments over whether Virginia Woolf was a 'political' writer or not.

* * *

1983 was a pivotal year in the debate over Virginia Woolf's politics. In this year tensions that had been bubbling between Woolf scholars and the estate exploded onto the pages of *Virginia Woolf Miscellany* and *Critical Inquiry*. In his introduction to an edition of *Virginia Woolf Miscellany* on the theme of Woolf's politics that year, Peter Stansky outlines the competing claims of the rival factions involved in this dispute over the nature of Woolf's political identity:

> I do not mean to be reductionist and to ascribe too much to the origins of the individuals involved in this debate, but on the whole those who are Woolfians – which I am using here to indicate those who tend to see Woolf's politics as less radical and less central to her being – are male, and frequently English. On the whole, those who are Lupines – who see Woolf as more to the left and argue that these political questions are more central to her being – are female, and frequently American.[25]

Stansky's characterisation of the battle for Woolf's politics as also a clash of cultures and genders was widely accepted and Lupines and Woolfians alike carefully cultivated these terms in their writing preceding the 1983 *VWM* debates.

Ellen Hawkes Rogat's critical review of Quentin Bell's 1972 biography of Woolf is one such example. Rogat was highly critical of what she felt was Bell's failure to properly interrogate the feminist concerns of Woolf's life and his picture of his aunt as a distinctly 'unnatural' woman.[26] In a 1977 essay concerned with Woolf's views on art and propaganda, Jane Marcus reiterated this criticism and went further by placing Bell's biography within a male, English tradition – 'Leavis, Forster, Bell' – which, she argued, sought to de-emphasise and depoliticise Woolf's life and writing.[27] Marcus describes Woolf here as a 'genteel Marxist' with the ability in her work to combine 'a Marxian economics with Freudian psychological insights and Wollstonecraft's revolutionary feminism'.[28] While we can be sure that this account of Woolf as a radical political agent would have horrified Quentin Bell, it was Marcus's use of the term 'Marxist' that inspired his particular ire and became a specific bugbear in all Bell's contributions to this debate.[29]

Jane Marcus's 1979 essay 'Tintinnabulations' is a more sustained critique of what she describes as the 'Bloomsbury view' propagated by the Woolf estate and British scholars.[30] According to Marcus a new biography of Woolf was needed, one that would break her out of the 'Bloomsbury zoo' in which the Bells held her captive.[31] It would re-emphasise the significance of her relationships with political women including Janet Case and Margaret Llewelyn Davies and present a portrait of the 'socialist, pacifist, and feminist' Woolf that the Bells had suppressed.[32] In an article from the same year published in *Critical Inquiry,* Quentin Bell attempts to remedy some of 'the false generalisations that are made and the absurdities which are repeated' on the subject of Bloomsbury and its politics.[33] Although Marcus is not mentioned it is evident that the essay is designed to undermine the portrait of a Marxist, feminist Woolf she had cultivated. Bell only discusses Woolf in the closing pages of the essay, instead focusing the rest of the paper on an attempt to recuperate Clive Bell's reputation as a political thinker and pacifist during the First World War – he describes him as 'the bête noire of militant womanhood today'.[34] When Bell eventually reaches Virginia Woolf it is to express his amazement that she should be seen 'as a maker of political ideologies' comparable to John Maynard Keynes and goes on to insist 'Virginia's life was not devoted to the cause of feminism; she had other interests and specifically feminist writings form but a small part of her total oeuvre'.[35]

Bell's article did not succeed in putting Jane Marcus in her place. When it was reproduced in 1988 Marcus supplied a critical introduction to her 1982 essay 'Storming the Toolshed' that speaks directly to her disputes with Bell over Woolf's feminist politics: 'What it records most significantly is a moment of male resistance to feminist theory in 1982, as well as my own suspicion of academic cooption of the feminist movement'.[36] In this essay we find the clearest evidence of Woolf's iconic status within feminist criticism. The most striking example of this is an episode in which Marcus daydreams about what Woolf's responses to developments in feminist literary criticism might be. While this vision of Woolf moving around a 1980s MLA delighting in the work of feminist scholars is seductive, it is also an example of an impulse of some feminist Woolf scholarship to whitewash Woolf (or should I say paint her red?), ignoring evidence that contradicts a perfected image of her.[37]

Marcus's description of the 'collective and collaborative work' pursued by feminist scholars in the US – 'the sisterhood of feminist Woolf scholarship' – is justly celebratory.[38] However, it is important to note her pointed reminder that this is an American sisterhood, as British readers – for Marcus they seem to be a homogenous group – are still too much in the thrall of Leavis and his *Great Tradition* to see Woolf as 'anything but elitist and mad'.[39] Not only does this overlook the different positions from which British scholars might critique Woolf, but it also neglects the contribution made by British academics to the recognition of Woolf's political identity and her feminism, notably Gillian Beer, Julia Briggs and Michèle Barrett. In addition to Barrett's 1979 *Virginia Woolf: Women & Writing*, which Marcus allows as an exception to her rule about British Woolf scholarship,[40] an earlier 1978 essay by Barrett concerning the state of Virginia Woolf criticism also emphasises Woolf's 'historical materialist understanding' and her feminism.[41] *Towards a Sociology of Virginia Woolf Criticism* addresses the ways in which the development of a 'socialist feminism' could result in a more sophisticated understanding of Woolf's life and writing.

Returning to the fateful 1983 issue of *Virginia Woolf Miscellany*, Peter Stansky concludes his introduction with, what in hindsight sounds rather like a plea for collegiate spirit and constructive argument: 'But one should not think of it as a battle; rather, as sharing insights and views as Woolf enters her second century, more vital than ever.'[42] Quentin Bell's authoritatively titled article 'Virginia Woolf, Her Politics', however, brooks no contradiction. In this article

Bell outlines the nature of Woolf's politics as he sees them – she was doubtless a Labour voter and a feminist but also found 'politicians of her own sex [...] worthy but tedious' and could not be described as a socialist, but rather 'a kind of Fabian'.[43] In the course of the article Bell 'invent[s] an interruption' and in doing so gets to the crux of his argument:

> 'Surely she was a marxist? That learned and eloquent lady, Professor Marcus had said so; it must be true.' The matter is on my conscience. In my biography of Virginia I pointed out how close 'The Leaning Tower' comes to marxist theory. For reasons which will appear, I did not call her a marxist, but if she had lived longer she might have become a marxist.[44]

Bell's tone of mock-chivalry is grating, however his assessment of Woolf's politics, in particular his description of Woolf as 'a kind of Fabian', usefully gestures to the complexity of Woolf's engagement with the left. Bell's insistence that there is no evidence to support Woolf being described as a Marxist – he can find nothing of 'her reaction to the 1917 revolution and N.E.P., her views of Stalin and the General Strike' – not only offers a rather superior corrective to Jane Marcus but also, perhaps inadvertently, draws attention to the need for close and detailed research into the nature of Woolf's political engagements.[45]

In contrast to Bell's piece, replete with ironic flourishes, Jane Marcus's rival piece in the same edition, a review of Grace Radin's *Virginia Woolf: The Years,* is restrained but nonetheless constructs a subtle critique of the Woolf estate. Marcus begins by quoting the Bells' suggestion that Woolf scholars had reached the 'bottom of the barrel' in terms of primary sources, only to triumphantly cite not only Grace Radin's study of *The Years* manuscripts, but also Mitchell Leaska's edition of *The Pargiters* and Louise DeSalvo's *Melymsbrosia* as examples of this material yielding 'crisp and delicious fruit'.[46] However, the arguments of the 1983 *VWM* acted only as a prelude to the dispute that would break out during the following year in *Critical Inquiry*.

In his essay 'A "Radiant" Friendship' Quentin Bell once again engages with Jane Marcus's reading of Woolf as a Marxist. He combines this with an attempt to reinstate Bloomsbury's importance in

Woolf's social and psychic life by investigating Marcus's claim in 'Tintinnabulations' that:

> Bloomsbury fades into insignificance as an 'influence' next to the radiance of Woolf's relationships with Margaret Llewelyn Davies, head of the Co-operative Working Women's Guild, Janet Case, her Greek teacher, Violet Dickinson, Madge Vaughan, and her aunt Caroline Stephen, the Quaker whom she called 'nun.'[47]

Bell pursues his ends by putting forward the following proposition: 'At least one of the women who encouraged Virginia to "write, read, and think" must surely herself have been a Marxist'.[48] According to Bell, although close friends of Woolf's as a young woman, Violet Dickinson and Madge Vaughan were 'nonstarters' as Marxists.[49] Although he concedes that 'a much stronger case can be made for Margaret Llewelyn Davies', Bell concludes that she was not a Marxist either.[50]

Jane Marcus appears unimpressed by what she considers Bell's semantic wrangling in her reply in *Critical Inquiry* in 1985:

> Mr Bell knows perfectly well that my use of the word "marxist" to describe Woolf as a triple thinker and to compare her to Walter Benjamin is meant to describe her mind and her fiction, not, as the word is used in his culture, to denote a card-carrying member of the Communist party.[51]

Marcus continues to stress the transatlantic divide in Woolf scholarship but also creates a distinctive forward-looking quality: 'Perhaps the next generation of Woolf critics is sharpening even now the stars and swords which will rip away the veils and give us a real Virginia Woolf.'[52] Here Marcus recognises the mutability of Woolf and her ability to mean something very different, even contradictory, to different groups of readers and critics. In this self-conscious understanding of the unique function of Woolf within feminist criticism, Marcus looks forward to Brenda Silver's work on the 'versioning' of Woolf within criticism and culture. There is also humour and warmth in this reply to Quentin Bell in *Critical Inquiry* summed up in its conciliatory conclusion: 'let me end this response by saying "Brother" to Quentin Bell'.[53]

* * *

Throughout their debate Marcus and Bell pay remarkably little attention to the actual details of Woolf's political activism and social participation. Instead, as we have seen, the tenacity of the question of Woolf's purported Marxism eclipses any attention to the nuances of Woolf's political position, how she engaged with and was influenced by various different political and social organisations.

The red herring of Woolf's Marxism in these debates and the stubborn cross-purposes at which Bell and Marcus argue – he understanding Marxist as a historically and culturally specific position which must be read in terms of the Russian Revolution while Marcus seems, problematically, to identify Woolf's left-leaning politics in a totalising sweep as Marxist – arguably set a precedent in Woolf studies, which has tended to ignore the details of Woolf's activities and their historical contexts. There is no doubt that this argument between Marcus and Bell is exciting for its scholarly urgency and for the gripping style of its contributors. As we have seen, for Marcus it is clear that there was more than Virginia Woolf's political identity at stake in this debate; she positions herself as not simply defending Woolf but also the efficacy of a Marxist-feminist critical practice. With all this to defend it is easy to see why Woolf's practical politics may have been sidelined. This book, with its emphasis on the subtleties and ambivalences of Woolf's political practice, responds directly to these arguments and retrieves Woolf's activism from a debate in which 'Marxism' comes to stand in for politics.

Notes

1. '"To Crush Him in Our Own Country": The Political Thought of Virginia Woolf', *Feminist Studies*, 4 (1978), 99–132 (p. 101).
2. Zwerdling, *Virginia Woolf and the Real World* (Berkeley: University of California Press, 1986).
3. *Virginia Woolf* (London: Chatto and Windus, 1996).
4. *The Feminist Aesthetics of Virginia Woolf: Modernism, Post-Impressionism and the Politics of the Visual* (Cambridge: Cambridge University Press, 1998).
5. *Virginia Woolf, the Intellectual, and the Public Sphere* (Cambridge: Cambridge University Press, 2003), p. 2.

6. *Virginia Woolf: Public and Private Negotiations* (Basingstoke: Macmillan, 2000), p. 1; '"Tilting at Universities": Woolf at King's College London', *Woolf Studies Annual*, 16 (2010), 1–44; '"Wide Circles": The *Three Guineas* Letters', *Woolf Studies Annual*, 6 (2000), 1–168.
7. *Virginia Woolf's Late Cultural Criticism: The Genesis of* The Years, Three Guineas *and* Between the Acts (London: Bloomsbury Academic, 2013), p. 2.
8. David Bradshaw's work on Woolf's involvement with 1930s anti-fascist groups ('British Writers and Anti-Fascism in the 1930s, Part I: The Bray and Drone of Tortured Voices', *Woolf Studies Annual*, 3 (1997), 3–27; 'British Writers and Anti-Fascism in the 1930s, Part II: Under the Hawk's Wings', *Woolf Studies Annual*, 4 (1998), 41–66) and Naomi Black's survey of Woolf's relationship with the 'organized women's movement of her day' (*Virginia Woolf as Feminist* (Ithaca, NY: Cornell University Press, 2004), pp. 33–50 (p. 33)) are significant exceptions.
9. 'To Crush Him in Our Own Country', 100–1.
10. *Virginia Woolf and the Politics of Style* (New York: State University of New York Press, 1986), p. 2.
11. *Virginia Woolf* (London: Wishart, 1932), p. 33.
12. *Virginia Woolf and the Real World*, p. 4.
13. London, The Women's Library (LSE), Suffrage Pamphlets, Appeal for Funds, 4 March 1910, 324.6230941 PEO.
14. London, London School of Economics Archive Collection (LSE), *Women's Co-operative Guild Thirty-second Annual Report, May, 1914–May, 1915*, COLL MISC 0657, p. 2.
15. 'activism, n.', *OED Online*, June 2013, Oxford University Press, http://0-www.oed.com.catalogue.ulrls.lon.ac.uk/view/Entry/1957?redirectedFrom=activism [accessed 2 April 2015; requires membership].
16. *Modernist Fiction, Cosmopolitanism and the Politics of Community* (Cambridge: Cambridge University Press, 2001), p. 116.
17. *Downhill All the Way: An Autobiography of the Years 1919–1939* (London: Hogarth Press, 1967), p. 27.
18. *Virginia Woolf: The Common Ground* (Edinburgh: Edinburgh University Press, 1996).
19. *Virginia Woolf*, p. 461.
20. Rachel Bowlby, *Feminist Destinations and Further Essays on Virginia Woolf* (Edinburgh: Edinburgh University Press, 1997) p. 13.
21. *Feminist Destinations*, p. 13.
22. 'The Authority of Anger: *Three Guineas* as Case Study', *Signs*, 16 (1991), 340–70 (p. 361).
23. 'Woolf's Feminism and Feminism's Woolf', in Susan Sellers (ed.), *The Cambridge Companion to Virginia Woolf*, 2nd edn (Cambridge: Cambridge University Press, 2010), pp. 142–79 (p. 142).

24. Regina Marler offers an overview of this dispute between Jane Marcus and Quentin Bell in her searching and highly entertaining account of the growing Bloomsbury industry. *Bloomsbury Pie: The Making of the Bloomsbury Boom* (New York: Henry Holt, 1997), pp. 142–52.
25. 'To the Readers: An Editorial Comment on Woolfians and Lupines', *Virginia Woolf Miscellany (VWM)*, 20 (1983), 1 (p. 1).
26. 'The Virgin in the Bell Biography', *Twentieth Century Literature*, 20 (1974), 96–113 (p. 99).
27. 'No More Horses: Virginia Woolf on Art and Propaganda', *Women's Studies*, 4 (1977), 265–90 (p. 269).
28. 'No More Horses', 272 and 274.
29. While in subsequent articles Marcus continues to refer to Woolf as a 'Marxist' she is careful to use inverted commas or clarify that rather than using the term to suggest Woolf was in any practical sense a communist, it is used to suggest Woolf's 'revolutionary materialism'. 'The Niece of a Nun: Virginia Woolf, Caroline Stephen and the Cloistered Imagination', in Jane Marcus (ed.), *Virginia Woolf: A Feminist Slant* (Lincoln: Nebraska University Press, 1983), pp. 7–36 (p. 12). Elsewhere Marcus argues that 'Virginia Woolf, like Walter Benjamin, was both a "Marxist" and a mystic' using Benjamin as a touchstone for Woolf's political vision. 'Thinking Back through Our Mothers', in Jane Marcus (ed.), *New Feminist Essays on Virginia Woolf* (Lincoln: University of Nebraska Press, 1981), pp. 1–30 (p. 5).
30. 'Tintinnabulations', in *Art and Anger: Reading Like A Woman* (Columbus: Ohio State University Press, 1988), pp. 157–81 (p. 161) (first publ. in *Marxist Perspectives*, 2 (1979), 145–67).
31. Marcus, 'Tintinnabulations', p. 157.
32. Marcus, 'Tintinnabulations', p. 159.
33. 'Bloomsbury and "The Vulgar Passions"', *Critical Inquiry*, 6 (1979), 239–59 (p. 239).
34. Bell, 'Bloomsbury and "The Vulgar Passions"', 243.
35. Bell, 'Bloomsbury and "The Vulgar Passions"', 249–50.
36. 'Storming the Toolshed', in *Art and Anger*, pp. 182–202 (p. 182) (first publ. in *Signs*, 7 (1982), 622–40).
37. 'Storming the Toolshed', pp. 188–9. In a significant essay on Woolf and class, Mary M. Childers draws our attention to this 'personification and idealization' of Woolf by some feminist scholars and the degree to which this has prevented engagement with Woolf's often problematic class politics. 'Virginia Woolf on the Outside Looking Down: Reflections on the Class of Women', *Modern Fiction Studies*, 38 (1992), 61–79 (p. 62).
38. 'Storming the Toolshed', p. 189.

39. 'Storming the Toolshed', p. 191. Marcus casts the debate over Woolf's politics as a clash of cultures in the following articles: 'Wrapped in the Stars and Stripes: Virginia Woolf in the U.S.A', *The South Carolina Review*, 29, (1996), 17–23 and 'A Tale of Two Cultures', *The Women's Review of Books*, 11 (1994), 11–13.
40. 'Storming the Toolshed', p. 191.
41. 'Towards a Sociology of Virginia Woolf Criticism', in Diana Laurenson (ed.), *The Sociology of Literature: Applied Studies* (Keele: University of Keele, 1978), p. 156.
42. 'To the Readers', 1.
43. Bell, 'Virginia Woolf, Her Politics', *VWM*, 20 (1983), 2 (p. 2).
44. 'Virginia Woolf, Her Politics', 2.
45. 'Virginia Woolf, Her Politics', 2.
46. Marcus, 'Review of Grace Radin's *Virginia Woolf: The Years*', *VWM*, 20 (1993), 4–5 (p. 4).
47. 'Tintinnabulations', p. 165.
48. 'A "Radiant" Friendship', *Critical Inquiry*, 10 (1984), 557–66 (p. 558).
49. 'A "Radiant" Friendship', 558.
50. 'A "Radiant" Friendship', 559.
51. 'Quentin's Bogey', *Critical Inquiry*, 11 (1985), 486–97 (p. 490).
52. 'Quentin's Bogey', 488.
53. 'Quentin's Bogey', 495.

Chapter 1

Virginia Stephen and Morley College, 1905–7

Introduction

> The original [Mary] Sheepshanks wants me to go and see her, and talk over my views, which I aint none. She thinks I might combine amusement and instruction – a little gossip and sympathy, and then 'talks' about books and pictures. I'm sure I dont mind how much I talk, and I really dont see any limit to the things I might talk about. However as she is sure – the good Sheepshanks – that I shall be of the greatest use – I dont mind trying. (*L1* 172)

Virginia Stephen began corresponding with Mary Sheepshanks, the vice-principal of Morley College, in late December 1904 and took up a voluntary teaching post at the beginning of 1905. Over the course of her three years teaching once a week at Morley, Virginia Stephen taught history of art, history, English composition and poetry appreciation. When she first mentions voluntary teaching at Morley College to her then closest friend, Violet Dickinson, it is with a characteristic mixture of taciturnity and enthusiasm.

This January 1905 letter reveals the contradictory impulses that typified Virginia Stephen's attitude towards her work at Morley. Immediately striking is her reluctance to admit that she has any 'views' to 'talk over' with the college's vice-principal. The self-deprecating, mock-cockney aside, 'which I aint none', comically links Virginia Stephen to her future working-class students at Morley, however, it also registers some anxiety about her unfamiliarity with Mary Sheepshanks's world of voluntarism, public spirit and social enquiry. This is compounded by the confused way in which she relates what her role will entail. While her reference to 'a little gossip and sympathy' apparently reveals a dismissive attitude towards the demands of teaching, this lackadaisical tone is undermined by the uneasiness registered in the inverted commas enclosing 'talks'. In the final line she appears to be sending up Mary Sheepshanks through her parodic, Dickensian figuring of her as 'the good Sheepshanks'. This flippant aside encodes a key anxiety for Virginia Stephen throughout her work at Morley – her association of her voluntary teaching with what she perceived as the patronising, philanthropic activities of Victorian ladies, including her mother and half-sister, Stella Duckworth.

Both Julia Stephen and Stella Duckworth were committed followers of Victorian social reformer Octavia Hill and engaged in various philanthropic pursuits. Julia Stephen donated £10 a year to Hill's charity from 1871 until the year of her death, 1895, while Stella Duckworth went as far as commissioning a number of charitable cottages for the poor to be built on Lisson Grove near Hill's tenement buildings in Marylebone. Octavia Hill memorialises Stella Duckworth in a letter to her volunteers upon her death in 1897, commending her selfless work for the poor and stating: 'These cottages, her last work for us, will come with all solemn sense of trust from her and as dear for her sake.'[1] In her early journals Virginia Stephen mentions the plans for Stella's cottages, her own grudging visits to workhouses and, with a flash of irreverent protest, Octavia Hill herself: 'then to Miss Hill in Marylebone Rd. Jo [Fisher] was there discussing the plans for Stellas new cottages with Miss Hill. All three learnedly argued over them for half an hour, I sitting on a stool by the fire and surveying Miss Hills legs – ' (*PA* 21).[2]

Morley College was (and remains) a flourishing centre of adult education in London's borough of Lambeth. Morley's origins lie in the Coffee Palace Association, a late-Victorian temperance group, and its attempts to rehabilitate the iniquitous Old Vic theatre by providing more wholesome entertainment for its working-class patrons. Denis Richards describes how the theatre was transformed from a place identified with drunkenness and prostitution into a centre of recreation and learning for Lambeth's working classes, emphasising the pivotal role of Emma Cons, a social reformer and advocate of leisure for working people.[3] Cons began her working life as one of Octavia Hill's rent collectors in Hill's tenement buildings in Drury

Lane where she also organised lessons for the residents.[4] She soon saw that the Old Vic's educational lectures outstripped the variety shows and concerts, which also occupied the programme, in popularity and, using money donated by prominent philanthropist Samuel Morley, Cons established a fully-fledged college in its own premises around the corner from the theatre.[5]

The instrumental roles played by middle-class temperance campaigners and Emma Cons herself in the founding of Morley suggest that Virginia Stephen was not simply expressing personal prejudice when she refers to her work at Morley as 'philanthropy' in her letters. And while Morley College's roots certainly were in the social reform and philanthropic movements of the late-Victorian period, it was the concurrent adult education movement that informed Morley's identity as a centre of adult learning. Morley established itself along the lines of earlier institutions such as the Mechanics' Institutes and Working Men's Colleges, both founded earlier in the nineteenth century. The range of classes and the approach to learning promoted at Morley reflected a contemporary preference for a humanist syllabus with an emphasis on learning for its own sake.[6] Charles Roden Buxton, principal of Morley College while Virginia Stephen taught there, reiterates this agenda in his opening remarks to each edition of the college magazine – 'but we specialise in those subjects which provide a real liberal education; we try to promote learning and general development for their own sakes'.[7]

While both the Mechanics' Institutes and Working Men's Colleges attempted to elide the paternalism of Victorian philanthropy by encouraging their working-class students to participate in the organisation of their college, Roger Fieldhouse suggests that the middle-class leadership in both enterprises meant that '[m]uch of it suffered from being patronising and bourgeois, even if well intentioned'.[8] He goes on to argue that the elevated, classical syllabuses of these institutions, which emphasised human fellowship, were also intended to ameliorate class feeling among working-class students and 'to educate them to conform happily to their allotted roles in society'.[9]

When Albert Mansbridge came to form the Workers' Educational Association in 1903 he too recognised that the failure of the Mechanics' Institutes and the limited popularity of the Working Men's Colleges was due to their old-fashioned paternalism.[10] And although Mansbridge explains in his history of the WEA that '[f]ellowship was the keynote of it all'[11] and Jonathan Rose has noted '[t]he WEA disavowed propaganda in favor of "impartial" and "nonpartisan" education', Mansbridge was insistent that the association's working-class students had a greater say in what they studied.[12]

Virginia Stephen encountered the sharp end of contemporary ideological rows in adult education while at Morley College.[13] It seems that those managing Morley College, were, like Albert Mansbridge, uneasy about appearing too much the direct descendent of older institutions. While Buxton's introductory address to the Morley magazine promotes a similarly humanist syllabus, he is keen to distance Morley from the Mechanics' Institutes and other colleges that came before it: 'A word to begin with for those who are not acquainted with our work. Morley College is not an Institute or a Polytechnic. What then is it?'[14]

Morley did differ from these institutions in one crucial way – it allowed female students to enter on the same terms as male students.[15] Mary Sheepshanks was a committed suffragist and in her unpublished autobiography she recalls Morley as institutionally sympathetic to this cause and singles out its male students for particular praise in this regard: 'I found the young men at Morley more fair minded and liberal about women's rights than most young men of the upper classes.'[16] Sheepshanks also organised debates on the subject of women's suffrage with Christabel Pankhurst speaking in April 1907,[17] while Virginia Stephen was still teaching there, and later Amber Reeves in 1909.[18] While owing much to the mid-nineteenth-century adult education centres in terms of its syllabus, this was an inheritance Morley was uneasy with. Although maintaining a policy of political non-partisanship, Morley was run from 1897 by a vocal suffragist who agitated for innovation in the organisation of the college, clashing with the more conservative members of the management board.[19]

It was, then, a lively institution, although one troubled by internecine argument, which Virginia Stephen entered in January 1905 at the age of twenty-three.[20] Her letters reveal how her work at Morley College became both a significant part of her week's routine but also a source of pride; there is positive excitement when her doctor, Savage, gives the all-clear for her to start work: 'I am booked for Morley College!' (*L*1 174). Letters to Dickinson in the early months of her teaching include numerous references to her work there – casual but self-important: 'I am rushing off to my workers, so I cant write – ' (*L*1 175). Virginia Stephen's first classes at Morley wandered through topics as diverse and broad as prose, Venice and ancient Greek history before she was eventually begged by her students to 'lecture steadily at English History next term "from the beginning"' (*PA* 255). These accounts of her lessons also glimmer with a mixture of possessive pride and humour. She tells Dickinson in one letter: 'You will have to come down and talk to them one week – lots of jokes is what they like – and then they blossom out – and say how they have written poetry since the age of 11!' (*L*1 177).

Virginia Stephen's teacherly enthusiasm and commitment to her work at Morley had to compete with her literary aspirations and cultivation of her fledgling career in journalism. Two months before her first correspondence with Morley College on the subject of teaching, Virginia Stephen took her first steps in her early career as a journalist with a modest proposition to the women's pages of the clerical *Guardian*: 'Would Mrs Lyttelton like a description of a Q. Meeting from my gifted pen, d'you think. I dont know if I shall have time, but it might be amusing' (*L*1 148). Although her first attempt at an article appears to have been less than successful, her desire to be published and more importantly her desire to be paid for her work meant she strove on and eventually received a commission: '1,500 words rather appals me [...] However I am too delighted to have a chance of turning an honest penny to mind what I do for it – and she [Mrs Lyttelton] is very generous to allow me any subject – as that gives me a large field' (*L*1 155).

Virginia Stephen's letters and diary entries throughout this period reveal these parallel pedagogic and literary pursuits to be consuming and often linked in her imagination: 'Ella [Crum] asks me to meet Mr Buxton the Principal of Morley: so I am rising in philanthropic circles, as I sink in literary ones. No books whatever to review, and I grind at my history with a sense of utterly unrequited energy' (*L*1 193). Here, with characteristic bathetic humour, Virginia Stephen's work at Morley College is locked in an uneasy tension with her journalistic pursuits, creating a precedent in her treatment of these distinct but concurrent enterprises.

Beth Rigel Daugherty's significant research has drawn attention to Virginia Stephen's work at Morley and its relationship to her journalism; she describes these pursuits collectively as 'an extraordinary apprenticeship'.[21] Daugherty also rightly identifies Virginia Stephen's first face-to-face encounter with working-class men and women at Morley as important, although I am keen to complicate her suggestion that at Morley she learnt 'to transcend class difference and identify with her students'.[22] Melba Cuddy-Keane has located Virginia Stephen's uneasiness regarding the syllabus at Morley and has begun the important work of contextualising her voluntary teaching within the broader development of adult education and the rise of the WEA.[23] There is more work to be done in order to establish the significant ways in which Virginia Stephen's experiences at Morley shaped her political thinking and her literary practice. While Cuddy-Keane and Daugherty have plotted the ways in which Virginia Stephen's time as a teacher influenced her inclusive, demotic techniques as an essayist, here I focus on how this early activity was formative to the development not only of her idiosyncratic brand of political and social thought, but also some of the key concerns of her early fiction.

'Report on Teaching at Morley College'[24]

Written in July 1905, seven months into her time at Morley College, Virginia Stephen's heavily drafted description of her experiences there possesses a distinctly teacherly tone. Assuming the voice of an at once put-upon but authoritative pedagogue, the exercise's opening lines go some way to explaining why this intriguing text has been read straightforwardly as a 'teaching report':

> This is the season for another report upon that class of working women {which I led there} <whom I> have already {once before this} mentioned.
>
> It was to be a class of history this time; in spite of the fact that those in authority looked rather coldly on it; history they told me, was the least popular subject in the college; at the same time they could not confute me when I asserted that it was also one of the most important.

Far from registering the formality that a reader would expect from a mandatory institutional exercise, there is a playful performativity in Virginia Stephen's stiff reference to 'those in authority' and her pompous choice of words like 'confute' and 'assert'. The ceremony of the opening passage and the text's claimed status as a report are undermined when we notice the month in which it was written. Right in the middle of the Morley College summer holiday, July would hardly be the month when reports were required. A journal entry on 25 March sheds some light on the character of this text. Virginia Stephen describes how she '[w]rote at a kind of sketch of my Morley College proceedings, to amuse myself – & possibly this may be of interest in future terms – so that I may see how I started, & which girls came' (*PA* 256). This entry describes a lost initial piece of writing on Morley to which she refers in the deleted section in the passage quoted above. This entry also provides us with an alternative way of naming the text. Referring to this text as the 'Morley Sketch' rather than 'Report on Teaching at Morley College', the title Quentin Bell settled on when producing his transcription of this text as an appendix to his 1972 biography of Woolf, recognises its literariness and allows for a more nuanced reading.[25] The sketch from July encourages this when it momentarily breaks in its performance, admitting a connection with the earlier sketch: 'my remarks this time are merely a development of that tentative sketch'.

In July 1905 Virginia Stephen was preoccupied with thoughts about the nature of her work at Morley. In a letter to Violet Dickinson she seems proud but vaguely uneasy about a dinner invitation from Morley's principal:

> I am going to dine with the Buxtons to discuss my good – would be good at any rate – works – Letters are not literature! It is so odd to plunge into philanthropic society, living on the other side of the river of a sudden. (*L1* 198)

This anxiety seems to have all but disappeared in a letter to Emma Vaughan a few days later, which almost bristles with superior satisfaction:

> Marny threw out cryptic hints the other day that you are on the look out for a profession and might possibly take some work at Morley. I am dining with the Principal, Mr Buxton, on Monday, and if you liked, I could offer him your invaluable services. (*L1* 199)

Virginia Stephen's evident pride at being invited into the inner philanthropic sanctum – she also received a letter from Ella Crum in July telling her 'what a wonderful thing it is to have [her] at Morley' (*L*1 201) – coupled with her concurrent feelings of dejection about her reviewing, could explain her drafting of this sketch and the way in which in it she tries out the various roles of dedicated teacher, social investigator and anti-authoritarian maverick. In the 'Morley Sketch' she is seeing if any of these fit; prompted by all this positive attention from the Buxtons and Ella Crum she wonders whether or not really 'to plunge into philanthropic society'.

Miss Stephen and Miss Williams

The curious quality of the narrative voice in the first passage of the sketch sets the tone for what is at once a playful and uneasy text wrought with deletions and insertions. The sketch concentrates first on the characters and occupations of the four women who attended Virginia Stephen's history class and then in the second half reflects on her approach to teaching. Although she writes about all of her students, Virginia Stephen pays by far the greatest attention to Miss Williams, a newspaper reporter, and it is during her reflections on Miss Williams that Virginia Stephen's deletions are at their most profuse and revealing.

This disproportionate attention paid to Miss Williams is qualified not only because 'she was certainly of a higher {level} level of intelligence than the other women', but perhaps more importantly because Virginia Stephen admits she 'must reconsider [her] judgment' of her. Having previously described her, we assume in the lost March sketch, as 'rather handsome & well dressed' but also 'inattentive & critical', Virginia Stephen allows that Miss Williams's attendance is good and is clearly fascinated to discover that 'she was a reporter on the staff of a Religious paper – reported {?} sermons in shorthand – {&} did typewriting, & also wrote reviews of books'.

Virginia Stephen's observation that Miss Williams was 'rather handsome & well-dressed' registers interest but also a competitive impulse, which is worth bearing in mind when assessing her treatment of Miss Williams's profession. Melba Cuddy-Keane has rightly recognised that Miss Williams gave Virginia Stephen 'insight into the pragmatic world of writing for money', one she herself was fast gaining first-hand experience of.[26] Virginia Stephen's letters from the period at which she began her reviewing show a preoccupation with when and what she will be paid for her work; in a letter to Emma Vaughan she describes making money from reviewing as 'our old ambition' (*L*1 160). Virginia Stephen did not identify with Miss Williams in any unproblematic way, but the surface similarities between herself and her student may have prompted self-assessment and been responsible for the uneasiness of this sketch.

In the 1904–5 Morley College annual report the list of the occupations of students that year includes one 'Reporter' who we can assume is Miss Williams.[27] There is more evidence of Miss Williams in the 1905 college magazine, which could further explain Virginia Stephen's curious mixture of animosity and curiosity towards her. In the list of certificate winners for 1905 under the 'College Examination' heading, we find one Annie Williams awarded a first-class certificate for her elocution exam.[28] Although we cannot be sure that this Annie Williams and the Miss Williams of Virginia Stephen's sketch are one and the same, this first-class award for elocution seems a fitting attribute for a 'rather handsome & well dressed' woman reporter wishing to 'get on' in her career. An honours certificate in elocution also implies a drive for social mobility, from which Virginia Stephen may have instinctively recoiled given her distaste for what she considered the pushiness of the lower-middle classes.

The fact that both Virginia Stephen and Miss Williams were not only cutting their journalistic teeth but also gaining their first experiences of literary reviewing in religious newspapers is significant. Virginia Stephen's first articles and reviews were published in the High Church newspaper the *Guardian*, with the help of Violet Dickinson who had put her in touch with Mrs Lyttelton, the editor of the newspaper's women's pages. In his introduction to the first volume of Woolf's essays – many of which were originally book reviews – Andrew McNeillie admits that, while the *Guardian* took an admirable interest in the arts, it was nonetheless a 'pretty dull clerical newspaper, replete with articles on such subjects as "Episcopal Visitations"' (*E*1 xii). It was certainly the most prominent and well respected of what Joseph Hatton describes as the 'numerous class' of Church papers. Hatton describes it as a 'carefully written and scholarly publication' and goes on to single out its book reviews for particular praise: 'Its reviews of books are, as a rule, thoughtful and well-written essays.'[29] It is telling that the *Guardian* is the only church paper Hatton mentions by name in his short section on religious newspapers in his 1882 survey of *Journalistic London*.

Arnold Bennett's description of the state of Church newspapers in his irascible guidebook *Journalism for Women* provides some of the detail, which Hatton's section politely leaves out. Bennett is dismissive of the 'vast hordes of religious papers' that were in circulation in London around the time Virginia Stephen and Miss Williams were working; he warns that the majority are impoverished and amateurish and thus paid poorly if at all.[30] In her guide for aspiring journalists, *Press Work for Women,* Frances H. Low recommends local religious newspapers as a good place to send speculative contributions and advises that the best way for 'the novice' to hone her craft is to attend meetings and sermons and then write reports of them.[31] This is exactly how Jane T. Stoddart, journalist on the *British Weekly* at the turn of the century, recalls beginning her career: 'I sent from Clifton descriptive accounts of the Octave services, with outlines of the sermons. I was careful to make my quotations in the preachers' exact words'.[32] To have obtained a position on the staff of a newspaper, however lowly, was a great achievement according to Low's guide and to be responsible for reviews the greatest of honours as, Low points out, '[r]eviewing can, as a rule, only be secured through a literary reputation or by intimate acquaintance with an editor'.[33] This was most certainly true of Virginia Stephen, who as Leila Brosnan has noted, exploited all of the 'opportunities afforded her by her privileged position at the heart of literary culture'.[34]

Reference to the layout and quality of the literary review pages of the various popular religious newspapers concurs with Virginia Stephen's presentation of a homogenised and clichéd method of reviewing in the 'Morley Sketch', which she attributes to the reporter's lack of time. What she describes in a deleted passage of the sketch as 'useful phrases which can [...] apply to any book' abound in the review pages of *The Church Family Newspaper* and *The British Weekly*. More interestingly, the short reviews in the 'Notices' section of these papers often quote reviews from other papers, including the authoritative *Guardian*.[35] Virginia Stephen alludes to this practice in the sketch when she notes that for the most part these reviews were 'quotations picked up at random' and her indignant conclusion that 'the column was filled out of someone else's pocket' registers a suspicious fear that her own reviews may have been plundered in this way. There is something pleasing in the thought of one of Virginia Stephen's painstakingly drafted reviews for the *Guardian*, often of what she considered bland and boring books, being trawled for expedient quotes by her 'hack' student Miss Williams. While this imagined challenge to Virginia Stephen's schoolroom authority might seem fanciful, it usefully foregrounds what she clearly felt was an uncomfortable and invasive parity between herself and Miss Williams.

The 'Morley Sketch's' characterisation of Miss Williams as a 'writing machine' and her work as mindless and mechanical also register class-based snobbery about religion. Virginia Stephen's description of the 'rapid turning of the pages' and 'quotations picked up at random', from which Miss Williams's notice emerges, inverts the traditional image of the theological student carefully scrutinising scripture, and encodes an association of religion with the unthinking, over-zealous lower orders, which we also find in Woolf's fiction, particularly her first novel *The Voyage Out*.[36]

Vincent P. Pecora has argued that *The Voyage Out* 'exhibits her critical appropriation of her religious inheritance' more clearly than any of Woolf's subsequent novels.[37] And in *The Voyage Out* class and religion are identified with each other in revealing ways.[38] Helen Ambrose's anxiety that while she is voyaging to South America the nurse with whom she has left her children may, against her wishes, teach them how to pray makes this connection only obliquely, but in a later episode where a sermon is given for the community of English tourists at the hotel, this conflation of religious faith with class position is striking. Having protested her Christianity in the face of her aunt's urbane atheism earlier in the novel, Rachel quickly renounces her faith when she is confronted with the classed bodies of her fellow worshipers. Most damning is the treatment of the 'hospital nurse' whose 'little round red face' and 'weak blue eyes' (*VO* 216) connote her low-class status just as Mrs Chailey's thick-set body in its 'sober black dress' (*VO* 21) mean she could be nothing else but a servant. Rachel feels increasingly horrified by what she considers the nurse's sheep-like acceptance of the sermon and of Christianity:

> she came to the conclusion that the hospital nurse was only slavishly acquiescent, and that the look of satisfaction was produced by no

splendid conception of God within her. How, indeed, could she conceive anything far outside her own experience [...] She was adoring something shallow and smug, clinging to it, so the obstinate mouth witnessed, with the assiduity of a limpet. (*VO* 216)

Here, Rachel's criticism of the nurse's religious acquiescence echoes the spirit of Virginia Stephen's comments about Miss Williams's unchallenging and mechanical method of reviewing. The aquatic comparison of the nurse with a limpet recalls the tentacles that Virginia Stephen imagines stretching from her working-class students' minds as they grappled with education in the 'Morley Sketch'. This marine imagery is employed in both episodes in order to demonstrate the women's otherness and their ignorance of cultural standards represented by an understanding of history or a healthy scepticism about religion. Rachel's querying note in the passage above – 'How, indeed, could she conceive anything far outside her own experience' – reiterates Virginia Stephen's question in the 'Morley Sketch': 'So thin is the present to them; {how can I} <must not the> past remain a spectre always?'

English history 'from the beginning': Virginia Stephen's history syllabus

Just two months before writing the 'Morley Sketch', Virginia Stephen excitedly reframed her authorial ambition in a letter to Violet Dickinson:

> By the way, I am going to write history one of these days. I always did love it; if I could find the bit I want. I have got a ticket for Dr Williams Library across the square, and describe myself as a 'journalist who wants to read history' and so I do feel a professional Lady. (*L1* 190)

The problem of finding 'the bit' of history that she wanted to write was one that consumed Woolf throughout her literary career. Werner J. Deiman has suggested that: 'Historical perspectives begin appearing [...] much earlier in Virginia Woolf's life and career than most commentators have sufficiently emphasised'.[39] This extract from

Virginia Stephen's letter reveals an early example of this impulse and, what is more interesting, an awareness of the difficulties surrounding it.

In the 'Morley Sketch' we arguably find an enactment of the key tension expressed in Virginia Stephen's somewhat rueful statement in the above quotation. Its surface polemic on the inherent and indisputable value of learning history is persistently undercut by Virginia Stephen's anxiety about her ability as a teacher to convey the 'right bit', 'the one good "scene"' that would spark her four students' dormant historical imaginations. Her statement: 'I do not know how many of the phantoms that passed through that dreary school room left any image of themselves upon the {four listening} women' can be read as a wistful reflection on her failings as a teacher as well as a reference to her students' shortcomings. As well as operating on a pedagogical level, Virginia Stephen's positioning of herself as a custodian of a quite particular historical narrative and her specific preoccupation with 'English history' ought to encourage us to consider the implications of what exactly was on Virginia Stephen's self-styled history syllabus.

Although her writing was frequently labelled ahistorical by early critics, in recent decades feminist scholars have emphasised not only the historical complexion of Woolf's writing, but also her own self-conscious historiographical concerns. Melba Cuddy-Keane has explored the ways in which Woolf engaged with contemporary theories of history, including R. G. Collingwood's progressive understanding of history as provisional.[40] Beth Carole Rosenberg has suggested that 'By viewing Woolf's historical project as postmodern – that is, as a method removed from time and the historical moment – we are freed from the burden of trying to establish the "truth" of Woolf's writing of the past'.[41] Quentin Bell wondered in his biography of his aunt if this sense of play could be traced back to her history classes at Morley: 'was she perhaps a little too imaginative? Was her version of English History rather too close to that which was later to fill the pages of *Orlando*?'[42]

By contrast, Sabine Hotho-Jackson has argued that running alongside Woolf's interest in modern developments in historiography 'was a much simpler streak in her thinking about history' and an allegiance to 'a traditional concept of history as a story'.[43] And it is true that Virginia Stephen's account of the systematic way in which she progressed through 'a {certain} reign or two {of} in Freeman or Green' in each class does not appear consistent with a radical challenge to historical metanarratives, and neither does her appraisal of Freeman, in particular, as 'a good manly writer with no nonsense about him' (*PA* 272). It is not only Virginia Stephen's recourse to historians such as E. A. Freeman and J. R. Green[44] as models for her own classroom narrative of English history, but also her dogmatic emphasis on the need for history to be seen 'as a whole' that reveal a certain attachment to a progressivist story of England, which is rarely addressed in accounts of her theory of history.[45]

If we assess the character of Virginia Stephen's reading as a young woman and her firm grounding in conventional and for the most part Whig history, her dissemination of a traditional, linear narrative of English history in her classes at Morley seems less remarkable. Virginia Stephen's early journals are replete with references to her intensive but pleasurable course of historical reading, much of it recommended by her father.[46] In 1897, when she was fifteen, she tackled J. A. Froude's *Life of Carlyle* and *History of England*, Thomas Carlyle's *Reminiscences* and *Life of Cromwell* and Thomas Arnold's *The History of Rome*. On 18 May Virginia Stephen gleefully records the developments in her reading, proclaiming her expertise and ambition:

> I have now got Carlyle's French Revolution – the 5th volume of Macaulay being restored to its place. In this way I shall become surfeited with history. Already I am an expert upon William (Hear Hear!) & when I have mastered C's 2 vols. I shall be eligible for the first B.A. degree – if the ladies succeed. (*PA* 87)

This quote reveals Virginia Stephen's systematic approach to becoming 'surfeited with history'. Her reference to 'the ladies' and her mention of her eligibility for 'the first B.A.' encourages us to see this reading, as well as Virginia Stephen's later teaching of history at Morley, in the context of her own formal instruction in the subject between 1897 and 1899 in the Ladies' Department at King's College London, where she studied under Professor J. K. Laughton, naval historian, confirmed liberal imperialist and, significantly, an acolyte of E. A. Freeman.

Despite Woolf's later insistence that she was virtually self-educated, Anna Snaith and Christine Kenyon-Jones have discovered that Virginia Stephen in fact 'studied at King's College Ladies' Department between 1897 and 1901, between the ages of 15 and 19'.[47] For the first two years, before focusing exclusively on Latin and Greek, Virginia Stephen attended English and Continental history lectures covering 'historical periods from 1660–1702, 1702–1748, and 1748–1789'.[48] Unfortunately the syllabuses for these two years do not include details of recommended reading; however, reference to the syllabus of 1900, the year after Virginia Stephen ceased her history studies, gives some idea of the approach taken by Professor Laughton. For a course covering the accession of Edward II to the coronation of Henry VII, Laughton recommends Samuel Rawson Gardiner's *Student's History of England* and Cyril Ransome's *Advanced History of England*.[49] While these general textbooks seem rather unchallenging in contrast to Virginia Stephen's precocious consumption of Froude, Carlyle and Arnold, Laughton's choices are revealing in terms of his own professional values. Samuel Rawson Gardiner was an historian Laughton admired and who had previously held the role of Professor of Modern History at King's College London. Gardiner, like Freeman, was politically liberal and an exponent of a 'scientific' approach to history. Laughton's biographer has described the 'huge impact' both Gardiner and Freeman had on Laughton's historical practice: 'Laughton's historical studies matched Freeman's specification, they were directed at the present, they took the form of foundation building from archival sources, and were "scientific" in their rigour'.[50]

We need not rely entirely upon Laughton's recommended reading to confirm that he was disseminating a Whiggish narrative of history to his students in the Ladies' Department of King's. Historian G. P. Gooch, who studied with Laughton at King's for three years before going to Cambridge, gives a mixed account of his mentor in his memoir:

> The brightest luminary was Sir John Laughton, the leading British authority on sea power and founder of the Navy Records Society. His lectures were rather uninspiring, for he conceived of history as a record of events rather than a panorama of the many-sided life of humanity.[51]

Gooch's criticism of Laughton's lectures provides an insight into the sort of historical narrative Virginia Stephen would have encountered at King's and perhaps offers an explanation for her own approach to history at Morley. Something of Laughton's conception of 'history as a record of events' is surely identifiable in Virginia Stephen's desire to teach English history 'from the beginning' (*PA* 255). Snaith and Kenyon-Jones suggest in their article that their research:

> alters not only Daugherty's claim that 'Virginia Woolf basically educates herself,' but also that she has 'next to no experience as a student' […] by the time she started teaching [at Morley], Woolf would have had a fair amount of exposure to different teaching styles and methods.[52]

While Laughton's 'uninspiring' teaching style may have influenced Virginia Stephen's decision to avoid lecturing in favour of a more conversational approach to teaching at Morley, as well as sealing her lifelong dislike of this form of teaching, it is equally true that his linear approach to history influenced her syllabus at Morley.

While it would be unwise to overstate the degree to which Virginia Stephen was formally trained in history, it is certainly true that her particular (and somewhat sentimental) devotion to the work of historians Thomas Carlyle and Thomas Babington Macaulay – her 'cherished Macaulay' – is almost exactly mirrored in historian G. M. Trevelyan's account of his youthful reading matter. He refers specifically to 'the sweet cake of Gibbon, Macaulay, Carlyle, etc., on which I was gorging myself'.[53] This parity between Virginia Stephen's and Trevelyan's adolescent reading usefully reminds us of their shared late-Victorian historical moment; however, Trevelyan figures in the story of Virginia Stephen's period at Morley and in the 'Morley Sketch' for other more intriguing reasons.

Born in 1876, G. M. Trevelyan was the great-nephew of Thomas Babington Macaulay, the forefather of the Whig historians, and as such belonged to the intellectual, as well as the landed, aristocracy. We can see from his account of his own practice as an historian that Trevelyan considered it a 'family tradition'.[54] With mock-judiciousness Trevelyan insists 'I have not been an original but a traditional kind of historian' and goes on to suggest that his primary preoccupation as an historian has been to maintain the literary quality of written histories, which distinguished the work of his great-uncle, and so offer a 'counterpoise' to the 'scientific' works of history that were then in vogue.[55] After studying and then lecturing at Cambridge until 1903, where he encountered many of the young men who would later make up the Bloomsbury group (whom he loathed), Trevelyan moved to London in order to write history and, as S. P. Rosenbaum has noted, to engage in various good works, including lecturing in history at Morley College.[56]

As a resident of Kensington, the son-in-law of the dreaded Mrs Humphry Ward and a thoroughly establishment figure, G. M. Trevelyan must have embodied all that Virginia Stephen in 1905 would have most despised. Indeed, her account of her first visit to Morley College in her diary includes a barbed reference to Trevelyan that jars with her enthusiastic description of her future students: 'In the evening to Morley College soirée in the Waterloo Road: where I discussed a class with nice enthusiastic working women who say they love books [...] G.[eorge] Trevelyan made a dull & raucous speech' (*PA* 218). The instinctive dislike revealed in this passage only sharpened during her time at Morley. In the 'Morley Sketch' we see this conflict coming to a head. Virginia Stephen furiously records the details of the curtailment of her history class; her arguments with Morley's management and her incredulity and scorn for the series of popular, Saturday lectures on the French Revolution that were replacing her history lessons and which were to be given by George Trevelyan himself.[57]

While the fact that it was Trevelyan who presented this series of lectures is superficially interesting, in that it appears to lend authority to the popular depiction of the early Bloomsbury group as a tremendous palimpsest of social relations and antagonisms, I am less interested in this biographical intrigue than in the way in which this connection with Trevelyan encourages us to read the 'Morley Sketch' as engaging in historically specific, theoretical debates about the value of history and the historical imagination.[58]

In light of this, Virginia Stephen's austere tone in the 'Morley Sketch' takes on new meaning. This is particularly true of the sketch's final paragraph where she expresses her profound objection to the cancellation of her course:

> Accordingly I am to stop at {H} <King> John: & turn my mind next term to essay writing & the expression of ideas. Meanwhile, my four women, {are to be} <can> hear eight lectures on the French Revolution if they wish to continue their historical learning: {& then? Which from a knowledge of the state of their minds I conceive will be wholly useless to them. It will be another temptation to them to.} And what, I ask, will be the use of that? Eight lectures dropped into their minds, {without any <which are wholly unable to>} like meteors from another sphere infringing on this planet, {& which [has has] merely time to gape for a moment & ask what are you to whence? before they} <dissolving into dust again>. {So fragmentary and disconnected will these eight} Such disconnected fragments will these eight lectures be: to people who{se mind} <have> absolutely no power of receiving them as part of a whole, & {applying the} applying them {in} to their proper ends.

This outrage is certainly evidence of Virginia Stephen's hurt pride and her insistence on her students' inability to engage with Trevelyan's lectures might seem like proof of her belief in their intellectual inferiority. Her understanding of history as a 'whole' and her suggestive reference to the 'proper ends' of historical learning also appear to suggest a commitment to the Whig values of continuity and progress expressed by E. A. Freeman and J. R. Green.

Virginia Stephen's use of language in the 'Morley Sketch' links it to Freeman's compendious *History of the Norman Conquest*, upon which she relied heavily when planning her lessons and whose rigorous style she admired (*PA* 278–9). Her distinctive planetary and scientific language in the passage above echoes that used in Freeman's introduction. Virginia Stephen's description of the lectures as 'dissolving', 'disconnected fragments' recalls Freeman's use of the word 'fused' in the following description of the state of European society at the time of the conquest:

> Those elements, Roman, Teutonic, Imperial and Ecclesiastical, which stood, as it were, side by side in the system of the early middle age, were then being fused together into the later system of feudal, papal, crusading Europe.[59]

That Virginia Stephen's criticisms of Trevelyan's lecture series in the 'Morley Sketch' are delivered using phrases that not only ape

Freeman's prose style, but also, more generally, call upon scientific tropes of astronomy and chemistry, allows us to read her objections to the lectures not simply as an expression of personal dislike but as signalling her alliance with current 'scientific' approaches to history against Trevelyan's populist efforts in his public Saturday lectures. In a letter to Violet Dickinson, just a few weeks before drafting the 'Morley Sketch', she asks: 'Do you feel convinced I *can* write? I am going to produce a real historical work this summer; for which I have solidly read and annotated 4 volumes of medieval English' (*L1* 202). Virginia Stephen's determination to 'produce a real historical work' encourages us to return to the element of performativity in the narrative voice of the 'Morley Sketch' and consider whether the dogmatic tone of this final paragraph could also be read as preparatory work on her authoritative, historian's voice for the work she was planning.

Despite her theoretical criticisms of Trevelyan's lectures, Virginia Stephen's line of argument in her 'Morley Sketch' is very similar to the one executed by Trevelyan in his lecture series. In his introductory lecture on 'England at the time of the French Revolution', Trevelyan states: 'It is my business as an historian, to show you that the past has been responsible for you; it is your own business to deduce from this the corresponding fact that you are responsible for the future.'[60] Not only does the title of Trevelyan's lecture recall the 'Morley Sketch's' prized emphasis on English history, his core, almost spiritual, belief in the direct connection between the past and present also chimes with Virginia Stephen's conviction that a knowledge of English history is a kind of moral entitlement and one that can 'give them a new interest in life'.

Reading the 'Morley Sketch' in the context of Virginia Stephen's contemporary reading of history and theoretical disputes within the discipline at the time, we can see that her alignment with Whig history ran deeper than just an adolescent devotion to Macaulay's romantic, grand narratives. While I would argue that the sketch reveals a commitment to English history and a conservative attachment to a unified English story, exemplified in her account of her weekly subject matter – 'So we {tramped through} made our way through Early British, & Roman, & Angles Saxons & Danes, & Normans, till we {had} were on the more substantial ground of the Plantagenet Kings' – through her concurrent efforts to get her female students to explore and inscribe their own personal histories, Virginia Stephen also inaugurates a different, competing mode of everyday, feminist history.

When introducing her student, Miss Burke, Virginia Stephen refers to the biographical account the latter has been writing:

> This sister, Burke was her name, had been as I found, writing that account of her own life which I had suggested before. It {was} <did> not take up many pages & only described certain {&} memories of childhood; it was a curious little production, {as it} <floundering> among long words, {&} involved {sentences} <periods,> with {an [?] tendency sprinkling of sententious remarks <through> like} <sudden ponderous> {reflections thrown} moral sentiments thrown into the {middle} <midst>. But she could write grammatical sentences, which followed each other {logical} logically enough; and she had evidently some facility of expression; in other circumstances I suppose, she would have been a writer!

Although Virginia Stephen's efforts to get her students to record the details of their lives may be dismissed as a standard schoolroom exercise, it is important to consider this project as operating in conjunction with her rigorous course in English history. The way Virginia Stephen describes and critiques Miss Burke's autobiographical writing in the passage above encourages us to see these as complementary pursuits. While her deleted reference to Miss Burke's 'sprinkling of sententious remarks' and the disparaging comment about 'moral sentiments thrown into the {middle} <midst>' that replaces it, can be read as rather superior, aesthetic complaints on Virginia Stephen's part, her desire to purge Miss Burke's writing of its sentimentality and moralising also reveals Virginia Stephen's desire to train her students to be sensitive but accurate historians of their own lives.[61] The instruction in English history 'from the beginning' these four women received, then, was not simply a patriotic exercise but a form of historiographical training; by conveying a traditional, linear narrative of English history, Virginia Stephen was preparing her students to intervene with their own personal histories.[62]

Daugherty has argued that Virginia Stephen's approach to teaching and the strategies she employed in her classroom represent a consistent effort on her part to 'empower' her students.[63] I agree that her history classes and her evangelical and possessive determination that her 'four women' should know the history of England is linked to Virginia Stephen's belief in the enfranchising possibilities of understanding a collective past. The distinctive coupling of grand narratives and personal, everyday stories – which is so striking in the juxtaposing in the 'Morley Sketch' of the 'solid ground of the Plantagenet Kings' with Miss Burke's personal history, her 'curious little production' – give us a vital insight into the heterodox character of Virginia Stephen's historical imagination.

While the 'Morley Sketch' arguably celebrates diverse historical narratives, attempting to synthesise the claims of both establishment and marginalised histories, it would be unwise to ignore the tension that accompanies this project. This is most evident in the close of the 'Morley Sketch'. Virginia Stephen's anxious references to fragmentation and dissolving not only register her commitment to the idea of history as a whole but also point to her fears that her efforts to fuse two registers of history are now just so much 'dust'. We encounter this tension in a variety of different incarnations throughout Virginia Woolf's writing where it continues to complicate but also animate her thinking about history. It is at the heart of Woolf's dialogue on the value of life writing and biography throughout her essays and is evident in her grappling with the role of history in fiction and vice versa.[64] This tension is also central to Virginia Stephen's early short story 'The Journal of Mistress Joan Martyn', in which it manifests itself in the ambivalent figure of historian and antiquarian Rosamond Merridew and her quest for original materials.

'The Journal of Mistress Joan Martyn' (1906)

Written during the summer of 1906, 'The Journal of Mistress Joan Martyn' shares many of the abiding concerns of the 'Morley Sketch', drafted almost exactly one year before it.[65] The first half of the 'The Journal' tells the story of the historian Rosamond Merridew, whose search for primary source material brings her to the ramshackle country hall of the Martyn family and their wealth of family papers, including the diary of their fifteenth-century ancestor Joan Martyn. The second half of the story contains a transcription of the antiquarian's discovery, the eponymous journal.

The text opens with Rosamond Merridew's reflections on the nature of history and a defence of her approach to the subject, for which she has received much criticism. Although primarily focusing on 'the system of land tenure in the 13th[,] 14th and 15th Centuries' (*CSF* 34), Merridew has:

> not scrupled to devote several pages [...] to an attempt to show, vividly as in a picture, some scene from the life of the time; here I knock at the serf's door, and find him roasting rabbits he has poached. (*CSF* 34)

As well as recalling Woolf's teaching techniques and her attempt to create a 'vivid' 'scene', Merridew's emphasis on the historical value of everyday life may be read as an articulation of what is explored in the 'Morley Sketch'. It is tempting to read the discovery of Joan Martyn's diary and its peculiar but subtle expressiveness as inspired by Miss Burke's 'curious little production'.

Melba Cuddy-Keane has also pointed out the connection between this early story's historical themes and Virginia Stephen's period of teaching at Morley. She describes it as early evidence of Virginia Stephen's conception of 'history as a dialogic interaction between the historical text and the historian's understanding'.[66] Going further, some critics have identified Rosamond Merridew's views on history as expressing those of her creator. While Louise DeSalvo argues that 'Rosamond Merridew's quest for a female past' encodes Virginia Stephen's 'own epic quest for a mythic mother as muse',[67] Sabine Hotho-Jackson suggests that Merridew's views about writing history are 'clearly Virginia Stephen's own'.[68] Emphasising the grating quality of Merridew's narrative voice, however, Leena Kore Schröder has challenged those who would identify this character too strongly with her author, suggesting that such an analysis 'begs the question of why Merridew isn't therefore a more attractive character?'[69]

Much has been made of the female-centred history that Merridew appears to promote. However, I would argue that the story deploys subtle strategies that encourage the reader to question Rosamond Merridew's reliability as a narrator as well as her credibility as an historian. From the very beginning of the story we are aware of a narrative wariness towards Merridew and her heraldic account of her career as an historian:

> My readers may not know, perhaps, who I am. Therefore, although such a practice is unusual and unnatural [...] I will not hesitate to explain that I am Rosamond Merridew [...] and that I have won considerable fame among my profession for the researches I have made into the system of land tenure in mediaeval England. Berlin has heard my name; Frankfurt would give a soirée in my honour; and I am not absolutely unknown in one or two secluded rooms in Oxford and in Cambridge. (*CSF* 33)

We might read this passage's curious mixture of mock-humility and sheer boastfulness as a humorous attempt at characterisation; however, there is a certain jarring quality that runs beneath this. Merridew's initial reluctance to introduce herself and her peculiar suggestion that 'such a practice is unusual and unnatural' is not only inconsistent with her clear delight in setting out her professional credentials but also introduces the terms 'unusual' and 'unnatural' at an early stage, meaning that they hang ominously over Merridew's subsequent explanation of her historical practice. This first and representative example of the way in which Virginia Stephen's pointed use of language disrupts Merridew's determinedly jolly narrative is just enough to assure moments of doubt in her readers' minds.

Similarly, the decision for Merridew's area of historical expertise to be medieval systems of land tenure may be read as a barbed and ironic choice that implicitly links Merridew's professional preoccupation with feudalism with her unscrupulous, even exploitative, methods of attaining historical documents. There is certainly an air of lordly entitlement in Merridew's description of her 'enterprise':

> I present myself at old farm houses, decayed halls, parsonages, church vestries always with the same demand. Have you any old papers to show me? As you may imagine the palmy days for this kind of sport are over; age has become the most merchantable of qualities; and the state moreover with its Commissions has put an end for the most part to the enterprise of individuals. (*CSF* 33)

Although Merridew complains that her 'poor private voice' is robbed of its 'persuasion' by the new state interest in the old documents she hunts for, this passage reveals that it is Merridew who often holds the upper hand in her endeavours. Far from characterising herself as a scholarly researcher, Merridew's use of the language of commerce, exchange and, again with an apt feudal inflection, the language of the hunt, casts her instead as a cross between a wayward cavalier and highwayman. Her description of her research as an 'enterprise' and her interest in the 'merchantable qualities' of the material she tracks down, coupled with the humble places she pillages them from, seem to undermine Merridew's self-portrait of a diligent and authoritative historian.

The inconsistency of Merridew's story and her slips into the language of commerce, hint that her drives and intentions are rather more complex and less noble than we may initially think. In his discussion of the story Engler Bernd also suggests that Rosamond Merridew's narrative is unreliable.[70] Bernd argues that this story is a 'sophisticated satire on the authority of both traditional and revisionist views of historiography' and that Merridew 'is an embarrassingly incompetent woman historian'; however, he overlooks the fact that Merridew is actually very effective in her acquisition of the antique journal and the significant political implications of Virginia Stephen's critique of Merridew's practice.

This dubious element of Merridew's activity becomes increasingly clear during the first half of the story and is especially pronounced during her dealings with the Martyns. Merridew's observation on discovering the house is telling:

> Here was one of those humble little old halls, then, which survive almost untouched, and practically unknown for centuries and centuries, because they are too insignificant to be pulled down or rebuilt; and their owners are too poor to be ambitious. (*CSF* 35–6)

The emphasis on both the seclusion of the location and the poverty Merridew anticipates in its owners hints at the power imbalance she depends upon to access hidden family treasures. This exploitation is made explicit in Merridew's excited aside:

> This is the kind of place, I thought, as I stood with my hand on the bell, where the owners are likely to possess exquisite manuscripts, and sell them as easily [to] the first rag man who comes along, as they would sell their pig wash. (*CSF* 36)

And then in her admission that: 'There are certain rules in the game of the antiquary, of which the first and simplest is that you must not state your object at the first encounter' (*CSF* 36).

While Merridew excuses these mercenary impulses by congratulating the hall's owners in advance for their lack of sentimentality and self-consciousness about their ancient home, her quick eye for markers of class in the Martyns' appearance and home reveals the significance of their relative poverty to her scheme, for example, her observations that Mrs Martyn had been 'using a machine on a pair of trousers' and that she 'looked like a housekeeper' (*CSF* 36) and her sensitivity to the inflections of both Mr and Mrs Martyn's speech – 'tinged' with dialect (*CSF* 37). It is precisely the Martyns' 'present poverty' (*CSF* 37), a fact repeated throughout the first half of the story, that encourages Merridew to pursue possible family papers in the belief she could get them for a 'good' price.

The Martyns' rosy faces and their Norfolk accents denote their low-class status and link them within the imaginative logic of the story not to their land-owning Martyn ancestors but rather to the 'bruised and battered' fifteenth-century family servants William and Anne, with Mrs Martyn's sewing machine having replaced Anne's needle and thread (*CSF* 46). Likewise, Merridew, travelling through the countryside in her own carriage, is reminiscent of a feudal baron in the process of collecting tithes. The two halves of the story are linked in other ways that collectively work to expose the exploitative workings of Merridew's antiquarianism. The most striking example of this is the way in which Merridew's desire to strike a deal with Mr Martyn for his precious hoard of manuscripts is mirrored in the fifteenth-century Martyns' efforts to marry their daughter Joan off to their neighbour, Sir Amyas. Joan is ambivalent about the prospect of her marriage and her use of the language of brokering and bargaining – 'I lose my youth however, and it is high time that a bargain were struck' (*CSF* 51) – recalls both Merridew's talk of buying and selling and the present-day Mr Martyn's ominous statement: 'We deal in grandfathers here' (*CSF* 39). In this way, Merridew's intention to buy the Martyn papers is obliquely linked to the exchange of Joan Martyn in a marriage contract negotiated by her parents that she describes in her journal. By stripping both procedures of any romance and revealing their purely transactional character, Virginia

Stephen encodes a critique of Merridew's self-serving professional practice.

Merridew's theory of history is as problematic in terms of its dismissive and reductive construction of class as her practice. In one of the 'vivid' digressions that distinguish her historical work, 'The Manor Rolls', Merridew shows a remarkably sentimentalised and nostalgic vision of life and class relations in medieval England:

> here I knock at the serf's door, and find him roasting rabbits he has poached; I show you the Lord of the Manor setting out on some journey [...] In another room I show you Dame Elinor, at work with her needle. (*CSF* 34)

Not only does the movement from one cosy vignette to another recall the nursery-rhyme rhythm of 'Sing a song of sixpence', the temperate movement from one scene to another implies an ease and equality between the actors – serf, Lord of the Manor and Dame Elinor. The depiction of the jolly serf about to enjoy a feast of rabbit is revealed to be particularly specious by an episode in the journal section of the story in which Joan Martyn records a visit to some of her father's tenants:

> Beatrice Somers, and her husband Peter live here, and they have children; but it was more like the burrow of some rabbit on the heath than the house of a man [...] There was but a rotten log on which a woman sat, nursing a baby [...] But she did not move or speak; and I doubt whether she could have spoken, or whether snarling and howling was her only language. (*CSF* 52–3)

Particularly striking is the recurrence of the rabbit imagery we encounter earlier in Merridew's description of the serf preparing his dinner. By comparing the Somers' home to 'the burrow of some rabbit', Virginia Stephen transforms the peasant into the hunted, non-verbal creature that Merridew had blithely imagined him cooking a few pages earlier. Joan Martyn's sneering description of the woman's speech as 'snarling and howling' obscurely recalls Merridew's references to the Martyns' Norfolk dialect but also, more interestingly, signals the peasantry's lack of agency. In the following passage this is made even clearer:

> These are the people we must rule; and tread under foot, and scourge them to do the only work they are fitted to do; as they will tear us to pieces with their fangs. Thus Anthony spoke as he took us away [...] Still the sight of that ugly face spoilt the rest of the walk; since it seemed that even my dear country bred pests like these. (*CSF* 53)

The brutality and contempt of this passage and the one above are inconsistent with the dream-like quality of the rest of the journal section of the story. The uncharacteristic digression on the need to 'rule', 'scourge' and stamp out any signs of insurrection among the peasantry, coupled with the emphasis on their lack of language, allows Virginia Stephen to present a brief but haunting picture of a suppressed and voiceless class, far too obscure and too deeply buried to be written into Merridew's 'The Manor Rolls'.

'The Journal of Mistress Martyn' has traditionally been read as inaugurating Virginia Woolf's life-long preoccupation with obscure lives and, as DeSalvo suggests,

> presag[ing] many of the central concerns of Woolf's later works: the role of women in the process of history; the opportunities denied women in centuries past; the institutions of marriage; the inadequacy of histories as they are traditionally written; the necessity of seeing history in terms of individuals.[71]

The glimmer of the hidden history of class in the extracts above not only acts as an internal reproach to Merridew's failure to properly account for these lives in her histories, but perhaps also reveals that Virginia Stephen recognised this as a wider failure in contemporary historiography.

I began by suggesting it is possible to read 'The Journal' as an extension of Virginia Stephen's desire for her students at Morley College to write their own life stories, to intervene in traditional histories with their own. What I have characterised as Virginia Stephen's critically sidelined interest in the relationship between history and social class in 'The Journal' should also be read as an albeit ambivalent response to her time at Morley College. Merridew's reliance on the power structures inherent in the class system and the brutal exclusion of the voice of Beatrice Somers from Joan Martyn's journal represent a change in Virginia Stephen's thinking about the sanctity of the English story 'from the beginning' that we find in the 'Morley Sketch'. 'The Journal' engages in an intertextual commentary and critique of Virginia Stephen's sketch from a year earlier – flagging up this previous work's blithe treatment of class and uncritical commitment to grand narratives of English history. The 'Morley Sketch' is also a significant intertext for Woolf's first novel, *The Voyage Out*, a text that is similarly marked with the imaginative legacies of Woolf's experiences at Morley College.

The Voyage Out (1915)

The Voyage Out opens with a chaotic tour of central London's 'mass of streets, squares, and public buildings' (*VO* 5) from the Strand to the Embankment and finally reaching the glowering spectacle of Waterloo Bridge. Helen Ambrose, whose perspective we assume, recognises the realities of everyday London life for the 'innumerable poor people' (*VO* 6) who populate the city. Her momentary alarm is, however, neutralised as Helen passes 'a building put up by the London County Council for Night Schools' (*VO* 6). This night school constitutes not only the most striking reference to Morley College throughout Woolf's fiction but also registers a deeply ambivalent message. The night school represents a beacon of humanity and progress illuminating the otherwise 'gloomy' west-end, just as the electric lamps lighting windows appear to Helen Ambrose as 'a small golden tassel on the edge of a vast black cloak' (*VO* 6). It is unwise to take this saintly and reassuring presence too much for granted. The positioning of the night school and Helen Ambrose's 'great relief' at coming across it also seem to indicate an element of satirical mistrust of the building's symbolic power. The London County Council and its night schools are implicitly linked to a bourgeois horror of 'the poor' and their authorised means of improving them. As such, it appears that what scholars have recognised as *The Voyage Out*'s central critique of Edwardian English society is from the novel's opening bound up with the contradictory figure of the night school.[72]

Virginia Woolf began drafting the novel that was eventually published as *The Voyage Out* in 1915, in mid-1907, while she was still (albeit unhappily) teaching at Morley College and still Virginia Stephen. The protracted process of drafting and revision that characterised Woolf's writing of *The Voyage Out* distances the final version from her experiences at Morley by too many years for the connection between these pursuits to share the immediacy of her early story. The ways in which *The Voyage Out* responds to and engages with Woolf's experiences of teaching at Morley are more oblique, existing as linguistic echoes and haunting motifs. It is the subtle gestures to Woolf's only half-remembered classroom and her attempts to enunciate more fully the anxieties about gender and class that emerged there that concern this discussion of *The Voyage Out*.

Returning to the intriguing deletions of the 'Morley Sketch' is a good place to start. As I mentioned earlier, the part of this sketch concerned with Virginia Stephen's student Miss Williams is a mess of deletions and insertions. She stumbles in particular over the subject of Miss Williams's profession; however, in one deleted half-sentence she expresses some of the curious mixture of hostility, curiosity and fellowship that defined her relationship to her working-class student: 'So we made much of this [having] we found we had a good deal in common; & I explored some of the more rather subterranean passages of my own profession'. As well as evoking all the grime and sordid dealings of Grub Street and striking a superior tone, her reference to the 'subterranean passages of my own profession' shows how she imaginatively identified with Miss Williams. 'Subterranean passages' is also a phrase that rings with sinister associations, recalling sewers, dungeons and catacombs and suggesting imprisonment, confinement and even death. From the terrible, dank tunnel of Rachel Vinrace's nightmare to the apparently innocent passages of the *Euphrosyne* and the numerous corridors of the hotel in Santa Marina peopled by comic Brits abroad, the motif of the passage recurs throughout *The Voyage Out*,[73] animating Woolf's critique of contemporary class and gender politics in this novel.

The Voyage Out tells the story of a young English woman, Rachel Vinrace, and her journey on her father's trading ship, the *Euphrosyne*, to a colonial town in South America where she accompanies her aunt and uncle, Helen and Ridley Ambrose.[74] Disparagingly described as 'an unlicked girl' (*VO* 16) by her aunt, Rachel has been brought up in isolation and ignorance by two spinster aunts in Richmond and much is made of her lack of a proper education (*VO* 26, 27, 71). Once in Santa Marina, Helen sets about educating Rachel and shaping her into a 'reasonable human being' (*VO* 86).

She enlists the help of two young men, the misogynist and Gibbon-loving St John Hirst, and Terence Hewett, an insouciant, aspiring novelist, both of whom are staying, along with a community of other English tourists, at Santa Marina's only hotel. After becoming engaged to Hewett during a boat trip into the jungle, Rachel dies suddenly of a mystery illness.

The imagery of the passage and the attendant suggestions of constriction, intolerance and menace that accompany it throughout *The Voyage Out* are introduced in the very first sentence of the novel: 'As the streets that lead from the Strand to the Embankment are very narrow, it is better not to walk down them arm-in-arm' (VO 3). The note of warning in this passage and the depiction of single-minded office workers intolerant of eccentricity are significant. Coupled with Helen Ambrose's recognition of the grimy 'skeleton' of poverty that exists 'beneath' the bustling beauty of the city, the novel's first few pages evoke 'subterranean passages' and announce the novel's preoccupation with what is concealed beneath convention and the performance of social roles.

This theme of narrowness frames the novel's first chapter as it concludes with a scene that directly recalls this first one. Having reached the *Euphrosyne* and been reintroduced to her niece after a gap of some years, Helen Ambrose reflects with annoyance that 'her worst suspicions' about her niece's dependence and lack of sophistication are confirmed as she struggles down a passage: 'she went down the passage lurching from side to side, and fending off the wall now with her right arm, now with her left; at each lurch she exclaimed emphatically, "Damn!"' (VO 16). This is both humorous and unsettling. Although we are perhaps meant to admire Helen's feistiness and honesty, there is something in the presentation of her struggle in the passage which evokes not only the narrowness of Rachel's outlook but also of Helen's – it is worth noting that this passage scene concludes a chapter in which Helen has done her best to 'promote' male talk at dinner and found her niece's skills as a hostess wanting. This image of Helen fighting her way down the passage, like several other key episodes that invoke the motif of the passage, is absent from the earlier draft of the novel *Melymbrosia*, where the relative chapter ends instead with a bird's eye view of the *Euphrosyne* moving down the Thames towards the sea. This is not the only instance in which some of the more explicit social critique that Louise DeSalvo admires in

Melymbrosia appears to have been channelled into a reference to a passage in *The Voyage Out*.

The motif of the passage remains prominent throughout the novel's account of the physical passage to South America and it continues to be used to illuminate and critique social conventions and gender roles. A key example of this appears in a description of a nightmare Rachel has early in the journey:

> She dreamt that she was walking down a long tunnel, which grew so narrow by degrees that she could touch the damp bricks on either side. At length the tunnel opened and became a vault; she found herself trapped in it, bricks meeting her wherever she turned, alone with a little deformed man who squatted on the floor gibbering, with long nails. His face was pitted and like the face of an animal.[75] (*VO* 68)

This dream takes place almost immediately after Rachel has been aggressively kissed by another passenger on the *Euphrosyne*, ex-Tory MP Richard Dalloway, an experience she finds deeply disturbing (*VO* 67). Suzette Henke has noted the way in which the dream is charged with 'male sexual brutality' and it seems clear that the dream's central threat of entrapment, coupled with the menacing and bestial figure of the gibbering man, can be read as an encoded critique of the patriarchal domination Rachel experienced throughout her censored and circumscribed upbringing in Richmond. Rachel's response in the dream of lying 'still and cold as death' (*VO* 68) also echoes her reaction to Dalloway's kiss – 'a chill of body and mind crept over her' (*VO* 67).[76] Along similar lines, Marianne DeKoven has persuasively read the tunnel and vault in this episode as 'vagina and womb', arguing that the deformed man is 'a figure of the distortion of the female in patriarchal culture: as Freud reveals, woman in patriarchy can only be visible or explicable as a "deformed man"'.[77]

The language of enclosure, the vaults and, crucially, underground passages that fill the dream sequence are not just Rachel's unconscious responses to Dalloway's aggressive overture but also represent a confused amalgam of this and another invasive episode experienced by Rachel during the voyage – her encounter with Mrs Chailey, the Vinraces' loyal servant. Elaborating on the suggestive motif of the 'subterranean passages' of the 'Morley Sketch', Rachel's dream sequence not only articulates the novel's wider critique of patriarchal society but also expresses in tandem anxieties about social class and status.

Close inspection reveals that Rachel's dream is a far more accurate re-staging of her encounter with Mrs Chailey than an unconscious rendering of the Richard Dalloway episode. Determined to have a new room aboard the ship, Mrs Chailey blocks Rachel's path down one of the boat's passages: 'But just as she was turning with a view perhaps to finding some employment, she was intercepted by a woman who was so broad and so thick that to be intercepted by her was inevitable' (*VO* 21). Not only does this instance, with its daunting repetition of the word 'intercepted', a flourish absent from the version of this scene in *Melymbrosia*, anticipate Rachel's overwhelming sense of being 'trapped' in her dream, it also harks back to a key episode in the 'Morley Sketch' where Miss Williams is 'cornered' by Virginia Stephen and forced to 'reveal herself'. With Rachel at the mercy of Mrs Chailey's 'rock-like' constitution and compelled 'to descend and inspect a large pile of linen heaped upon a table' (*VO* 21), the class-based power dynamic so forcefully illustrated in the 'Morley Sketch', in which Woolf occupies the superior position and Miss Williams the inferior one, is inverted and problematised in *The Voyage Out*. Rachel's lack of interest in the linen and her consternation that 'a woman of fifty should behave like a child and come cringing to a girl because she wanted to sit where she had not leave to sit' (*VO* 22) reflect her discomfort with her position as mistress in the infantilising binary of servant and mistress.

Rachel flees from her altercation with Mrs Chailey 'up on to the deck' (*VO* 22) and much of the discomfort of this scene, and certainly the desire for flight, are reiterated later in the dream sequence. As Andrea Lewis has noted in her discussion of the politics of empire and gender in *The Voyage Out*, the 'little deformed man' (*VO* 68) with whom Rachel is confined in her dream 'calls to mind Mrs Chailey's disproportionate body'.[78] I would add that the 'squatting' position he occupies also affects something of the servility of the servant's body, forever hunched in a bow. And while the creature's 'long nails' and 'pitted face' do register the threat that Henke implies, this is ameliorated by the pathetic adjectives used to describe him: 'little' and 'deformed'. The man's proportions share much with the pitiful curiosities that decorate Mrs Chailey's cabin – 'china pugs, tea-sets in miniature, cups stamped floridly with the arms of the city of Bristol, hair-pin boxes crusted with shamrock' (*VO* 22). It is then possible to read Rachel's horror at being enclosed with this figure, not as the rigid terror some critics have suggested, but rather as a reproduction of her instinctive recoil from Mrs Chailey and her desire to escape from the ideological binds that connect them as mistress and servant.

More interesting still are the ways in which Rachel herself is identified with the terrible creature of her dreams. After her dream and after the Dalloways have disembarked, Rachel has a revelation during a discussion with her aunt, in which Helen explains a woman's (inferior) role in sexual politics by way of an explanation for Mr Dalloway's kiss: 'By this new light she saw her life for the first time a creeping hedged-in thing, driven cautiously between high walls, here turned aside, there plunged into darkness, made dull and crippled for ever' (*VO* 72). There is the obvious recurring imagery of the passage in this extract, however by describing her life as a 'creeping, hedged-in thing' (*VO* 72) Woolf recalls not only the little man trapped in his vault but also the 'barbarian men' who Rachel imagines coming 'scuffling down the passages [...] to snuffle at her door' (*VO* 68). This provocative passage does not feature in *Melymbrosia* and so the ambivalent identification between the dream creature and Rachel herself is not so clear. This is an instance in which the imagery of the passage is used in a way that complicates the political implications of Woolf's novel, enriching rather than obscuring them.

The dream sequence's re-enactment of Rachel's encounter with Mrs Chailey and the interesting ways in which the language and imagery of the dream recur in Rachel's view of her own life mean it is an episode charged with the competing impulses of recognition and resistance. The mirroring also supports Jane Wheare's reading of Woolf's use of repetition in *The Voyage Out* as the key way in which she 'directs our reading of her narrative'.[79] Here the 'long tunnel, which grew so narrow by degrees' (*VO* 68) reminds us not only of the narrowness of the ship's passages which both Rachel and Mrs Chailey must negotiate, but also gestures to the measured circumscription of both women's lives.

As we have seen through the discussion of Rachel's relationship with Mrs Chailey, the passage is a particularly apt motif for both the experience of servants, obliged to occupy literally the 'subterranean passages' of their below-stairs realm, and also the experience of middle-class daughters compelled by bourgeois values and the tyranny of the 'private house' to remain within its upper network of passages, while its sons escaped to school. In spite of its prominent exotic setting, the world of *The Voyage Out* and its characters is conceived very much in what Woolf would later describe in *Three Guineas* as 'the shadow of the private house' and its strict social codes and values (*TG* 184).

Although none of the action of the novel takes place in the Richmond house Rachel shares with her two aunts, its symbolic significance is confirmed through frequent references and Rachel's own need to mentally revisit it. Immediately after the exchange between Rachel and Mrs Chailey, Rachel retires to her room and during a reverie 'upon the characters of her aunts, their views, and the way they lived' (*VO* 28) recalls an overheard snatch of conversation between her aunts:

> 'And, of course, at half-past ten in the morning one expects to find the housemaid brushing the stairs.' How odd! How unspeakably odd! But she could not explain to herself why suddenly as her aunt spoke the whole system in which they lived had appeared before her eyes as something quite unfamiliar and inexplicable. (*VO* 28)

It is telling that it is Aunt Lucy's complacent assumption about her housemaid's role in the mechanics of her middle-class home and the implied moral rightness of this state of affairs that prompts the opposite response in Rachel, who finds 'the whole system in which they lived' suddenly strange. The expectations and prescriptive roles allotted by her aunt to the housemaid shock Rachel momentarily out of her usually languorous state and force this attempt to enunciate the 'unfamiliar and inexplicable' condition of their lives. Rachel's repeated utterance – 'How odd!' – as well as emphasising the sudden strangeness of the imagined scene with the housemaid also, with its exclamatory punctuation, implies a note of surprised recognition that, again, recalls the contradictory feelings of otherness and familiarity I identified in Woolf's encounter with Miss Williams in the 'Morley Sketch'.

This equivocal quality and its class implications are more pronounced in the earlier draft of the novel, where Rachel explicitly connects the oddness she senses with her aunt's expectations about the housemaid: 'It seemed odd […] that one should ever expect to find a housemaid brushing the stairs' (*M* 39). In the ensuing conversation

Rachel's aunts resist an honest discussion about 'the organisation of labour' (*M* 39), preferring Christian platitudes instead:

> As became Christian ladies, the Misses Vinrace maintained that no human being if she is doing her duty is either ugly or inferior.
> 'What is the mud on your boots Rachel,' Miss Clara explained, 'is good earth in the street.' Therefore it followed that one's feeling to a housemaid was as good a feeling as one could get.
> 'I shudder when I pass them' Rachel confessed. 'I'd rather have a tooth out than speak.' (*M* 39–40)

In this version, Woolf's criticism of Rachel's aunts is stark. They fail to recognise the radical implications of their niece's suggestion that one person expecting another to brush their stairs is odd, with the unsaid implication that it is also wrong, instead assuming she is being snobbish and admonishing her for lack of Christian feeling. Although both aunts are characterised as rather vague, kind and ineffectual, a note of disciplinary warning sounds in their explanation that 'no human being if she is doing her duty is either ugly or inferior' (*M* 39). Their inclusive reference to human beings is undermined by the immediate use of gendered pronouns, making this statement loaded with patriarchal expectations.

And while Rachel's admission that she 'shudders' as she passes the housemaid on the stairs and that she would 'rather have a tooth out than speak' may be interpreted simply as snobbish diffidence, when read in relation to the taut cross-purposes at which she and her aunts are speaking it requires some deeper consideration. The use of the word 'shudder' again registers the faltering recognition, which I would argue defines Woolf's construction of inter-class relations between women in *Melymbrosia* and also *The Voyage Out*. Shuddering seems to be the instinctive response of someone who has been shocked or, more interestingly, someone who has seen a ghost. This conspicuous use of 'shudder' with all its supernatural connotations implies that as she passes the housemaid on the stairs – another of these prominent domestic passages – Rachel indeed sees the maid as her own ghostly double. The housemaid is Rachel's double in terms of their shared experience of patriarchal oppression, which polices their movements and assigns the private house as their proper place. However, both Rachel's and the housemaid's encounters with patriarchy are mediated by their differing class positions; for instance, while it is Rachel's duty to become a 'highly trained' hostess adept at 'promoting men's talk without listening to it' (VO 10) or participating, the housemaid must silently brush the stairs at half-past ten. The housemaid, then, takes on a removed and ghostly quality for Rachel, in order to reflect this slippage.

Gender and class dynamics continue to be explored and critiqued on the stage of the passage when the action of the novel moves to South America.[80] The corridors of Santa Marina's hotel and the activities of its occupants within them are particularly intriguing. Jane Wheare has highlighted the significant insight that characters such as Miss Allan and Mrs Thornbury give us into the unrecorded lives of women.[81] What we discover about these peripheral female characters – their relationships and their values – is dramatised in the network of corridors. David Bradshaw suggests that it is through repeated '[f]igures of circulation' and a 'chain of images concerned with rotation' that Woolf inscribes the 'restricted and unfulfilling' roles assigned to women in Edwardian society – for example, the circuits Rachel and Mrs Dalloway walk around the deck of the *Euphrosyne*.[82] This argument is compelling; however, I will show that from almost our first glimpse of the hotel and its inhabitants it is the space of the passage which becomes symbolic of the enclosed and inhibited quality of women's lives.

At the beginning of chapter 9 the reader encounters a number of the female tourist characters in succession as the narrative winds its way down the hotel's corridor, peering in room after room. We start with Miss Allan, a school mistress engaged in writing a *Primer of English Literature,* as she reads Wordsworth's *Prelude*. She is distracted by the sounds coming from the room next to hers – 'she then became aware of a swishing sound next door – a woman, clearly, putting away her dress' (VO 93) – and speculates on the thinness of the hotel's walls, 'only matchboard' (VO 93). As Miss Allan switches off her light we move to the room next door, which we are told is 'as like in shape as one egg-box is like another' (VO 93). Susan Warrington brushes her hair before a mirror and reflects anxiously on her marital prospects: 'She was thirty years of age, and owing to the number of sisters and the seclusion of life in a country parsonage had as yet had no proposal of marriage' (VO 94). The feeling of progressing down the corridor is then reinforced by the narrator's check-list of room numbers: 'Thirty-six, thirty-seven, thirty-eight' until we come to '[t]hirty-nine [...] a corner room, at the end of the passage', where Mrs Elliot cannot sleep and scolds her husband when he comes to bed late: 'But you know that I never can sleep when I'm waiting for you' (*VO* 95).

From the melancholy of Miss Allan's 'grey petticoats', through the poignant banality of Susan Warrington's diary entry, to the desperation of Mrs Elliot's one-sided conversation with her husband, this episode sympathetically draws out the similarities between the lives of these differently aged women. However, what appears to be a straightforward critique of the circumscribed, egg-box-like nature of explicitly middle-class women's lives is once again complicated by the ghostly figure of the maid:

> The faint but penetrating pulse of an electric bell could now be heard in the corridor. Old Mrs Paley, having woken hungry but without her spectacles, was summoning her maid to find the biscuit-box. The maid having answered the bell, drearily respectful even at this hour though muffled in a mackintosh, the passage was left in silence. (*VO* 95)

Just as Woolf implies Rachel Vinrace's complicity in maintaining an oppressive class system in her dealings with Mrs Chailey, here our sympathy for Miss Allan, Susan Warrington and Mrs Elliot is cut short by this insight into old Mrs Paley's selfish sense of entitlement, which is enhanced by her pure but banal greediness for a biscuit. Woolf again wrangles with the ways in which class mediates women's encounters with patriarchy.

Like the maid for whom the passage is intimately linked to her low-class position and her servitude – in the episode above she must rush down the corridor to wait on her mistress and earlier she is confined to the staircase she must sweep – this space is also the province of the hotel's resident prostitute who seems to be perpetually, furtively wandering down its corridors. Hewett sees her 'crossing from one room to another' in the 'dimly lighted' passage, and she is finally evicted after she is noticed by Mr Thornbury, who 'was doddering about the passages very late' one night (*VO* 178, 290).[83]

Woolf returns repeatedly to the liminal space of the passage in order to make critical points not only about the position of women in society, but crucially their relationships with one another. In *The Voyage Out* women are constantly meeting each other, getting in each other's way and misunderstanding each other in this space. A good example of this comes after the sermon in the hotel when Rachel spends her afternoon moving between rooms of female guests and encountering others in the corridors. Rachel and Miss Allan, 'completely equipped for Sunday tea', make their way downstairs but are impeded by Mrs Paley in her bath chair. The old woman fails to hear or understand Miss Allan's platitude 'that people are so like their boots', forcing Miss Allan to repeat the joke four times leading to Rachel's exasperated flight from the corridor: 'This misunderstanding, which involved a complete block in the passage, seemed to her unbearable' (*VO* 244). Rachel's guttural and furious response to being trapped by 'old Mrs Paley blocking up the passage' recalls her reaction to being intercepted by Mrs Chailey on the *Euphrosyne*. In both episodes it is the failure of honest communication between women that upsets her – Mrs Chailey's subterfuge with the sheets and Miss Allan's well-meaning but insipid adage.

One of the last evocations of the passage comes in Rachel's feverish nightmare just before her death:

> Rachel again shut her eyes, and found herself walking through a tunnel under the Thames, where there were little deformed women sitting in archways playing cards, while the bricks of which the wall was made oozed with damp, which collected into drops and slid down the wall. But the little old women became Helen and Nurse McInnis after a time, standing in the window whispering, whispering incessantly. (*VO* 313)

The 'little deformed women' in this dream of course recall the terrible creature of Rachel's nightmare earlier in the book, but this dream sequence has a greater significance than simply recalling this earlier episode. It is important that the 'little deformed man' should have turned into two women playing cards. This dream clearly reveals Rachel's instinctive recoil from working-class women, but also reflects the novel's wider anxiety about relationships between women. The arches beneath the river Thames in which the women huddle remind us of the lingering look at Waterloo Bridge at the beginning of novel and represent a striking manifestation of the 'subterranean passages' referred to in the 'Morley Sketch'. Throughout *The Voyage Out* Woolf uses the imagery and trajectory of the passage to investigate the intersections of class and gender in an effort to develop the collective critique of both which she initiated in the 1905 'Morley Sketch'. If the sinister alienation of Rachel's final dream appears to register only despair rather than critique or challenge, the last instance in which Woolf calls upon the image of the passage also acts as a powerful indictment of gender and class structures.

As Hewett makes his last visit to Rachel's sickbed before she dies, he encounters Mrs Chailey in the corridor: 'Chailey was in the passage outside, repeating over and over again, "It's wicked – it's wicked". Terence paid her no attention; he heard what she was saying, but it conveyed no meaning to his mind' (VO 332). The ambivalence of Mrs Chailey's distraught cry and Hewett's failure to pay her any attention is telling. Ostensibly only performing her duty as a loyal servant, Mrs Chailey's cry also rings with a chilling indictment. Throughout the novel Rachel has had difficulty in expressing her criticisms of the social system, frequently resorting to strings of words: 'It *is* terrifying – it *is* disgusting' (VO 72) and 'Mr Bax, hospital nurses, old men, prostitutes, disgusting – ' (VO 220). Mrs Chailey's cry, then, echoes these critical, if inarticulate, stabs made by Rachel against patriarchal society.

Notes

1. *Octavia Hill's Letters to Fellow Workers, 1872–1911*, ed. Robert Whelan (London: Kyrle Books, 2005), p. 401.
2. Little has been written about Virginia Stephen's, and later Woolf's, fractious relationship to the world of late-Victorian philanthropy. However, Hermione Lee has recognised the way in which her voluntary work at Morley 'linked her to her mother's and Stella's world of late-Victorian good works' (*Virginia Woolf*, p. 222) and Milena Radeva has begun the work of exploring how the discourse of philanthropy influences Woolf's presentation of the public sphere in her novels and informs her critique of bourgeois London society ('Re-Visioning Philanthropy and Women's Roles: Virginia Woolf, Professionalization, and the

Philanthropy Debates', in Eleanor McNees and Sara Veglahn (eds), *Woolf Editing/Editing Woolf: Selected Papers from the Eighteenth Annual Conference on Virginia Woolf* (Clemson: Clemson University Digital Press, 2009), pp. 206–14).
3. For the history of Morley College, see Denis Richards, *Offspring of the Vic* (London: Routledge & Kegan Paul, 1958).
4. David Owen, *English Philanthropy, 1660–1960* (Cambridge, MA: Belknap Press of Harvard, 1965), p. 406.
5. For more on Samuel Morley, see Owen, *English Philanthropy, 1660–1960*, pp. 406–8.
6. For accounts of the syllabus and approaches of other adult education colleges, see *A History of Modern British Adult Education*, ed. Roger Fieldhouse (Leicester: National Institute of Adult Continuing Education, 1996).
7. London, Morley College Library, *Morley College Report for 1904–1905*, p. 1.
8. *A History of Modern British Adult Education*, p. 44.
9. *A History of Modern British Adult Education*, p. 44.
10. Albert Mansbridge's primary aim through the Workers' Educational Association was to bring a university style education to working people and this was achieved through the University Tutorial Class in which tutors, predominantly from Oxford and Cambridge, gave courses lasting three years to WEA students. Morley College was one of the first institutions to work in association with the WEA and to implement its University Tutorial Class. Richards, *Offspring of the Vic*, p. 155. For more on the WEA, see Jonathan Rose, *The Intellectual Life of the British Working Classes* (New Haven, CT: Yale University Press, 2001), pp. 256–97. Virginia Woolf would later become involved with the WEA, giving various lectures, including one in 1941 in Brighton upon which her essay 'The Leaning Tower' was based. For more on her involvement, see Cuddy-Keane, *Virginia Woolf, the Intellectual and the Public Sphere*, pp. 86–92.
11. Mansbridge, *An Adventure in Working-Class Education Being the Story of the Workers' Educational Association* (London: Longmans, 1920), p. 5.
12. Rose, *The Intellectual Life of the British Working Classes*, p. 266.
13. The fact that Virginia Stephen is mentioned by name in the official executive committee meeting minutes suggests she would have been aware of the institutional workings of Morley College. In the minutes of a meeting on 3 May 1907 under the subheading 'Literature Circles' it is stated: 'It was reported that Miss Stephen would take one Literature Circle and it was decided that Mr Trevelyan should be asked to take the other.' London, Lambeth Archives, Minet Library, Morley

College Executive Committee Minutes, vol. 3, 1901–12. A full discussion of Mr Trevelyan and Virginia Stephen's encounter with him inside and outside Morley College will come later in this chapter.
14. Morley College Library, *Morley College Report for 1904–1905*, p. 1.
15. According to Fieldhouse, women were marginalised by the ethos of the Working Men's Colleges: 'Maurice believed it would not be possible to create a sense of fellowship if women were present.' *A History of Modern British Adult Education*, p. 31.
16. London, The Women's Library (LSE), Papers of Mary Sheepshanks, *The Long Day Ended*, 7MSH, p. 49.
17. London, Morley College Library, *Morley College Magazine*, May 1907, p. 115.
18. Sybil Oldfield, *Spinsters of this Parish: The Life and Times of F. M. Mayor and Mary Sheepshanks* (London: Virago, 1984), p. 93.
19. In her autobiography Sheepshanks describes the ideological battles that took place between members of the college council, usually sparked by Emma Cons's attempts to resist change. Papers of Mary Sheepshanks, *The Long Day Ended*, 7MSH, p. 29a.
20. How Mary Sheepshanks came to make contact with Virginia Stephen and suggest her volunteering as a teacher is impossible to establish, as Sheepshanks's letters have not survived; however, there are various possible explanations. Mary Sheepshanks formed friendships with Bertrand Russell and Theodore Llewelyn Davies while at Cambridge, so that when she moved to London she came into contact with an extended circle of acquaintances, among whom she counted 'the Leslie Stephen brothers and sisters'. Papers of Mary Sheepshanks, *The Long Day Ended*, 7MSH, p. 40. While it is likely that Sheepshanks and Virginia Stephen encountered each other in the post-Apostolic London scene, it is also possible that Sheepshanks came to make contact with Woolf through a quite different avenue. Woolf had suffered a nervous breakdown upon the death of her father in February 1904 and had spent much of the year recovering at the country home of her friend Violet Dickinson. It would be quite characteristic of the older and protective Dickinson to attempt through her friend and London neighbour in Manchester Street, Ella Crum, who happened to be a vice-president on the Morley College council, to find some distracting and pleasurable activity for her friend to become absorbed in upon her return to London.
21. 'Virginia Woolf Teaching/ Virginia Woolf Learning: Morley College and the Common Reader', in Helen Wussow (ed.), *New Essays on Virginia Woolf* (Dallas: Contemporary Research Press, 1995), pp. 61–78 (p. 61).

22. 'Virginia Woolf Teaching/ Virginia Woolf Learning', p. 63.
23. *Virginia Woolf, the Intellectual, and the Public Sphere*, pp. 82–5.
24. A full transcription, including deleted phrases, is included as an appendix to this book and all quotations come from this version.
25. The very fact of the so-called report's inclusion in Bell's appendices is curious and even contradictory, given the cursory treatment Woolf's teaching receives in that book.
26. *Virginia Woolf, the Intellectual, and the Public Sphere*, p. 82. Quentin Bell also suggests that her encounter with Miss Williams gave Virginia Stephen her 'first view of Grub Street [...] the demi-monde of letters, a region that was to loom large in her imagination'. *Virginia Woolf: A Biography*, vol. 1, pp. 106–7. For more on Woolf's early career as a reviewer, see Jeanne Dubino, 'From Book Reviewer to Literary Critic, 1904–1918', in Beth Carole Rosenberg and Jeanne Dubino (eds), *Virginia Woolf and the Essay* (New York: St Martin's Press, 1997), pp. 25–40, and Beth Rigel Daugherty, 'Reading, Taking Notes, and Writing: Virginia Stephen's Reviewing Practice', in Jeanne Dubino (ed.), *Virginia Woolf and the Literary Marketplace* (Basingstoke: Palgrave Macmillan, 2010), pp. 27–42.
27. Morley College Library, *Morley College Report for 1904–1905*, p. 9.
28. Morley College Library, *Morley College Magazine*, September–October 1905, p. 11.
29. *Journalistic London* (1882) (London: Routledge, 1998), p. 210. A rather stern entry for the *Guardian* in *The Writers' Year-Book* for 1904 supports McNeillie's assessment: 'A paper dealing only with Church and theological matters' (London: Writers' Year-Book Company, 1904), p. 25.
30. *Journalism for Women: A Practical Guide* (London: John Lane The Bodley Head, 1898), p. 84.
31. *Press Work for Women* (London: L. Upcott Gill, 1904), p. 14.
32. *My Years of the Harvest* (London: Hodder and Stoughton, 1938), p. 50.
33. *Press Work for Women*, p. 13.
34. *Reading Virginia Woolf's Essays and Journalism: Breaking the Surface of Silence* (Edinburgh: Edinburgh University Press, 1997), p. 49.
35. *The Church Family Newspaper*, 13 January 1905, p. 818; *The British Weekly*, 6 July 1905, p. 315.
36. In his discussion of Virginia Woolf and religion Pericles Lewis has noted this tendency to attribute religious zeal to her working-class and lower-middle-class characters. *Religious Experience and the Modernist Novel* (Cambridge: Cambridge University Press, 2010), p. 154.

37. *Secularization and Cultural Criticism: Religion, Nation, & Modernity* (Chicago: University of Chicago Press, 2006), p. 173.
38. *Secularization and Cultural Criticism*, p. 176.
39. 'History, Pattern, and Continuity in Virginia Woolf', *Contemporary Literature*, 15 (1974), 49–66 (p. 50).
40. Cuddy-Keane, *Virginia Woolf, the Intellectual, and the Public Sphere*, pp. 146–67.
41. 'Virginia Woolf's Postmodern Literary History', *MLN*, 115 (2000), 1112–30 (p. 1115).
42. *Virginia Woolf: A Biography*, vol. 1, p. 106.
43. Hotho-Jackson, 'Virginia Woolf on History: Between Tradition and Modernity', *Forum for Modern Language Studies*, 27.4 (1991), 293–312 (p. 296).
44. Michael Bentley positions E. A. Freeman and J. R. Green as, albeit critical, inheritors of the Whig historical tradition which originated in the works of Thomas Babington Macaulay, among others. Bentley, however, uses the idea of this Whig tradition advisedly, stressing the differences that existed between different generations and different individual historians. For example, the emulation of the German school in a move towards scientific methods of research and collation of findings among historians such as E. A. Freeman, J. R. Green and J. A Froude, which led to criticism of the romantic style of Macaulay and Thomas Carlyle. In spite of these stylistic and technical departures, however, Freeman and Green certainly did not break with the patriotic belief in the sanctity and superiority of English history or the notion of history as progress that was at the core of Whig theories of history. *Modernizing England's Past: English Historiography in the Age of Modernism, 1870–1970* (Cambridge: Cambridge University Press, 2005), p. 23.
45. For biographies of E. A. Freeman and J. R. Green and expositions of their historical approaches, see B. Norton's *Freeman's Life: Highlights, Chronology, Letters and Works* (Farnborough: Norton, 1993), and Anthony Brundage, *The People's Historian John Richard Green and the Writing of History in Victorian England* (London: Greenwood Press, 1994). For a more critical account of Freeman's work, see Marilyn Lake, 'Essentially Teutonic: E. A. Freeman, Liberal Race Historian: A Transnational Perspective', in Catherine Hall and Keith McClelland (ed.), *Race, Nation and Empire: Making Histories, 1750 to the Present* (Manchester: Manchester University Press, 2010), pp. 56–73.
46. For Leslie Stephen's influence on his daughter's early historical reading, see Katherine C. Hill's 'Virginia Woolf and Leslie Stephen: History and Literary Revolution', *PMLA*, 96 (1981), 351–62.

47. Kenyon-Jones and Snaith, '"Tilting at Universities"', 4.
48. '"Tilting at Universities"', 14.
49. London, King's College London Archives, *King's College Ladies' Department Syllabus of Lectures 1899–1900*, KW/SYL 8, p. 16.
50. Andrew Lambert, *The Foundations of Naval History: John Knox Laughton, the Royal Navy and the Historical Profession* (London: Chatham, 1998), p. 87.
51. *Under Six Reigns* (London: Longmans, 1958), p. 11.
52. '"Tilting at Universities"', 35.
53. *An Autobiography & Other Essays* (London: Longmans, 1949), p. 12.
54. *An Autobiography & Other Essays*, p. 1.
55. *An Autobiography & Other Essays*, p. 1. For a discussion of Trevelyan's political and historical practice with particular reference to his attitudes towards the British Empire, see Bill Schwarz's 'Englishry: G. M. Trevelyan's Histories', in Hall and McClelland (eds), *Race, Nation and Empire: Making Histories, 1750 to the Present*, pp. 117–32.
56. *Edwardian Bloomsbury: The Early Literary History of the Bloomsbury Group, Volume Two* (Basingstoke: Macmillan, 1994), p. 167.
57. London, Morley College Library, *Morley College Magazine*, March 1906, p. 111.
58. In an article on Virginia Stephen's 1907 biographical tribute to Violet Dickinson, 'Friendships Gallery', Karin E. Westman has noted the way in which Virginia Stephen both emulates and parodies G. M. Trevelyan's flamboyant style. 'The First *Orlando*: The Laugh of the Comic Spirit in Virginia Woolf's "Friendships Gallery"', *Twentieth Century Literature*, 47 (2001), 39–71.
59. Edward. A. Freeman, *The History of the Norman Conquest, its Causes and its Results*, vol. 1 (Oxford: Clarendon, 1870), p. 3.
60. Morley College Library, *Morley College Magazine*, March 1906, p. 111.
61. Anna Snaith's research on the letters Woolf received after the publication of *Three Guineas* show that she later encouraged Agnes Smith, a working-class weaver with whom she corresponded, to publish an autobiography with the Hogarth Press. (Snaith, '*Three Guineas* Letters', *Woolf Studies Annual*, 6 (2000), 17–168 (p. 103).
62. It is interesting to note that later in *A Room of One's Own* it is Trevelyan's *History of England* that Woolf's narrator turns to in search of the historical details of women's lives only to find accounts of her subordination and abuse: 'she was locked up, beaten and flung about the room' (*AROO* 40). Indeed, it is in reaction to Trevelyan's history that the narrator suggests that students at Girton and Newnham ought to 'rewrite history' or rather 'add a supplement to history' (*AROO* 41).

63. 'Taking a Leaf from Virginia Woolf's Book: Empowering the Student', in Mark Hussey and Vara Neverow-Turk (eds), *Virginia Woolf Miscellanies: Proceedings of the First Annual Conference on Virginia Woolf* (New York: Pace University Press, 1992), pp. 31–9.
64. See 'The New Biography' (*E4* 473–9). For a powerful defence of what Woolf calls the 'truth of fiction', see the 'First Essay' in *The Pargiters* (*P* 9).
65. This is the title given by Louise DeSalvo and Susan M. Squier, who edited and introduced the story when it was first published in *Twentieth Century Literature*, 25 (1979), 237–69. I will be using the version printed in Susan Dick's *The Complete Shorter Fiction of Virginia Woolf*, as previously indicated.
66. *Virginia Woolf, the Intellectual, and the Public Sphere*, p. 149.
67. 'Shakespeare's *Other* Sister', in Jane Marcus (ed.), *New Feminist Essays on Virginia Woolf*, pp. 61–81 (p. 79).
68. 'Woolf on History: Between Tradition and Modernity', 297.
69. 'Who's Afraid of Rosamond Merridew?: Reading Medieval History in "The Journal of Mistress Joan Martyn"', *Journal of the Short Story in English*, 50 (2008), 2–12 (p. 2).
70. 'Imagining Her-Story: Virginia Woolf's "The Journal of Mistress Joan Martyn" as Historiographical Metafiction', *Journal of the Short Story in English*, 20 (1993), 9–26 (p. 9).
71. 'Shakespeare's *Other* Sister', p. 63.
72. See Emily O. Wittman, 'The Decline and Fall of Rachel Vinrace: Reading Gibbon in Virginia Woolf's *The Voyage Out*', in Helen Southworth and Elisa Kay Sparks (eds), *Woolf and the Art of Exploration: Selected Papers from the Fifteenth International Conference on Virginia Woolf* (Clemson, SC: Clemson University Digital Press, 2006), pp. 160–8 and David Bradshaw, 'Vicious Circles: Hegel, Bosanquet and *The Voyage Out*', in Diane F. Gillespie and Leslie K. Hankins (eds), *Virginia Woolf and the Arts: Selected Papers from the Sixth Annual Conference on Virginia Woolf* (New York: Pace University Press, 1997), pp. 183–90.
73. In her essay exploring the parallels between Conrad's *Heart of Darkness* and *The Voyage Out*, Marianne DeKoven also emphasises the significance of passages and the ways in which these figure in Woolf's critique of 'hegemonic gender, economic and narrative structures'. *Rich and Strange* (Princeton: Princeton University Press, 1991), p. 90.
74. The critical reception of Woolf's first novel has been less positive than that of her later work. A combination of its deceptively conventional *Bildungsroman* plotting and the band of comic English tourists who populate the hotel are partly responsible for this suspicion of *The Voyage Out*. Pamela Transue argues it is a novel 'hindered by

[Woolf's] attempt to work within traditional novelistic conventions' (*Virginia Woolf and the Politics of Style*, p. 17), while Hermione Lee is impatient with the 'feebly satiric' minor characters and suggests that '[t]he mass of undigested literary allusions in *The Voyage Out* compares badly with their more integrated use in the later novels' (*The Novels of Virginia Woolf* (London: Methuen, 1977), pp. 38 and 41). Vincent Pecora's analysis of the novel also positions it in relation to Woolf's later more sophisticated work by describing *The Voyage Out* as 'an awkwardly managed storehouse of imagery and characters on which most of Woolf's mature work would draw' (*Secularization and Cultural Criticism*, p. 160). By contrast, Louise DeSalvo suggests that the published version of *The Voyage Out* compares unfavourably with an earlier draft of the novel, entitled *Melymbrosia*, edited and published by DeSalvo in 1982. DeSalvo suggests that *Melymbrosia* 'is, in many ways, a bolder rendering of the later work', with its political and social satire appearing more prominently (*M* xxii). Chene Heady ('Accidents of Political Life: Satire and Edwardian Anti-Colonial Politics in *The Voyage Out*', in Jessica Berman and Jane Goldman (eds), *Virginia Woolf Out of Bounds: Selected Papers from the Tenth Annual Conference on Virginia Woolf* (New York: Pace University Press, 2001, pp. 97–104), David Bradshaw ('Vicious Circles', pp. 183–90) and Kathy Phillips (*Virginia Woolf Against Empire* (Knoxville: The University of Tennessee Press, 1994)) have produced valuable readings of *The Voyage Out*, which aim to foreground the political dimensions of the novel.

75. Louise DeSalvo has read this dream sequence as expressing Rachel's unconscious memories of sexual abuse at the hands of her father, Willoughby Vinrace, whose brutality and excessively controlling behaviour are referred to elsewhere in the novel (*VO* 14 and 17). DeSalvo also suggests that Woolf writes her own experiences of sexual abuse into the text and that the novel 'is extremely realistic in its portrait of the deadly effects of sexual abuse upon a young woman, who is not even fully aware of what has happened to her, who only becomes aware in the images that crowd her dreams'. *Virginia Woolf: The Impact of Childhood Sexual Abuse on Her Life and Work* (London: The Women's Press, 1989), p. 168. Both Diana L. Swanson and Lisa Tyler have also suggested that Rachel shows characteristics of someone who has suffered from sexual abuse, as well as arguing that her 'old-fashioned father' (*VO* 14) Willoughby Vinrace, with his overbearing manner, behaves in a way that is consistent with an incestuous father. '"My Boldness Terrifies Me": Sexual Abuse and Female Subjectivity in *The Voyage Out*', *Twentieth Century Literature*, 41 (1995), 284–309;

'"Nameless Atrocities" and the Name of the Father: Literary Allusion and Incest in Virginia Woolf's *The Voyage Out*', *Woolf Studies Annual*, 1 (1995), 26–46.
76. 'De/Colonizing the Subject in Virginia Woolf's *The Voyage Out:* Rachel Vinrace as *La Mysterique*', in Mark Hussey and Vara Neverow (eds), *Virginia Woolf: Emerging Perspectives: Selected Papers from the Third Annual Conference on Virginia Woolf* (New York: Pace University Press, 1994), pp. 103–8 (p. 104).
77. *Rich and Strange*, p. 106.
78. 'The Visual Politics of Empire and Gender in Virginia Woolf's *The Voyage Out*', *Woolf Studies Annual*, 1 (1995), 106–19 (p. 111).
79. *Virginia Woolf: Dramatic Novelist* (Basingstoke: Macmillan, 1989), p. 37.
80. Although not the focus of the present project, colonial politics are also an important lens through which to read *The Voyage Out*. As scholars have noted, throughout the novel Woolf demonstrates a critical awareness of the procedures of imperialism, as when she satirises Richard Dalloway's conservative imagination, 'a lasso that opened and caught things, enormous chunks of the habitable globe' (*VO* 43), or spoofs Clarissa Dalloway's histrionic jingoism as she reflects on 'our navies, and the people in India and Africa' and concludes 'it makes one feel as if one couldn't bear *not* to be English!' (*VO* 42). Andrea Lewis has explored the complicated ways in which discourses of race, class and gender intersect in the novel to produce what she reads as an ambivalent critique of imperialism ('The Visual Politics of Empire and Gender in Virginia Woolf's *The Voyage Out*', *Woolf Studies Annual*, 1 (1995), 106–19), while Jed Esty has argued that Woolf's failure to observe the 'generic protocols of the bildungsroman' in *The Voyage Out* can be read as a formal expression of 'Woolf's intertwined [...] suspicion of imperialism and patriarchy' (*Unseasonable Youth: Modernism, Colonialism, and the Fiction of Development* (Oxford: Oxford University Press, 2012), p. 128). In a recent article on Virginia and Leonard Woolf's anti-imperialism, Anna Snaith explores 'the Woolfs' shared articulation of economic imperialism' in *The Voyage Out* and *Empire and Commerce in Africa* (1920), investigating the ways in which the anti-imperialist politics of Virginia Woolf's first novel may have influenced her husband's subsequent work of non-fiction. ('Leonard and Virginia Woolf: Writing Against Empire', *The Journal of Commonwealth Literature*, 50 (2015), 19–32 (p. 22).)
81. *Virginia Woolf: Dramatic Novelist*, p. 38
82. 'Vicious Circles', pp. 188–9.

83. Patricia Morgne Cramer has suggested that 'the prostitute wafting from "one room to another" [...] appears as Rachel's ghosted double'. 'Virginia Woolf and Sexuality', in Sellers (ed.), *The Cambridge Companion to Virginia Woolf*, 2nd edn, pp. 180–96 (p. 183).

Chapter 2

Virginia Stephen and the People's Suffrage Federation, 1910

Introduction

> By the way, are you an Adult Suffragist? This is a real question. (*L1* 426)

Unlike the voluminous correspondence with Margaret Llewelyn Davies and the self-critical diary entries that illuminate Virginia Woolf's enduring relationship with the Women's Co-operative Guild, we have only scattered references to her voluntary work for the suffrage and to the movement in general from January to November 1910.[1] Although they may appear to speak only of Virginia Stephen's initial enthusiasm rapidly transformed into impatient criticism, these seemingly throwaway references have the potential to alter our understanding of Virginia Stephen's encounter with suffragism and contribute usefully to the wider narrative of the suffrage campaign at a pivotal moment in this battle.

This chapter's opening quotation is a significant example of this dual historical potency. The last line of a typically playful letter to her close friend and fellow reviewer Lady Eleanor Cecil, this provocative question is consistent with Virginia Stephen's affectionate but challenging style. Its startling appearance at the conclusion of a letter otherwise concerned with personal matters, and the striking contrast between the urgency of Stephen's statement – 'This is a real question' – and the teasing and in-jokes that precede it, suggest more might be at stake in this curious correspondence than first appears.

The daughter of the Earl of Durham and the wife of Lord Robert Cecil, the Conservative MP, Nelly Cecil, as Virginia Stephen affectionately addressed her, was from the aristocracy proper and an important friend to Virginia Stephen when she was in her early twenties. During her period at Morley College, Virginia Stephen's letters to Nelly Cecil show her at her most snobbishly detached – when describing the adverse effects of teaching composition to a 'Milkman' (*L1* 281) – but also her most committed; she appealed to Nelly Cecil on behalf of one of her students, Cyril Zeldwyn, an enthusiastic socialist in need of employment (*L1* 321). This second example demonstrates Virginia Stephen's willingness to reveal her social commitment to Nelly Cecil and also her awareness of the powers and privileges that accompanied her friend's aristocratic status. Nigel Nicolson suggests that Virginia Stephen's letters to her friend recognise Nelly Cecil's high-class position but also gently mock this grandness: 'behind Virginia's letters is the suggestion that Nelly is nicer than all this implies' (*L* 1 xix).

This letter from June 1910 is certainly shot through with a playful mixture of deference and spoof. It is, in fact, a very silly letter in which Stephen extravagantly bemoans the time that has elapsed since the two women met: 'Where have you been all this time? and has your view of the world changed? Are you still an aristocrat? are you exquisite or shabby?' (*L1* 426). Virginia Stephen's challenging question about Nelly Cecil's position on the suffrage at the end of this letter appears to represent a distinct shift in tone, and yet it is possible to read these apparently light-hearted questions, dotted throughout the letter, as building towards it. Virginia Stephen's enquiries about her friend's possibly altered view of the world – 'Are you much changed by contact with the world?' and later 'has your view of the world changed?' – can be read as skirting around the issue of the suffrage, which was in 1910, along with the question of home rule in Ireland, the most compelling political story of the moment.[2]

Even if this strange letter contains coded references to the suffrage campaign throughout, this does not account for the peculiar, abrupt tone of this final question – 'By the way, are you an Adult Suffragist? – or the pressing seriousness of her closing statement – 'This is a real question'. Virginia Stephen would have been aware that her friend's politician husband was a prominent and vocal supporter of votes for women in Parliament and that Nelly Cecil shared his views.[3] But what is crucial here is to recognise that to be an 'Adult Suffragist' was something quite different from being in favour of women's suffrage and this letter, with its strange sniping, is shot through with Virginia Stephen's awareness of this distinction.

In his discussion of Virginia Stephen's involvement with the suffrage campaign, Alex Zwerdling has noted the consistent way in which she identifies the cause she is working for as that of the suffragists:

> 'Suffragist,' it should be noted, not 'Suffragette'. The distinction between the constitutional methods of the former and the extralegal tactics of the latter had by this time been clearly established, and Woolf's decision to join the nonviolent section of the movement is characteristic and important.[4]

While Zwerdling is right to pay close attention to the semantic specificities of Virginia Stephen's references to the suffrage, recent historians of the movement have made efforts to complicate a received narrative in which the distinctions between constitutional suffragist and militant suffragette are accepted. Sandra Stanley Holton has argued that such rigid classifications are 'difficult to apply in any consistent way' and 'tend to obscure those currents within the suffrage movement which cut across it'.[5] Holton focuses on the neglected contribution of what she calls 'democratic suffragists', a phrase coined by Margaret Llewelyn Davies.[6] These campaigners sought women's suffrage 'as part of a more general democratisation of British society', often believing that uniting socialist and feminist causes was the most effective way of achieving this.[7] These campaigners frequently identified their cause as that of adult suffrage.

While Virginia Stephen's moment of suffragism is frequently referenced, her repeated self-identification as an adult suffragist has been neglected. Perhaps on account of her references to attending two rallies for women's suffrage at the Royal Albert Hall in November 1910 (L1 438), scholars have assumed that Virginia Stephen's voluntary work earlier that year was with the predominantly middle-class and constitutionalist National Union of Women's Suffrage Societies.[8] This assumption not only overlooks her persistent self-identification as an adult suffragist,[9] but also the vexed relationship that existed between the NUWSS and adult suffragists.

Naomi Black's book *Virginia Woolf as Feminist* is the exception, providing the most detailed and valuable analysis of Virginia Stephen's involvement in adultist campaigning to date. Black speculates about which group she volunteered for, suggesting that '[t]he People's Suffrage Federation is the only group that we can identify with any probability from such scrappy, incomplete evidence'.[10] While making a convincing case for her connection with the People's Suffrage Federation, Black discounts the adult suffrage platform of this group, suggesting it was in 'practice a woman suffrage group that used the desirability of full adult suffrage as an argument for the inclusion of women in any measure designed to expand the franchise'.[11] Black's efforts to preserve the connection between Woolf's early suffragism and the women's movement are consistent with her book's aim of establishing Virginia Woolf as feminist, but also risk overlooking the contentious position of adult suffragists, and in particular the PSF, within the movement.

Building on Black's argument for her connection with the PSF, this chapter rethinks Virginia Stephen's involvement in the suffrage campaign in 1910 focusing on the adultist context of this activism and challenging certain critical orthodoxies that have built up around the issue of Woolf and the suffrage. This emphasis on Virginia Stephen's adult suffrage credentials also responds to an increasing effort in histories of the suffrage to dismantle the prevailing binaries of militant/constitutionalist and suffragist/suffragette and instead produce a more nuanced, but also more complicated account of the British suffrage movement.[12]

The People's Suffrage Federation

George Dangerfield's description of the PSF as 'an extremely shadowy organisation' in his account of the suffrage movement is inaccurate and telling.[13] The PSF was far from secretive about either its political aims or its activity; prominent members promoted the cause of universal adult suffrage in national newspapers, while numerous self-published pamphlets and newsletters reiterated the Federation's emphatic slogan: 'One Man, One Vote; One Woman, One Vote'. Holton describes the efforts the PSF made to mobilise other 'universal suffragists who had been driven to focus on women's exclusion from the franchise because of the luke-warm commitment to sexual equality they had encountered in Labour, socialist and Liberal circles'.[14] Dangerfield's dismissive reference to the PSF reveals more about his own reluctance to veer from the received narrative of the suffrage movement and his related wariness of addressing the complicated position of adult suffragists within this campaign.[15]

The PSF was constituted in October 1909[16] with the object of 'obtain[ing] the Parliamentary suffrage for every adult man and woman on a short residential qualification'.[17] In this it broke with the NUWSS, which campaigned for votes for women on equal terms with men. By contrast, the PSF's inaugural pamphlet argues that 'the present franchise law favours property and penalises labour, and the real voice of the people will never be heard until manhood and womanhood are the qualifications for voting'.[18] This commitment to a universalist agenda for electoral reform represented the interests of both women and, what this pamphlet refers to as, 'the disenfranchised millions' and reflected the diversity of the individual members and the industrial and political bodies affiliated to the PSF.[19] In a letter appealing for funds in March 1910, the PSF recognises that 'being based on a broad democratic principle, uniting men and women in a common object' its 'field of work differ[ed] from other suffrage societies'.[20] In practice, the PSF recruited members from existing suffrage societies insisting there was no need to leave their current body: 'We do not ask those who become members of the Federation to leave other suffrage societies, but we offer the opportunity for men and women to work together for complete political freedom.'[21] While the PSF maintained this inclusive message, in some notable instances members of women's suffrage groups left them in order to join the PSF. Bertrand Russell felt it necessary to resign his position on the executive of the NUWSS in order to join the PSF, as was bitterly recorded in *The Common Cause* in December 1909.[22]

Margaret Llewelyn Davies played a central role in the formation of the PSF and acted as secretary to the executive committee.[23] As the president of the Women's Co-operative Guild, Llewelyn Davies was keenly aware of the need for an organisation agitating on a universal suffrage platform. As her private letters testify, she believed that adult suffrage was the only just course for electoral reform. In a letter to her friend, Dorothea Ponsonby, Llewelyn Davies complained:

It has been very boring of Lloyd George not going straight for adult suffrage. The only way of really conquering the ridiculous bogey of a majority of women is to face it [...] The majority of people cd. be won just as easily for adult as for any of these absurd compromises.[24]

Llewelyn Davies believed that working-class women – whose interests were not necessarily represented by women's suffrage societies, which were prepared to back a limited reform bill from which working women would be excluded – needed an organisation that would agitate on their behalf.[25] In an interview with *The Woman Worker* in November 1910, Llewelyn Davies was candid and critical about the prospect of limited reform: 'The Limited Bill is so obnoxious to us [...] We feel that a personal, and not a property basis, is the only democratic one'.[26]

The PSF's inaugural executive committee included a number of other prominent representatives from the women's arm of the Labour Movement. Mary R. Macarthur, who was at that time also the secretary of the Women's Trade Union League, was joint-secretary of the PSF with Llewelyn Davies. Margaret Bondfield, a prominent trade union activist, was the PSF's chairman, while Arthur Henderson, the chairman of the Labour Party, was its honorary treasurer.[27] The general committee also included members of the Independent Labour Party (ILP), George Lansbury and Frank Rose.[28] Branches of the WCG, the ILP, the Liberal Association, Trade Unions and the Women's Labour League were affiliated to the PSF, and it boasted a number of high-profile individual members.

The obscure light in which the PSF is cast in some histories of the suffrage campaign is surprising then, not only when we consider the variety of its members, but also when we regard the range and wealth of its pamphlets. Titles included Bertrand Russell's 1910 *Anti-Suffragist Anxieties*, an attempt to get to the root of opposition to women's suffrage and an interrogation of what he describes as the fear of dangerous feminine emotion being introduced into politics.[29] F. D. Acland's *Adult Suffrage: An Address to Democrats* was based on a speech made in 1911, while Maud M. A. Ward's *Adult Suffrage in Other Countries*, another pamphlet advertised in the back of Acland's publication, is perhaps what Rosalind Nash had in mind when she told Virginia Stephen in her January 1910 letter that there 'was a good deal to be got up about the franchise (not only women's) in other countries'.[30]

While Naomi Black is understandably cautious about stating categorically that it was the PSF with which Virginia Stephen volunteered, there is convincing evidence to support this. Beyond the telling emphasis on 'Adult' in her June 1910 letter to Nelly Cecil and the peculiarly combative tone of her sign-off, there is substantial circumstantial evidence that suggests Virginia Stephen was involved with the PSF. Virginia Stephen's letter to her former Greek tutor, Janet Case, where she first offers her help to the cause, gestures to the PSF in several specific ways.

> Would it be any use if I spent an afternoon or two weekly in addressing envelopes for the Adult Suffragists?
> I dont know anything about the question. Perhaps you could send me a pamphlet, or give me the address of the office. I could neither do sums or argue, or speak, but I could do the humbler work if that is any good. You impressed me so much the other night with the wrongness of the present state of affairs that I feel that action is necessary. Your position seemed to me intolerable. The only way to better it is to do some thing I suppose. How melancholy it is that conversation isn't enough! (*L1* 421)

My introduction outlined the ways in which this letter is significant to this book's broader concern with the nature of Virginia Woolf's attitudes towards political action. However, the moment at which this letter was written and the person to whom it was addressed are both significant in other, more material ways. They draw our attention to the public, political story behind this letter: the formation of the People's Suffrage Federation.

A progressive teacher, Janet Case was also committed to social and democratic reform and sympathetic to the struggle for female enfranchisement.[31] When the PSF was formed in October 1909, through the combined efforts of various groups outlined above, Case was on the executive committee.[32] That Case was a prominent member of this new organisation and the fact that Virginia Stephen's letter was sent so soon after the PSF's formation establishes with fair certainty that it was the PSF with which Virginia Stephen was affiliated. It is also worth noting that a number of Virginia Stephen's close acquaintances were listed among the individual members of the PSF in January 1910. Among them were Lady Ottoline Morrell, John Maynard

Keynes, Mary Sheepshanks, Sydney Waterlow and Desmond and Mary (Molly) MacCarthy.[33]

Morrell's membership is of particular interest as she lived locally to Virginia Stephen, who was particularly impressed by the aristocratic Morrell in these early years of their friendship. While Morrell's diary does not refer to the PSF specifically, she makes frequent references to her enjoyable discussions with Virginia Stephen at this time. In an entry in November 1909, only weeks after the constitution of the PSF, Morrell describes a disappointing visit to the House of Commons to hear Lloyd George's Budget debated. She is, however, cheered up by a visit to Virginia Stephen's house: 'After the house was over we went on to Miss Virginia Stephen and had amusing talk there on Politics etc. — Really one gets more amusing talk there than anywhere I think. She is so clever.'[34]

Morrell's characterisation of Virginia Stephen as an active and engaged participant in political discussion strengthens my sense of her as alert to the nuances and internal tensions of the suffrage movement.

To return to the Janet Case correspondence, Case appears to have passed Virginia Stephen's letter on to her PSF colleague and neighbour in Hampstead, Margaret Llewelyn Davies, who, in turn, passed this correspondence on to another member of the executive council for consideration, as later in the month Virginia Stephen received a letter from Rosalind Nash making various suggestions of what she might like to spend her time with the PSF working on. From its opening lines we are left in little doubt that the organisation Nash represents is the PSF:

> Dear Miss Stephen,
> I promised Margaret ll. Davies to write you about People's Suffrage, last Thursday, and have been much too long in doing it. I was so glad to hear you were going to do some work for us.[35]

Along with Nash's reference to 'People's Suffrage', there are several other features of this letter that collectively suggest it was the PSF with which Virginia Stephen was affiliated and point to its uncompromising adultist agenda. Later in the letter when Nash outlines the various tasks Virginia Stephen may like to undertake as a volunteer, she writes: 'There is a great deal to be got up about the franchise (not only women's) in other countries but that would be a dull business which perhaps some legal person might enjoy.'[36] Nash's parenthetical assertion – 'not only women's' – recalls the PSF's universal campaigning platform and was perhaps included by Nash in order to discreetly remind her prospective young volunteer of this fact.

At the letter's close we are again put fixedly in mind of the PSF. Earlier in the letter Nash had suggested that Virginia Stephen might want to put together a book of 'good extracts on representation' and she finishes her correspondence by returning to this idea as the most promising: 'I think it [the collection of extracts] would be a great help. The labour people, who have a touchingly exaggerated reverence for book learning, would really get some good from it.'[37] This reference to the 'labour people' reminds us of the 'feminist-labour alliance'[38] that Holton describes as at the heart of the PSF, while the satirical edge to Nash's reference to their 'reverence for book learning' also hints at the particular sort of tensions that necessarily exist in such a coalition and the kinds of compromises that must be effected in order for it to function.

As with this letter from Nash, Virginia Stephen's initial letter to Janet Case points to the PSF in several significant ways. The suggestive phrasing of the letter reveal it to be concerned with the contentious position of adult suffragists, particularly members of the PSF, within the wider community of suffrage campaigners. Virginia Stephen's reference to 'the wrongness of the present state of affairs' appears to be a broad allusion to the exclusion of women from the voting system and the hostility with which the demands of suffrage campaigners were met by the establishment. However, it is also possible to read 'the present state of affairs' as referring more particularly to the internal situation within the suffrage movement itself. Such a reading hinges on the ambiguity of the word 'present' in this context. It is quite possible that Virginia Stephen is referring not to the 'present' situation of women denied the vote, but rather the specific and uncomfortable position occupied by members of the PSF at that time.

The formation of the PSF in 1909 inspired hostility from other suffrage groups, who believed that campaigning on an adult suffrage platform could compromise the chances of passing the comparatively moderate reform they were pressing for.[39] The clipped tone of the editorial of *The Common Cause*, the organ of the NUWSS, throughout the early months of the PSF's existence hints at this antagonism. The editor's response to a letter from Margaret Llewelyn Davies, defending the PSF and adult suffragists against the criticism they had received since their formation, is particularly icy and provides a useful insight into the nature of suffragist anxiety over adult suffragism:

> We do not think it likely that Suffragists will feel reassured by vague aspirations like these. Women before now have felt quite confident that men would not desert them. We do not doubt Miss Llewelyn Davies' confidence, but we are not yet satisfied that she has any ground for it, and the answers of the candidate supported by the People's Federation in Bermondsey were not reassuring – Ed., 'CC'.[40]

The January 1910 issue of *The Englishwoman*, a journal sympathetic to the cause of women's enfranchisement, reveals similar tension. In an article considering 'The Year's Progress in the Women's Suffrage Movement', Clementina Black refers darkly to the formation of the PSF as the single most damaging development in the campaign for women's suffrage:

> At this point some reader will certainly exclaim in amazement, 'But why "damaging?" Are not these people fighting your battle, and merely asking more than you venture to ask?' In answer I can but repeat and expand the weighty words written last February by the Executive of the National Union of Women's Suffrage Societies, when it opposed Mr Geoffrey Howard's Adult Suffrage Bill 'on the grounds, among others, that it will seriously complicate the position, alienate many supporters, goes far beyond any demand in the country, and is not asked for by any organized body of women who have worked for the suffrage'.[41]

Black expands on these points and concludes her discussion of the PSF by suggesting that its demand for radical voting reform goes against England's 'custom' of making 'political changes gradually'.[42] In light of this, Virginia Stephen's reference to the 'wrongness of the present state of affairs' reads as both an allusion to the hostile reception of the PSF from existing suffrage societies and an early, admittedly oblique, critique of the implacability of single-issue suffrage campaigners.

A reading of Virginia Stephen's letter as peculiarly concerned with the situation of the PSF appears to be supported later in the letter where she writes: 'Your position seemed to me intolerable.' It is possible that she is referring to Case's individual position as an unmarried, self-supporting, middle-class woman. Certainly, Constance Rover has suggested that the campaign for women's suffrage had emerged out of a particular late-Victorian concern with the 'plight' of middle-class women forced to find work in order to support themselves and their need for proper political representation.[43]

And yet Virginia Stephen's reference to 'your position' may be another gesture to the problematic position of the PSF in early 1910. Still in its infancy, this organisation not only had to contend with the mistrust of the NUWSS. The much-anticipated 1910 Conciliation Bill was likely to recommend limited voting reform rather than the universal suffrage the PSF campaigned for. The coming bill then put the PSF in the queasy position of having to decide whether to publicly support a bill which was not likely to run along adultist lines.[44] The PSF annual report for October 1909 to October 1910 recalls that 'the position was a very difficult one for Adult Suffragists, as the Liberal Party had not officially given any pledge for a larger measure'.[45] The PSF's reluctance to put their wholehearted support behind the Conciliation Bill was the source of further internecine quarrelling, in particular with the NUWSS.

After tentatively committing their support to the 1910 Bill in the early stages of its drafting, the PSF were forced, due to what they considered the untenably limited character of the Bill, to 'officially neither support[s] nor oppose[s] the Conciliation Bill' and instead continue to campaign for electoral reform along adult suffrage lines.[46] By the second reading of the 1911 Conciliation Bill we can assume that Margaret Llewelyn Davies's hostility to its limited terms was representative of the PSF more broadly. Dorothea Ponsonby, friend of Llewelyn Davies and wife of Liberal (and later Labour) MP Arthur Ponsonby, recorded in her diary in August 1911: 'She [Llewellyn Davies] looked very worn & tired & beautiful [...] I listened to her putting her case to Arthur against the Suffrage Conciliation Bill & it was so interesting & so extraordinarily well put'.[47]

Virginia Stephen's letter to Janet Case encourages us to situate her voluntary work with the PSF in 1910 within the context of a specific and fraught moment in the campaign for the suffrage. Other letters from this period register Virginia Stephen's awareness of the suspicion the PSF was met with. When she writes self-deprecatingly of her voluntary work to Violet Dickinson in February her choice of words is telling: 'People say that Adult Suffrage is a bad thing; but they will never get it owing to my efforts' (*L1* 422). Most often cited as an example of her dismissive attitude towards activism, in this letter we again see the degree to which Virginia Stephen was aware of the dim view taken of adult suffragist claims.

It is worth considering in greater depth the reason for this hostility towards adult suffrage from mainstream women's suffrage societies, and the marginal position of the PSF within the suffrage movement. So far in this discussion the primary reasons to emerge for these groups' resistance to the idea of adult suffrage have been what Holton describes as the 'class-antagonism' of woman suffragists towards the broader formulation of adult suffrage, but also woman suffragists' conviction that adultist demands for a radical overhaul of the franchise laws would be harder to achieve and so compromise the passage of a limited bill, which gave the vote to some women on a property qualification.[48]

It would be inaccurate to cast this antagonism towards adult suffrage and the PSF as exclusively inspired by a desire to protect middle-class interests. The very concept of adult suffrage was deeply ambiguous. As Holton has observed, it could suggest either 'universal franchise with both the property and sex disqualifications removed, or merely the extension of the existing sexually exclusive franchise to all adult males'.[49] For some parties, then, adult suffrage did not include any provision for women and so could quite rightly be seen as operating in opposition to the cause of votes for women. While we can see from their campaign slogan – 'One Man, One Vote: One Woman One Vote'[50] – that the PSF certainly interpreted adult suffrage as synonymous with universal suffrage, adult suffrage had a rather more contested history within the Labour Movement, from where the PSF drew several of its most prominent members. While some key figures in the Labour Party, notably Keir Hardie, supported the suffrage movement, others considered it to be driven by the self-interest of middle-class women and were openly hostile towards the idea of votes for women.[51] In light of this, the NUWSS's suspicion of the PSF, a group not only working under the banner of adult suffrage but one which depended upon a 'feminist-labour alliance',[52] is more understandable.[53]

* * *

Even a brief account of this particular factional debate within the suffrage movement and the contentious position of adult suffragists encourages a cautious approach to Virginia Stephen's often-celebrated early moment of suffragism. That she was aligned with what was a fairly marginal group and one with an at least ambiguous relationship to the mainstream of the suffrage movement should make us think differently about this voluntary work and reassess the ways in which Virginia Stephen's early allegiance to the PSF influenced her presentation of the suffrage campaign throughout her literary career.

Adultist agendas: *Night and Day* (1919), *The Years* (1937) and *Three Guineas* (1938)

Night and Day focuses on Katharine Hilbery, a fully-fledged member of the intellectual aristocracy whose days are filled with a combination of domestic management and helping her mother write a biography of 'the poet' (*ND* 71), her grandfather.[54] Katharine is engaged to the pompous and highly-strung William Rodney and the novel charts her break with Rodney and the transfer of her, albeit problematic, affections to Ralph Denham, a brilliant but dissatisfied middle-class solicitor. *Night and Day* also tells the parallel story of Mary Datchet, friend to Katharine and Ralph and volunteer for 'a society for woman's suffrage' (*ND* 62) in Russell Square. Alongside the central romance plot between Katharine and Ralph runs the story of Mary's profound and unrequited love for Ralph, her decision to relinquish this and her renewed commitment to democratic social reform at the end of the novel.

The appearance of conventionality in both the novel's plotting and its narrative style have led to scholarly suspicion of *Night and Day*. In order to defend it against the dismissive charge of being an 'apprentice novel',[55] some critics have highlighted *Night and Day*'s distinctive modernist features[56] or linked its concerns to her later safely modernist works.[57] Although this critical wrangling over

Night and Day's stylistic status has often dominated discussion of this novel, scholars have recently begun the work of exploring its intriguing political and social content.[58]

Although eighteen and nineteen years separate *Night and Day* from the publication of *The Years* and *Three Guineas* respectively, these works, which Woolf initially conceived of as a single project, wedding fiction and polemic, reprise many of the debates and preoccupations of this early novel. Woolf herself makes the connection between these projects in her diary: 'after abstaining from the novel of fact all these years – since 1919 – & N[ight] & D[ay]. indeed, I find myself infinitely delighting in facts for a change, & in possession of quantities beyond counting' (D4 129). Some of the facts and ideas that Woolf explores in these later works must have been stored up not just since she wrote *Night and Day* but since her early activism with the PSF. These companion texts show Woolf still committed to adultist principles and still thinking through the political and social legacies of the campaign for women's suffrage.

* * *

Although published on 20 October 1919,[59] almost a decade after Woolf's voluntary work with the PSF, *Night and Day* is shot through with the imaginative significance of this activism. This preoccupation with the suffrage is less surprising when we consider the gains made by the movement during the years Woolf was drafting the novel. In February 1918 a proportion of women (including Woolf) were granted the franchise by the Representation of the People Act, which also opened up the franchise to all men over the age of twenty-one. And although, as Snaith and Whitworth have noted,[60] it is difficult to tell exactly when Woolf's second novel is set, a number of features, among them Mary Datchet's activism, confirm that it is set in pre-war London, most probably around 1909 or 1910.[61]

In *Night and Day* we encounter a tribute to the equality politics of the PSF and an engagement with its adultist agenda. While the satirical rendering of Mary Datchet's suffrage office and her committed, if comic, colleagues Mrs Seal and Mr Clacton is frequently accepted as evidence of Woolf's contempt for activism, Alex Zwerdling suggests it is a 'mistake to take such passages as Woolf's declarations of independence from the women's movement' and insists that they give voice to Woolf's frustration with 'the narrowly political focus the Suffragette agitation had created'.[62] Zwerdling is right to note the element of critique in Woolf's presentation of Mrs Seal's belligerent devotion to 'the cause' and what is cast as her naive belief in the transformative effects of the franchise (*ND* 141). However, rather than being prompted by a belief that the votes for women campaign had overshadowed other significant 'women's movement' issues, I would argue that the criticisms levelled against suffrage campaigners in the novel can be read as expressions of Woolf's adultist sympathies and her alliance to those campaigners Margaret Llewelyn Davies described as 'democratic suffragists'.

The reader's first glimpse of the office of 'Mary's society for woman's suffrage' in chapter 6 comes in bathetic conclusion to the account of Mary's walk to work 'across Lincoln's Inn Fields and up Kingsway' (*ND* 62), during which she happily identifies with the anonymous tide of workers moving into the city. Mary's perambulatory reflections are rapidly undercut when she reaches her office:

> The suffrage office was at the top of one of the large Russell Square houses, which [...] was now let out in slices to a number of societies which displayed assorted initials upon doors of ground glass, and kept, each of them, a typewriter which clicked busily all day long [...] The noise of the different typewriters already at work, disseminating their views upon the protection of native races, or the value of cereals as foodstuffs, quickened Mary's steps, and she always ran up the last flight of steps which led to her own landing, at whatever hour she came, so as to get her typewriter to take its place in competition with the rest. (*ND* 63)

The preponderance of societies housed in the building and the diversity of their views begin to undo the feeling of cohesion and identification that characterised Mary's walk to work. The description of the building divided up into different 'slices', the busy and inharmonious 'clicking' of 'different typewriters' and Mary's panicked sprint 'up the last flight of stairs' so that her own typewriter can 'take its place in competition with the rest', cumulatively work to create a sense of disunity and contention. More troubling still is the underlying suggestion in this passage that the distinctions between these societies rest only in 'the assorted initials' that appear on their doors. A similar impression of arbitrariness is created by references throughout the novel to the anonymous but manifold leaflets produced by Mary's society – 'a pyramid of leaflets' (*ND* 64); 'Leaflet No. 3' (*ND* 137); 'the lemon-coloured leaflets' (*ND* 215). While this narrative scepticism about Mary's society and its dismissiveness of pressure groups in general may be put down to Woolf's oft-discussed mistrust of societies and groups, this critique in *Night and Day* is, at least in part, informed by her experience of volunteering with the PSF. This becomes all the more clear when we encounter Mary's co-workers.

Mrs Seal's unbridled enthusiasm for the 'cause' of women's suffrage is treated with both comic flippancy and critical impatience. Jane Wheare reads this caricaturing of Mrs Seal as an 'over-zealous philanthropist' as reflecting Woolf's belief, 'one which she repeatedly voices elsewhere against philanthropists, namely, that all too often dedication to a "cause" is accompanied by a lack of sympathy for individual human beings'.[63] Woolf's vexed attitudes towards philanthropy are touched on in chapter 1; however, the portraits of philanthropists we encounter in Woolf's fiction are rather more varied than Wheare suggests. While Miss Willatt in her early story 'Memoirs of a Novelist' is cast in the mould of Mrs Humphry Ward, Eleanor Pargiter in *The Years*, whose visits to the poor and sick of East London and whose philanthropic cottages are surely based on Stella Duckworth's charitable enterprises, is a sympathetic character whose commitment to social reform is tempered by personal misgivings about the value of her work. In *Night and Day* there is a pointed and historically situated critique that operates through Mrs Seal and her face, 'permanently flushed with philanthropic enthusiasm' (*ND* 64).

Mrs Seal's excited listing of her social reforming credentials to Katharine over tea in the suffrage office is evidence of this historical potency: 'I think I've been on as many committees as most people. Waifs and Strays, Rescue Work, Church Work, C.O.S., – local branch – besides the usual civic duties which fall to one as a householder' (*ND* 69). While Pamela Transue argues that Mrs Seal's numerous philanthropic commitments characterise her as 'a ludicrous figure, a perpetual enthusiast who loves a cause, any cause', Mrs Seal's career in voluntarism reveals a more pointed, political function to her activities.[64] Mrs Seal's references to 'Waifs and Strays' and 'Church Work' suggest the activities of any middle-class lady do-gooder; however, the Charity Organisation Society (COS) holds rather more specific and contentious connotations. The COS was a late-Victorian private charity which collected information about the poor with the aim of discerning between the deserving and undeserving.[65] Virginia Stephen was sceptical about the COS, as we can see from her references to her cousin Marny's work for them in her early letters. In a letter to Emma Vaughan, Virginia Stephen suggests her own work at Morley is preferable to 'the poverty and crime in which Marny's lurid soul delights' (L1 200), implying that there was some sinister power-play involved in her cousin's slumming in East London. Leonard Woolf, who for a time in 1912 volunteered with Marny at the COS, expresses similar reservations about its aims and methods in his autobiography, crediting his experiences on the COS care committee with converting him to socialism.[66]

Mrs Seal's background in these paternalistic forms of late-Victorian philanthropy – the exact sort that Virginia Stephen had such reservations about – encourages us to see the suffrage office as similarly conservative and Woolf's antagonism towards it as rooted in the same anxiety about reactionary modes of social reform. This is reinforced by Mrs Seal's reference to 'the usual civic duties which fall to one as a householder'. This apparently throwaway remark has rich implications and succeeds in rooting *Night and Day*'s otherwise anonymous suffrage society not only within the politics of the movement, but specifically within the context of the PSF's manifesto. Mrs Seal's reference to her status as a householder recalls the terms of the limited bill that most suffrage societies campaigned for, which would extend the vote to women on the same terms as men with one of the primary conditions being ownership of property. For the PSF this prioritising of the rights of householders was undemocratic and inspired their slogan 'persons not property'.[67]

Rather than representing mere comic relief, Mrs Seal's teatime chatter importantly locates *Night and Day*'s treatment of the suffrage within the politics of the PSF. This is also evident in Mrs Seal's utter devotion to Miss Markham, one of the leaders of the society. We are told that only Mrs Seal's 'vast enthusiasm and her worship of Miss Markham, one of the pioneers of the society, kept her in her place, for which she had no sound qualification' (*ND* 64). While it might be tempting to focus on the second half of this quotation, on Mrs Seal's apparent unsuitability for her, albeit voluntary, role, the more revealing element in terms of Woolf's critique is certainly

Mrs Seal's 'worship of Miss Markham'. The way in which Mrs Seal's evangelical commitment to the cause is bound up with her devotion to its leader recalls the cult of personality that emerged around Emmeline and Christabel Pankhurst in the Women's Social and Political Union (WSPU), and encourages us to see the suffrage society in *Night and Day* as not only based on the WSPU, but also as sending up the Pankhursts in particular. The clearest example of this comes in chapter 13, where on arriving at her office Mary Datchet is greeted by Mrs Seal and Miss Markham's dog:

> She ran upstairs as usual, and was completely awakened to reality by the sight of Mrs Seal, on the landing outside the office, inducing a very large dog to drink water out of a tumbler.
> 'Miss Markham has already arrived,' Mrs Seal remarked, with due solemnity, 'and this is her dog'. (*ND* 135)

The bathetic substitution of Miss Markham with her dog undercuts our expectations of a grave and noble figure, while Mrs Seal's identification with the dog emphasises her hound-like loyalty. Here Woolf appears again to be rehearsing familiar criticisms levelled at women's suffrage groups, in particular the WSPU, that they were structured autocratically, while also hinting at the fundamentally undemocratic nature of the campaign for limited reform.

The PSF's campaigning platform for democratic suffrage reform was constructed in clear opposition to this and a critique of single-issue campaigning and limited reform was at the heart of all of its campaign material. This argument is set out most compellingly at the conclusion of the PSF's leaflet, *Facts about the Franchise*:

> As it is, it would be a mistake both of tactics and of principle to identify women's suffrage with a measure so unfair to working people. The right tactics for the true friends of women are to press for a democratic suffrage [...] and leave the limited Bill to its natural friends, the conservatives.[68]

Woolf's playful treatment of the campaign for women's suffrage in this episode and in the novel as a whole may be read as a more serious satire on the undemocratic strategies of these groups, a critique informed by her encounter with the PSF and its platform of democratic suffragism.

Furthermore, the choice of Miss Markham's name also encourages us to view Woolf's critique as historically rooted in the complex political landscape of the suffrage campaign in 1910. Violet Markham, along with Mrs Humphry Ward (again), was among the most prominent members of the Women's National Anti-Suffrage League, established in 1908.[69] And while it is possible to read this decision to name the leader of her fictional suffrage society after a notorious anti-suffragist as just another of Woolf's pranks in her effort to send up the suffrage movement, it has more serious implications and should be read as part of a calculated critique of women suffragists rather than as a wholesale spoof of the movement. By making Miss Markham in *Night and Day* share her name with Violet Markham, Woolf appears to muddy the boundaries between proponents of women's suffrage and its opponents, sinisterly hinting at the hypocrisy of the single-issue campaign.

This critique of the conservatism of women suffrage campaigners, and particularly the Pankhursts' suffragettes, is staged more explicitly in *The Years*. The adultist agenda at work in *The Years* is at its clearest in Woolf's characterisation of Rose Pargiter.[70] A committed suffragette who is imprisoned for smashing windows in the '1914' section of the book, by the 'Present Day' Rose has received a medal for her 'work in the war' (*TY* 263). Sowon Park has roundly challenged affirmative readings of Rose as heroic or symbolic of Woolf's feminist politics.[71] Identifying the military tropes that accompany Rose throughout the novel and her belligerent and possessive pride in 'her country', Park argues that the 'militant suffragism as practised by Rose Pargiter is not on the side of human progress', and that Woolf seeks to show that it 'is rather a section in the continuum of violence that has fascism and militarism as its extreme.'[72] Rose, with her soldierly bearing, love of speeches (*TY* 304) and taste for medals, should be read as a satire on the WSPU as Park suggests, but, as with Mrs Seal, her actions should also be read in the context of Woolf's adultist sympathies. A number of characters voice criticisms of Rose that echo the PSF position on women's suffrage. Martin refers to the speed with which suffragettes re-positioned themselves as friends to the government when war broke out and hints at the violent outcomes of their public embrace of jingoism during the First World War: ' "She smashed his window," Martin jeered at her [Rose], "and then she helped him to smash other people's windows" ' (*TY* 307).

Ostracised for their adultism in 1910, at the outbreak of war a number of former PSF members faced further rancour for their pacifism and continued commitment to forging international feminist links.[73] Woolf's native pacifism is now seen as a pillar of her politics, but Kitty Lasswade's insistence at the close of *The Years* – 'Rose is a fine fellow, [...] But Rose was wrong, [...] Force is always wrong,' (*TY* 307) – should encourage us to consider how far her work with PSF was a source of this commitment.

Woolf's satirical treatment of the suffrage campaigners in *Night and Day* and *The Years* is historically specific and inflected by the adultist platform of the PSF. This is also clear in the characterisation of Mr Clacton, Mary's other co-worker at the suffrage office in *Night and Day*. While Mrs Seal is depicted as essentially well meaning if misguided, Mr Clacton is an altogether more malevolent figure. He is a character through whom Woolf formulates her most striking criticisms, ones that would reverberate throughout her subsequent work. Little attention has been paid to the character of Mr Clacton; possibly the classed terms in which he is described (*ND* 64) and Woolf's unpleasant sneering at his desire for culture – signalled by 'the yellow-volume' (*ND* 65) in the crook of his arm – have led critics to dismiss Mr Clacton as a flight of snobbish fancy. And while class is an important lens through which to study Mr Clacton's character, it is also important to recognise the ways in which, through his gender and status as the only man in the society office in *Night and Day*, Woolf begins to develop the theories about masculinity, misogyny and the desire for power that are at the heart of her polemic writing. The description of Mr Clacton's preparations for a committee meeting is a striking example of this:

> Mr. Clacton was in his glory. The machinery which he had perfected and controlled was now about to turn out its bi-monthly product, a committee meeting; and his pride in the perfect structure of these assemblies was great. He loved the jargon of committee-rooms; he loved the way in which the door kept opening as the clock struck the hour, in obedience to a few strokes of his pen on a piece of paper; and when it had opened sufficiently often, he loved to issue from his inner chamber with documents in his hands, visibly important, with a preoccupied expression on his face that might have suited a Prime Minister advancing to meet his Cabinet. (*ND* 137)

The use of 'glory' in the first sentence is pointed, indicating Mr Clacton's hunger for distinction while obliquely recalling the rhetoric of the First World War. Having introduced this masculine culture of glory, Woolf proceeds in a controlled and systematic way to dismantle it through her account of what she characterises as Mr Clacton's perverse and performative pleasure in committee meetings. The reference to 'the machinery which he had perfected' not only implies Mr Clacton's authoritarian desire for control, but the conspicuous use of the words 'machinery' and then 'product' deny Mr Clacton's activities a deeper sense of purpose, suggesting it is precisely the mechanised, anonymous process he relishes. Later, the stifling uniformity of the opening of the door in 'obedience' to the 'strokes of his pen' shares an emphasis on process rather than end result and the telling use of the word 'obedience' also implies something sinister at work in Mr Clacton's 'pride' in his committee meetings.

The emphasis on Mr Clacton's instinctive desire for control and his need to be at the centre of events dictating procedure anticipates Woolf's critique of what she characterises as an essentially masculine desire for domination,[74] which exerts itself both in public and private life, in her 1938 feminist polemic, *Three Guineas*. In Mr Clacton's love of 'the jargon of committee-rooms' we find the stirrings of Woolf's profound mistrust of corrupt terminology. Mr Clacton's commitment to the ritual of the committee meeting, and the way in which he is made to feel 'visibly important' by these events, foreshadows Woolf's explicit critique of the egotism and pomposity behind public ceremonies and displays organised by bodies such as the Army and the University. In *Three Guineas* Woolf focuses on the 'symbolical meaning' of ceremonial dress, suggesting its prime purpose is to 'advertise' the social standing of its wearer; Mr Clacton's props of 'documents in his hands' and his 'preoccupied expression' represent early stand-ins for the rosettes and stripes Woolf describes in *Three Guineas* (*TG* 134–7).

While the legacy of the PSF is identifiable in the motifs and arguments of *Three Guineas*, it is worth noting that this group and indeed the cause of adult suffrage are not explicitly identified in Woolf's polemic. By contrast, Woolf engages directly, if ambivalently, with the heritage of the women's suffrage movement, referring to the WSPU and to its leader Emmeline Pankhurst (*TG* 166–7). And it would appear that by identifying herself as a spokeswoman for the daughters of educated men in *Three Guineas*, Woolf traces her lineage back to the middle-class, campaigning women who sought 'votes for women' rather than 'womanhood and manhood suffrage' on equal terms.[75]

In spite of this clear engagement with the history of the women's suffrage cause, Woolf's notorious rejection of what she describes as the 'vicious and corrupt word ... "feminist"' (*TG* 227) in *Three Guineas* can be usefully understood in terms of Virginia Stephen's involvement in the campaign for adult suffrage. Not only does Woolf's emphatic and repeated use of the word 'corrupt' to describe the word 'feminist' accord with her critique of the single-issue platform we encounter in *Night and Day*, her vision of a literally post-feminist mode of activism in *Three Guineas* is a striking echo of the PSF's universal platform: 'The word "feminist" is destroyed; the air is cleared; and in that clearer air what do we see? Men and women working together for the same cause' (*TG* 227).

Berenice Carroll has argued that Woolf's ritual destruction of the word 'feminist' in *Three Guineas* is an example of her often misunderstood 'biting sarcasm' and has suggested that for Woolf 'labels simply could not express the real meaning of feminist struggle'.[76] Carroll goes on to suggest that Woolf's suspicion of feminism can be read as reflecting her mistrust of 'organized suffrage groups' and their capacity for generating meaningful political change. Carroll touches briefly on Woolf's own involvement in the movement: 'and though she did some suffrage work before World War I, her attitude toward the suffrage societies is markedly ambivalent, as appears most clearly in *Night and Day*'.[77] Carroll's linking of *Three Guineas*, *Night and Day* and the suffrage is highly suggestive. To return to the quote above from *Three Guineas*, it seems clear that there we find not simply hostility to suffragism, but also a veiled expression of adultist resistance to the narrow and elitist demands of many women's suffrage societies. This is, of course, most clear in Woolf's revivification of PSF rhetoric in her bold statement: 'Men and women working together for the same cause'.

Night and Day contains other more direct gestures to the PSF itself. Mary Datchet's work-in-progress, a volume entitled 'Some Aspects of the Democratic State' (*ND* 226), which she surreptitiously works on after office hours, recalls the principles of the PSF. Likewise, a disguised version of the PSF appears towards the end of the novel in the form of Mr Basnett's 'Society for the Education of Democracy upon Capital', to which Mary eventually defects from the suffrage office. This society's 'scheme for the education of labour, for the amalgamation of the middle class and the working class, and for a joint assault of the two bodies' (*ND* 302) echoes the PSF's mission statement:

> The Federation's field of work differs from that of other suffrage societies. It has set itself to win the support of organised movements, industrial and political, men's and women's, so that its task is like that of several movements in one.[78]

Mary's decision to leave the narrow field of suffrage campaigning to work for this amalgamated body for democratic reform is characterised as progressive and directly contributes towards her ennobled position at the end of the novel, an imposing but 'serene' silhouette behind an illuminated window (*ND* 431).

* * *

There is certainly evidence of adultist agendas at work in *Night and Day*, *The Years* and *Three Guineas*, and while Virginia Stephen's early association with a body campaigning for the rights of both the working classes and women holds a great appeal, her engagement with this activity was by no means straightforward or celebratory. While it may be argued that Woolf concludes her second novel with an affectionate gesture to the ideals that inspired the PSF ten years earlier, her letter to Janet Case in late 1910 strikes an altogether more ambivalent note. In it she appears to declare an end to her year-long career as a PSF activist by way of an arch question, surely calculated to frustrate her earnest friend: 'Do you ever take that side of politics into account – the inhuman side, and how all the best feelings are shrivelled?' (*L1* 441).

Reading Woolf's hostile treatment of the suffrage office in *Night and Day* as an expression of her adultist convictions rather than as reflecting a general antagonism towards social and political activism is, for the most part, convincing. However, there remains running through the novel a vein of profound scepticism regarding political and social action, similar to the one we find in this 1910 letter to Janet Case.

While *Night and Day*'s presentation of Mrs Seal and Mr Clacton seems to operate straightforwardly as a form of adultist critique, by unpacking the ambiguous and often contradictory figure of Mary Datchet we access a simultaneous but subtextual debate about the value and viability of political action.[79] It is precisely the concurrency of these two strands of argument in *Night and Day* that lends it its peculiar combination of stylisation and conventionality, which has traditionally led to scholarly unease with this novel.

Mary Datchet is the most neglected character in a neglected novel. Those critics who do discuss her characterisation and role in the novel have gestured to the uneasy position she occupies in spite of her appearance of absolute straightforwardness.[80] In her reading of the novel's conclusion, Jane Marcus suggests: '[o]ne [...] has the odd feeling that the only really satisfactory ending to the novel would be in Katharine Hilbery's marriage, not to Ralph but to Mary Datchet'.[81] This reading interestingly uncovers sororal themes in the novel, and gestures to the unsatisfactory way in which Mary Datchet's story is cut short in *Night and Day*. Anna Snaith has also suggested there is greater significance to Mary's activism in the novel than being merely the standard attribute of any New Woman character, highlighting the degree to which she is 'ambivalent about the suffrage cause and the efficacy of the Society and its workers'.[82] Taking Snaith's evaluation of Mary Datchet as a point of departure, I consider here what Mary's political and social involvement and her profound ambivalence towards this work might mean. Following on from my suggestion that some of Woolf's most powerful feminist arguments put forward in *Three Guineas* are rehearsed in *Night and Day*, I want to make a case for *Night and Day* as a formative text in Woolf's development as a political thinker. Through the character of Mary Datchet Woolf reflects seriously on arguments about political action and, most importantly, the persistence of activism in the face of fundamental ambivalence.[83]

In her discussion of *Night and Day*, Jane Wheare suggests that 'the absence of caricature in Woolf's portrayal of Mary [...] lends authority to her world-view'.[84] It is certainly true that Mary is not mocked in the same pantomimic way that Mrs Seal and Mr Clacton are. However, it is worth noting that in the place of this caricature there is a more sophisticated form of narrative irony that dogs Mary throughout the novel, questioning her world-view and the value of her activism. This irony characterises the narrative's treatment of Mary Datchet's writing and of her manuscript in ways that reveal the complicated politics of the novel.

Mary's 'manuscript' represents a prominent gesture to the PSF in *Night and Day* but also operates in another quite distinct way. The first glimpse the reader has of this work-in-progress is in telling circumstances. Ralph Denham has just insisted 'you don't read enough, Mary [...] You ought to read more poetry' (*ND* 108) and then belittled her suffrage work, criticising its parochialism and narrowness. Reeling from this, Mary seeks out her manuscript:

> She then went to a drawer, which she had to unlock, and took from it certain deeply scored manuscript pages. She read them through, looking up from her reading every now and then and thinking very intently for a few seconds about Ralph [...] Then she looked back again at her manuscript, and decided that to write grammatical English prose is the hardest thing in the world. (*ND* 110)

It is easy to miss this passage. Yet there are some details in the language and punctuation of these sentences, which suggest their (subversive) significance. The parenthetical use of commas in the first sentence draws our attention to the fact the pages are secreted away in a locked drawer, while the phrase 'certain deeply scored manuscript pages' is deliberately evasive. While Mary's reflections on the difficulty of writing 'grammatical English prose' may be read as an attempt to lighten the introspective quality of the close of this chapter, this hyperbolic statement and the careful phrasing of this passage register a certain anxiety about writing that is explored in greater depth when the manuscript appears later in the novel.

Mary's manuscript does not appear again for over 100 pages until chapter 21 when she again seeks solace in her writing after rejecting Ralph's botched marriage proposal:

> Within a few minutes of opening her door, she was in trim for a hard evening's work. She unlocked a drawer and took out a manuscript, which consisted of a very few pages, entitled in a forcible hand, 'Some Aspects of the Democratic State'. (*ND* 225)

The reappearance of the manuscript is significant and perplexing. Although the ritual unlocking of the drawer and the recurrent use of the word 'manuscript' link this episode to the earlier one in chapter 10, leading the reader to assume both episodes refer to the same piece of writing, there are ways in which this passage subverts this assumption. The narrator refers to 'a very few pages' and 'a manuscript' as though this were the first time the reader had encountered them. While it is possible that the two manuscripts are indeed discrete projects, it is more interesting to read this as a lapse, as some telling forgetfulness on the part of the narrator,[85] and one which encourages us to think more deeply about what Woolf might be saying through Mary's project.

The description of Mary's work in this chapter also registers the vague snootiness levelled against it in the earlier chapter: 'The aspects dwindled out in a criss-cross of blotted lines in the very middle of a sentence, and suggested that the author had been interrupted, or convinced of the futility of proceeding' (*ND* 225). The narrator's dismissive references to the dwindling quality of Mary's writing and to the 'criss-cross of blotted lines' that blemish her pages not only suggest Mary's amateurism but also continue this peculiar but persistent narrative cloaking of the real contents and purpose of Mary's writing. It is worth noting that the presentation of Mary's writing lacks the warmth and charm that is reserved for Mrs Hilbery's 'will-o'-the wisp' (*ND* 30) efforts to write her father's biography. It is arguable that as Mary's text is a political tract rather than a work of literary biography it would doubtless inspire less sympathy from the novel's rather conservative narrator.[86] However, I would also suggest that the presentation of Mary's work has a more general, but perhaps more powerful point here. The way in which the manuscript bears the evidence that 'the author had been interrupted' registers an early example of Woolf's preoccupation with the conditions faced by women writers and anticipates her reflections on interruptions in *A Room of One's Own* (*AROO* 71). Likewise, using the word 'author' here, rather than identifying Mary specifically, generalises the terms of this passage in a way that encourages the reader to reflect on the situation of women writers more broadly. Conversely, this use of 'author' could imply particularity too. Indeed, it is possible to read this as an instance in which Woolf has written her own authorial anxiety into the text and that the author in this passage, so convinced of the 'futility' of their endeavours, is Woolf herself.[87]

Reading Mary's writing as reflecting Woolf's early concerns with the status of the woman writer, while at the same time being informed by her personal writerly anxieties, is borne out by the following excerpt:

> Ralph had told her once that she couldn't write English, which accounted for those frequent blots and insertions; but she put all that behind her, and drove ahead with such words as came her way, until she had accomplished half a page of generalization and might legitimately draw breath. (*ND* 225)

Ralph Denham's definitive statement that Mary 'couldn't write' is another example of Woolf rehearsing ideas about women and writing that would feature more prominently in later work. This male critique of women's creativity anticipates Charles Tansley's more famous indictment, whispered in Lily Briscoe's ear, 'women can't paint, women can't write' (*TTL* 54).

Woolf's decision to make Mary – the most overtly politically and socially engaged character in the novel – a conduit for her own introspective writerly anxiety is surprising and important. Woolf's anxiety about the value of her writing was informed by constant comparison with the social and political work undertaken by friends and by her husband. While she often saw them as contrasting, even oppositional activities, for Woolf they were certainly imaginatively associated with each other.

It seems strange, then, that Woolf should have fashioned this same feeling of futility and writerly struggle in the character of Mary Datchet. Sowon Park has suggested that in *Night and Day* Woolf represents the 'gulf between the world of high culture and the world of suffrage' each 'represented respectively by Katharine and Mary'.[88] While this concern with the clash of culture and politics is certainly present in *Night and Day*, the conflicting demands of literary and political identities are both played out in the character of Mary Datchet, who is not simply representative of a certain kind of political woman but also a character that speaks obliquely of Woolf's own insecurity as a writer.

This discussion of the ways in which Mary Datchet's authorial anxiety may mirror Woolf's own inner debate about the value of her writing brings us back to the question of Mary's ambivalence towards the suffrage and the degree to which this too is expressive of Woolf's own position. It seems clear that the sentiments Virginia Stephen expressed at the end of her time volunteering for the PSF in a 1910 letter to Janet Case ('Do you ever take that side of politics into account – the inhuman side, and how all the best feelings are shrivelled?') reverberate throughout the novel and can be found on the lips of a variety of characters including Ralph Denham (*ND* 108–9), Katharine Hilbery (*ND* 80), Mr Hilbery (*ND* 81) and also Mary Datchet (*ND* 156). It is also true that some years after her initial voluntary role with the PSF, Woolf encountered a group that had inherited the adultist platform of the PSF and counted among its members many ex-PSF campaigners. By way of a conclusion to this discussion of Mary Datchet and *Night and Day* I explore the ways in which Woolf's brief and sideways encounter with the National Council for Adult Suffrage may have informed the model of ambivalent activism she constructs through Mary Datchet and continues to wrangle with in *The Years*, almost two decades later.

* * *

Virginia Woolf's diary entry for 12 November 1917 is brief but replete with gossip: bumping into Roger Fry at the Omega studios and then an unexpected meeting with Clive Bell and Mary Hutchinson at Gordon Square and 'some Garsington gossip' (*D1* 75). After some light comments about the book she is reading, Woolf ends the entry by writing: 'L. is at the Suffrage; & I watch 3 fireballs glowing red hot' (*D1* 75). This shift in tone recalls the conclusion of Virginia Stephen's letter years earlier to Nelly Cecil where she demands: 'Are you an Adult Suffragist?' The ambiguous phrasing of this diary entry and its final image of Woolf brooding over '3 fireballs glowing red' encourage further reflection on the ways in which the suffrage campaign, although in its closing days, still preyed upon Woolf's mind.

Woolf's peculiarly worded reference to Leonard being 'at the Suffrage' interests me. In comparison to the precise and indicative nature of her references to adult suffrage in her 1910 letters, this use of 'the Suffrage' as a noun seems evasive. Although according to Leonard Woolf's diary he spent the evening of 12 November at a meeting of the executive committee of the League of Nations Society (*D1* 74) and Woolf's reference to 'the Suffrage' gives us few clues as to which suffrage group Leonard was affiliated with at this late stage in the campaign, it is clear from the limited records of the National Council for Adult Suffrage that in 1917 Leonard Woolf was a member of its executive committee.[89] Other members of the executive of the NCAS include familiar names from the PSF: Margaret Llewelyn Davies, J. S. Middleton and Margaret Bondfield.[90]

A brief look at the history of the NCAS reveals not only an overlap in membership with the PSF but that it was also campaigning along similar adultist lines. Born out of the Votes for All group, chaired by Helena Swanwick, the NCAS was officially formed at a conference on 22 September 1916, 'pulling together the left-wing campaign for adult suffrage'.[91] Just a month before the founding of the NCAS an open letter to the Prime Minister, H. H. Asquith, appeared in *The Yorkshire Post* under the heading 'A Demand for Adult Suffrage'.[92] This letter reiterates many of the claims and arguments at the centre of the PSF campaign and it makes use of a similar rhetoric of equality and democracy. The NCAS's chief legislative recommendation – 'to give the vote to every adult man and woman on a short residential qualification' – repeats exactly that of the PSF. Likewise, their desire to see 'Parliament truly representative of the nation' and the frequent references to the rights of all classes are reminiscent of the strong Labour Party influence within the campaign for adult suffrage.[93] The arguments put forward in this letter are lent greater urgency and poignancy by being repeatedly placed in the context of the war:

> They [the people] are prepared to say that the youth who had not so much as a latchkey wherewith to qualify, but who has been willing to risk his young life, has earned the right to a vote, and the use of it when he returns.[94]

By February 1917 the NCAS was under increasing pressure to accept the limited suffrage bill proposed by the 1917 Speaker's Conference. At a meeting organised by the NCAS at Kingsway, *The Christian Commonwealth* reported that it was grudgingly accepted that 'it would be a considerable gain to have even the illogical and timorous recommendations of the Speaker's Conference embodied in a Government Bill'.[95]

Woolf's ambivalent reference to 'the Suffrage' in her diary entry and the fact that Leonard appears to take up her adult suffragist activism are worth considering in more detail. Laura Moss Gottlieb has argued that Virginia and Leonard Woolf not only held divergent political views but that Leonard Woolf '[h]aving given up his strictly literary efforts early in their marriage [...] may have felt that, if his wife was going to be the literary genius in the family, he was entitled to be the sole political commentator'.[96] Leonard Woolf's co-option of the cause of adult suffrage, which Virginia Woolf had campaigned for ten years earlier, and Virginia Woolf's apparent lack of interest in the cause can be interestingly understood in the terms of Gottlieb's argument.

Yet Woolf's portrait of herself watching the 'fireballs' is expressive of more than a lack of interest. As well as being a statement of non-participation it is also an expression of self-recrimination. Such moments of intense and ambivalent reflection recur throughout *Night and Day* and are taken up as a motif in *The Years*. While Mary Datchet is presented throughout *Night and Day* as dynamic, strong and active – 'quite capable of lifting a kitchen table on her back, if need were' (*ND* 36) – the reader just as frequently catches her in moments of deep reverie or self-reflection not dissimilar from that which Woolf describes in her November 1917 diary entry. After a busy morning of work in the suffrage office, Mary spends her lunchtime gazing at the Elgin Marbles in the British Museum (*ND* 65) and once she has returned to the office, 'watching the flight of a bird' (*ND* 66). Later, in the midst of the committee meeting Mr Clacton has organised, we are told Mary 'was looking out of the window, and thinking of the colour of the sky, and of the decorations on the Imperial Hotel' (*ND* 138). While these may be read as instances of Mary being distracted from her work by thoughts of Ralph, there is something more focused and ultimately productive in Mary's 'watching'. These are moments in which her ambivalence towards the cause takes hold, requiring her to think more deeply about the nature and value of her activism.

Ann Ronchetti argues that 'Woolf's difficulty in portraying Mary lies in her ambivalence about Mary's work as a reformer and her status as a woman who lives without heterosexual love'.[97] This overlooks the more compelling and ultimately more illuminating question of Mary's ambivalence and what Woolf is saying through this.

By frequently showing Mary in moments of contemplation, Woolf suggests that this is a necessary accompaniment to her activism. *Night and Day*'s championing of Mary Datchet should not be read necessarily as a championing of the suffrage cause, but rather in the figure of Mary Datchet we find the inauguration of a form of political action that embraces self-questioning and accepts unease.

This model of ambivalent activism is also crucial to Woolf's later novel, *The Years*.[98] Eleanor Pargiter's thoughts during a suffrage meeting,[99] which takes place in the '1910' chapter of the novel, bear a striking resemblance to those of Mary Datchet during the committee meeting in *Night and Day*. Although Eleanor appears to be similarly distracted by the world outside the meeting, unlike Mary Datchet she is able to enunciate her contradictory feelings about the meeting and the value of the kind of political action it stands for:

> Why must we do it? Eleanor thought, drawing a spoke from the hole in the middle. She looked up. Someone was rattling a stick along the railings and whistling; the branches of a tree swung up and down in the garden outside. The leaves were already unfolding ... Miriam put down her papers; Mr Spicer rose.
> There's no other way, I suppose, she thought, taking up her pencil again. (*TY* 129)

This is a developed version of the earlier committee room episode from *Night and Day*.[100] But here Woolf is more explicit about her character's unease with the process in hand – this is clear in Eleanor's asking herself 'Why must we do it?' and her failure to concentrate on the meeting. This passage reflects Woolf's abiding interest in the nature of social and political participation, and Eleanor's wary conclusion that '[t]here's no other way' and her decision to take up her pencil hint at the distinctive place ambivalence held in Woolf's thinking about political practice.

The preoccupation with the value of activism – what it amounts to – we find in this relatively early episode in the novel transforms into a more urgent debate about the risks of taking action in the final, 'Present Day' chapter. Eleanor's refrain, 'Why must we do it?', repeated throughout the preceding chapters, finds itself transformed in the mouth of her dissatisfied nephew North who instead asks: 'What we ought to do? ... What ought we to do?' (*TY* 309).

Having sold his farm in Africa and returned to England, North is thoroughly out of sorts. His elderly relatives are incomprehensible to him, as are the thrusting, politically engaged young men he encounters at his aunt Delia's party (*TY* 295).[101] North rejects the models of engagement he sees around him, whether it is his uncle Patrick's and Kitty's debate about the 'old days' and social progress (*TY* 293) or what he sees as the brave new world of 'joining societies' and 'signing manifestos' (*TY* 296).

It is clear to North that there is something broken in the current practice of politics: 'Something's wrong, he thought; there's a gap, a dislocation, between the word and reality' (*TY* 296). In a rehearsal of a number of the arguments in *Three Guineas*, North locates the source of his unease in a gestural politics: 'There was the pump-handle gesture; the wringing-wet-clothes gesture; and then the voice, oddly detached from the little figure and tremendously magnified by the loudspeaker, went booming and bawling round the hall: Justice! Liberty!' (*TY* 296). This anxiety about a politics wedded to performance can be identified in the '1910' chapter of the novel. Eleanor is dismissive of the political types she sees around her at the meeting – 'There's the Judd type, there's the Lazenby Type' (*TY* 129) – and in a manuscript draft of this chapter Rose strategises on the bus on the way to the meeting and we are told 'she had rehearsed her speech in her bath that morning'.[102] Even so, in this final chapter North is far from completely disenchanted with politics. He and his sister Peggy struggle throughout with their desire to forge a new kind of political practice, clinging to the hope that they will one day 'live differently' (*TY* 309).

This is a different, perhaps more anxious debate than we find in *Night and Day*, which is certainly a result of its 1930s context. While appearing to sneer at the political young men and their responses to fascism in *The Years*, Woolf writes directly in response to the same threat. The fraught character of North's reflections speaks of an urgent need for new ways of thinking about and doing politics as Woolf saw it. And action is still necessary. The right kind of gesture, an authentic political gesture, a gesture of dissent, is still privileged here, in spite of, or rather because of, what North perceives to be the dominance of an empty gestural politics. This is clear in the portrayal of Eleanor's response to the photograph in the paper:

'Damned – ' Eleanor shot out suddenly, 'bully!' She tore the paper across with one sweep of her hand and flung it on the floor. Peggy was shocked. A little shiver ran over her skin as the paper tore. The word 'damned' on her aunt's lips had shocked her. (*TY* 242)

Although it is first the sound of the swear word on her aunt's lips that shocks and amuses her, it is Eleanor's gesture that impresses Peggy – 'And her gesture, tearing the paper ...' – and which she feels impelled to imitate, in spite of her laughter: 'And the way she tore it! she thought, half laughing, and she flung out her hand as Eleanor had flung hers.'

Throughout this syncopated chapter, which is punctuated by dozens of questions that characters ask themselves and ask each other, there remains a will to action demonstrated first in Eleanor's affirmative gesture and later in North's hesitant move to participate: 'He must make the effort. Yet he hesitated. He felt repelled and attracted, attracted and repelled. He began to rise; but before he had got on his feet somebody thumped on a table with a fork' (*TY* 303).

North's experience of these contradictory emotions, at once attracted and repelled, register an ambivalence that is the necessary accompaniment to action. In this chapter which is primarily about politics – as North self-defensively observes, all anyone talks about is 'money and politics' (*TY* 292) – Woolf and her characters continue to reflect on the efficacy of political activism and what form it should take. The self-examination and reticence in this quotation are at the heart of this politics. Like her characters in *Night and Day* and *The Years*, Virginia Woolf's persistent feelings of ambivalence and uncertainty did not compromise her political practice in her life and writing – they instead formed an invaluable, constituent part of it.

Notes

1. Virginia Woolf's later involvement with and contributions to the London Women's Service Library, founded by the London and National Society for Women's Suffrage have been explored by Anna Snaith in ' "Stray Guineas": Virginia Woolf and the Fawcett Library', *Literature and History*, 12 (2003), 16–35 and also by Barbara Green in *Spectacular Confessions: Autobiography, Performative Activism, and the Sites*

of Suffrage, 1905–1938 (Basingstoke: Macmillan, 1997), pp. 144–68. Jane Goldman has also foregrounded Woolf's awareness of the suffrage campaign and her interaction with its key figures. *The Feminist Aesthetics of Virginia Woolf*, pp. 29–30.

2. The year began with the story of Lady Constance Lytton's imprisonment in Walton Gaol in Liverpool under the assumed identity of Jane Warton, a seamstress. After going on hunger strike she was subjected to a brutal force-feeding regime, which she recalled in articles in *The Suffragette* and *The Times*. See Elizabeth Crawford's *The Women's Suffrage Movement: A Reference Guide, 1866–1928* (London: University College London Press, 1999), pp. 361–2. However, it was also a period of anticipation and optimism among both suffragists and suffragettes. In February a committee was formed to 'further the cause of women's suffrage' with Lord Lytton, brother of Constance and committed supporter of women's suffrage, at its head. This group of cross-party MPs formulated the first Conciliation Bill, which was to be introduced in Parliament on 14 June only a few days after this letter was written. For more on the Conciliation Bills of 1910 and 1911, see Roger Fulford, *Votes for Women* (London: Faber and Faber, 1957), pp. 221–34 and Sandra Stanley Holton, *Feminism and Democracy: Women's Suffrage and Reform Politics in Britain, 1900–1918* (Cambridge: Cambridge University Press, 1986), pp. 69–72.
3. David Morgan, *Suffragists and Liberals: The Politics of Women's Suffrage in Britain* (London: Basil Blackwell, 1991), pp. 43, 81.
4. *Virginia Woolf and the Real World*, p. 212.
5. *Feminism and Democracy*, p. 4.
6. *Feminism and Democracy*, p. 5.
7. *Feminism and Democracy*, p. 6.
8. In her otherwise excellent biography of Woolf, Hermione Lee describes this work as 'addressing envelopes in an NUWSS office'. *Virginia Woolf*, p. 279.
9. Jane Marcus has gestured to Virginia Stephen's adultism: 'Woolf had not been a militant suffragist, but had espoused the cause of adult suffrage [...] which stressed the solidarity of women and workers'. 'Art and Anger', *Feminist Studies*, 4 (1978), 68–98 (p. 90).
10. *Virginia Woolf as Feminist*, p. 37.
11. *Virginia Woolf as Feminist*, p. 37. Black has also flagged up Virginia Stephen's repeated use of 'adult suffrage' in her 1910 letters (p. 205).
12. Recent historians of the suffrage have focused on overlooked campaigning groups and bodies. Jo Vellacott has considered the campaigning by democratic suffragists, many of whom were also pacifists, during the First World War in her study *Pacifists, Patriots and the*

Vote: The Erosion of Democratic Suffragism in Britain During the First World War (Basingstoke: Palgrave Macmillan, 2007). Angela V. John and Claire Eustance have also explored the contributions of male suffragists to the campaign for the women's vote in their edited collection *The Men's Share?: Masculinities, Male Support and Women's Suffrage in Britain, 1890–1920* (London: Routledge, 1997).

13. *The Strange Death of Liberal England* (London: Serif, 1997), p. 139.
14. *Suffrage Days: Stories from the Women's Suffrage Movement* (London: Routledge, 1996), pp. 148–9.
15. In an otherwise groundbreaking study of the suffrage and party politics, Constance Rover provides a clipped, footnoted account of the PSF: 'The People's Suffrage Federation, claiming adult suffrage [...] conducted a very limited campaign. It was accused of a "dog in the manger" attitude, emerging only to oppose the Women's Enfranchisement Bill'. *Women's Suffrage and Party Politics in Britain, 1866–1914* (London: Routledge & Kegan Paul, 1967), p. 171.
16. The first mentions of the PSF in newspapers appear in late 1909 and its inaugural newsletter and list of members has written at its openning 'constituted in October 1909'. London, TUC Library, Gertrude Tuckwell Papers, People's Suffrage Federation [October 1909], 604/64, Box 25, Reel 12, p. 1. It is important to distinguish between the PSF and an earlier adult suffrage group named the Adult Suffrage Society with which it shared some members, including Margaret Bondfield, who, rather confusingly, refers to the PSF as the Adult Suffrage Society throughout her autobiography, *A Life's Work* (London: Hutchinson, 1948), pp. 81–2. The Gertrude Tuckwell Papers include two records of this earlier group: one December 1907 letter to its members from the acting secretary, Maud M. A. Ward, outlining proposed revisions to the constitution, and a document headed 'Proposed New Rules of the Adult Suffrage Society'. Gertrude Tuckwell Papers, 604/55 and 604/56, Box 25, Reel 12. However, the 10 November 1910 issue of *The Woman Worker* has short reports on both the PSF and the Adult Suffrage Society on the same page, suggesting they were campaigning independently at the same time (p. 445). It is also worth noting that the editorial on the Adult Suffrage Society notes that the group had agreed at a recent executive meeting that they would support no electoral reform bill that was 'based on a property qualification', unlike the PSF, which initially agreed to support the limited bill. Jill Liddington and Jill Norris provide a detailed account of the emergence of the Adult Suffrage Society in 1905 and characterise it as an attempt by some groups within the Labour Party to prevent a women's suffrage measure from being supported, revealing the tension that existed between woman suffragists

and adult suffragists in the early 1900s. *One Hand Tied Behind Us* (London: Virago, 1978), pp. 231–6.
17. London, The Women's Library (LSE), Suffrage Pamphlets, Appeal for Funds, 4 March 1910, 324.6230941 PEO.
18. Gertrude Tuckwell Papers, People's Suffrage Federation [October 1909], 604/64, Box 25, Reel 12, p. 3.
19. Gertrude Tuckwell Papers, People's Suffrage Federation [October 1909], 604/64, Box 25, Reel 12, p. 3.
20. Suffrage Pamphlets, Appeal for Funds, 4 March 1910, 324.6230941 PEO.
21. 'People's Suffrage Federation', *The Woman Worker*, 27 October 1909, p. 392.
22. 'Should Suffragists Welcome the People's Suffrage Federation?', *The Common Cause*, 9 December 1909, p. 463.
23. London, The Women's Library (LSE), Suffrage Pamphlets, *The First Annual Report of the People's Suffrage Federation. October 1909–1910*, PC/06/396-11/11.
24. Linchmere, Shulbrede Priory, Papers of Dorothea and Arthur Ponsonby, Margaret Llewelyn Davies to Dorothea Ponsonby, 2 January [n.y.]. Although this letter has no year it was certainly written pre-May 1916 as it refers to Llewelyn Davies's father as being in good health. (He died on 18 May 1916.)
25. For Holton's account of Llewelyn Davies's early attempts to alter the formulation of private members' bills on women's suffrage so that they would make some provision for working-class women, and the criticism this drew from women's suffrage groups, see *Feminism and Democracy*, p. 61. Holton suggests that the WCG, the WTUL and the WLL enthusiasm for a new adult suffrage enterprise was also inspired by the urgent need to unite the interests of Labour Party members, who demanded the extension of the franchise to working-class men, with those in favour of women's suffrage.
26. 'Miss Llewelyn Davies and The People's Suffrage Federation', *The Woman Worker*, 10 November 1909, p. 437.
27. Suffrage Pamphlets, *The First Annual Report of the People's Suffrage Federation. October 1909–191'*, PC/06/396-11/11.
28. Gertrude Tuckwell Papers, People's Suffrage Federation [October 1909], 604/64, Box 25, Reel 12, p. 2.
29. London, TUC Library, Gertrude Tuckwell Papers, *Anti-Suffragist Anxieties*, 1910, 604 II/ 152, Box 25, Reel 12.
30. London, The Women's Library (LSE), Suffrage Pamphlets, *Adult Suffrage: An Address to Democrats*, [1911], PC/06/396-11/20.

31. Bell, *Virginia Woolf: A Biography*, vol. 1, p. 161. In a sketch of 'Miss Case' in her 1903 diary, Virginia Stephen describes her tutor as 'a really valiant strong minded woman [...] possessed of clear strong views' (*PA* 183–4).
32. Suffrage Pamphlets, *The First Annual Report of the People's Suffrage Federation. October 1909–1910*, PC/06/396-11/11.
33. Gertrude Tuckwell Papers, People's Suffrage Federation, [October 1909], 604/64, Box 25, Reel 12, p. 7.
34. London, British Library, Lady Ottoline Morrell Papers, Transcription of Add MS 88886/4/6, Journal for September 1909-April 1910, Add MS 88886/6/7, p. 35.
35. Falmer, University of Sussex Special Collections at The Keep, Monks House Papers (MHP), General Correspondence of Virginia Woolf, Rosalind Nash to Virginia Stephen, 19 January 1910, SxMs18/1/D/101/1.
36. MHP, Rosalind Nash to Virginia Stephen, 19 January 1910, SxMs18/1/D/101/1.
37. MHP, Rosalind Nash to Virginia Stephen, 19 January 1910, SxMs18/1/D/101/1.
38. *Feminism and Democracy*, p. 6.
39. *Feminism and Democracy*, p. 64.
40. 'Letters', *The Common Cause*, 11 November 1909, p. 407.
41. *The Englishwoman*, January 1910, p. 257.
42. *The Englishwoman*, January 1910, p. 258.
43. *Women's Suffrage and Party Politics in Britain*, p. 14.
44. Holton has detailed how previous attempts to broaden the formulation of a women's suffrage measure, for example Margaret Llewelyn Davies's efforts to include 'a provision for the enfranchisement of married women on their husbands' property qualification' in 1907, which would have extended the vote to more working-class women, met with opposition from suffrage organisations which were 'opposed to the bill on the grounds that it was bad tactics', but many also resented the socialist principle behind it. *Feminism and Democracy*, p. 61.
45. Suffrage Pamphlets, *The First Annual Report of the People's Suffrage Federation. October 1909–1910*, PC/06/396-11/11, p. 2.
46. Suffrage Pamphlets, *The First Annual Report of the People's Suffrage Federation. October 1909–1910*, PC/06/396-11/11, p. 2.
47. Linchmere, Shulbrede Priory, Papers of Dorothea and Arthur Ponsonby, Diary of Dorothea Ponsonby, 5 August 1911, DPD1911, p. 11.
48. *Feminism and Democracy*, p. 61.
49. *Feminism and Democracy*, p. 54.

50. Suffrage Pamphlets, Appeal for Funds, 4 March 1910, 324.6230941 PEO.
51. For more on the ambiguous meaning and interpretations of 'adult suffrage' within the Labour Movement, see Holton, *Feminism and Democracy*, p. 60 and Holton, *Suffrage Days*, pp. 123–5. See also Liddington and Norris, *One Hand Tied Behind Us*, pp. 179–86, for a detailed and gripping account of the roots of 'the bitter wrangling between the adult suffragists and women suffragists' in the ILP, the nature of the resistance to any measure pressing for equal enfranchisement in the early 1900s and Emmeline Pankhurst's subsequent split with the ILP. Laura Ugolini covers similar ground, but paying particular attention to the male members of the ILP and their approach to this debate in ' "It Is Only Justice to Grant Women's Suffrage": Independent Labour Party Men and Women's Suffrage, 1893–1905', in Claire Eustance, Joan Ryan and Laura Ugolini (eds), *A Suffrage Reader: Charting Directions in British Suffrage History* (London: Leicester University Press, 2000), pp. 126–44.
52. Holton, *Feminism and Democracy*, p. 6.
53. The 'mutual suspicion' between the leadership of the NUWSS and the Labour Party eventually abated and in the wake of the three failed Conciliation Bills in 1912 the NUWSS increasingly supported Labour candidates during by-elections in order to undermine the Liberal government. For more on this later 'alliance' between suffragists and Labour, see Holton, *Feminism and Democracy*, pp. 76–96.
54. The similarities between Woolf's own life and that of her protagonist, particularly their social standing and their literary families, are worth noting. For more on these parallels, see Steve Ellis's discussion of *Night and Day* in *Virginia Woolf and the Victorians* (Cambridge: Cambridge University Press, 2007), pp. 12–42.
55. Ann Ronchetti, *The Artist, Society & Sexuality in Virginia Woolf's Novels* (New York: Routledge, 2004), p. 30.
56. Janis M. Paul suggests that the novel 'rebels thematically against its own conventional structure' through sustained questioning of the culture and principles of its Victorian setting. (*The Victorian Heritage of Virginia Woolf: The External World of Her Novels* (Oklahoma: Pilgrim Books, 1987), pp. 81). By contrast, Steve Ellis argues that Woolf's treatment of the Victorians in her novel is not antagonistic as Paul suggests, insisting that Paul's desire to 'retain its [*Night and Day's*] "true" Woolfian credentials' leads her to ignore the ways in which *Night and Day* seeks to establish a 'helpful relationship between the generations' (*Virginia Woolf and the Victorians*, pp. 33, 14).

57. See Randy Malamud's 'Splitting the Husks: Woolf's Modernist Language in *Night and Day*', *South Central Review*, 6 (1989), 32–45.
58. Jane Marcus ('Enchanted Organs, Magic Bells: *Night and Day* as Comic Opera', in *Virginia Woolf and the Languages of Patriarchy* (Bloomington: Indiana University Press, 1987), pp. 18–36), Jane Wheare (*Virginia Woolf: Dramatic Novelist*, pp. 84–110) and Susan M. Squier ('Tradition and Revision: The Classic City Novel and Virginia Woolf's *Night and Day*', in Susan M. Squier (ed.), *Women Writers and the City: Essays in Feminist Literary Criticism* (Knoxville: University of Tennessee Press, 1984), pp. 114–33) have all considered the novel as a feminist critique of Edwardian culture and society, and, more recently, Anna Snaith and Michael H. Whitworth ('Introduction: Approaches to Space and Place in Woolf', in Snaith and Whitworth (eds), *Locating Woolf: The Politics of Space and Place* (Basingstoke: Palgrave Macmillan, 2007), pp. 1–28 (pp. 8–17)) and David Bradshaw ('"Great Avenues of Civilization": The Victoria Embankment and Piccadilly Circus in the Novels of Virginia Woolf and Chelsea Embankment in *Howards End*', in *Transits: The Nomadic Geographies of Anglo-American Modernism* (Oxford: Peter Lang, 2010), pp. 189–210) have interrogated the ways in which an exploration of the politics of place and space in the novel allows for a more nuanced understanding of its social commentary, in particular in relation to imperialism.
59. B. J. Kirkpatrick and Stuart N. Clarke, *The Bibliography of Virginia Woolf* (Oxford: Oxford University Press, fourth edition, 1997), pp. 18–19.
60. 'Introduction: Approaches to Space and Place in Woolf', p. 14.
61. For example, the reference at the beginning at chapter 20 to 'some obscure Parliamentary manoeuvre' (*ND* 214) preventing women from obtaining the vote is suggestive of this period.
62. *Virginia Woolf and the Real World*, pp. 213–14.
63. *Virginia Woolf: Dramatic Novelist*, p. 93.
64. *Virginia Woolf and the Politics of Style*, p. 36.
65. For more on the COS, see Robert Humphrey's *Poor Relief and Charity 1869-1945: The London Charity Organization Society* (Basingstoke: Palgrave Macmillan, 2001).
66. *Beginning Again: An Autobiography of the Years 1911–1918* (London: Hogarth Press, 1964), p. 99.
67. Suffrage Pamphlets, Appeal for Funds, 4 March 1910, 324.6230941 PEO.
68. Gertrude Tuckwell Papers, *Facts about the Franchise*, Leaflet No. 1 [n.d.], 604/64, Box 25, Reel 12, p. 8.

69. For more on Markham's anti-suffrage politics, see Harold Smith, *The British Women's Suffrage Campaign, 1866–1928* (London: Longman, 1998), p. 29.
70. Susan M. Squier's essay on typescript drafts of *The Years* situates Woolf's presentation of Rose (and particularly her conversations with her cousins Elvira and Maggie) in the context of 'specific tactical disagreements within the women's movement' regarding militancy. 'A Track of Our Own: Typescript Drafts of *The Years*', in Jane Marcus (ed.), *Virginia Woolf: A Feminist Slant*, pp. 198–211 (p. 210).
71. 'Suffrage and Virginia Woolf: "The Mass Behind the Single Voice"', *Review of English Studies*, 56 (2005), 119–34 (p. 131).
72. 'Suffrage and Virginia Woolf', p. 132.
73. Vellacott, *Pacifists, Patriots and the Vote*, pp. 59–61.
74. Beverly Ann Schlack makes a similar observation in her discussion of Mr Clacton in 'Fathers in General: The Patriarchy in Virginia Woolf's Fiction', in Jane Marcus (ed.), *Virginia Woolf: A Feminist Slant*, pp. 52–77 (p. 71).
75. Both Vara Neverow and Naomi Black have identified the influence of the women's suffrage movement in *Three Guineas*. '"Tak[ing] Our Stand Openly Under the Lamps of Piccadilly Circus": Footnoting the Influence of Josephine Butler on *Three Guineas*', in Gillespie and Hankins (eds), *Virginia Woolf and the Arts*, pp. 13–24 and 'Virginia Woolf and the Women's Movement', in Jane Marcus (ed.), *Virginia Woolf: A Feminist Slant*, pp. 180–97 (pp. 190–3). Woolf was taken to task for the decision to speak for the daughters of educated men by a working-class reader of *Three Guineas*, Agnes Smith. In a letter to Woolf in 1938 Smith pointed out: 'the problems with which you deal are those of the working woman also, in fact those problems you outline affect the working woman in a far greater degree' (Snaith, '*Three Guineas* Letters', 99). Jane Marcus defends Woolf's decision to speak from such an apparently exclusive platform, drawing on the essay's detailed footnotes and Woolf's critique of the ill-informed and patronising, 'pro-proletarian' stance adopted by other writers of the period. 'No More Horses', 273.
76. 'To Crush Him in Our Own Country', 121.
77. 'To Crush Him in Our Own Country', 122.
78. Suffrage Pamphlets, Appeal for Funds, 4 March 1910, 324.6230941 PEO.
79. In her discussion of the politics of community and forms of subjectivity in Woolf's writing in the 1920s and early 1930s, Jessica Berman touches on questions relating to what she identifies as Woolf's concern with 'the limits and possibilities of real-world social and political

action' that are also central to my discussion of *Night and Day* here (*Modernist Fiction*, p. 117).

80. Scholars have put this down to Woolf's difficulty in writing a 'political' character. Eileen Sypher reads Mary Datchet as representing a type of socially conscious woman and argues that, although presented as noble and admirable, Mary does not inspire Woolf's '*aesthetic* imagination'. *Wisps of Violence: Producing Public and Private Politics in the Turn-of-the-Century British Novel* (London: Verso, 1993), p. 162. Sybil Oldfield has suggested that 'Mary Datchet's hardheaded, reformist political activism was precisely the kind of work that Virginia Woolf could not render convincingly from the inside'. 'From Rachel's Aunts to Miss La Trobe: Spinsters in the Fiction of Virginia Woolf', in Laura L. Doan (ed.), *Old Maids to Radical Spinsters: Unmarried Women in the Twentieth-Century Novel* (Urbana: University of Illinois Press, 1991), pp. 85–104 (p. 91).

81. 'Enchanted Organs, Magic Bells', p. 23.

82. *Virginia Woolf: Public and Private Negotiations*, p. 34.

83. Snaith argues, in a similar vein, that the novel is not simply preoccupied with Mary's commitment to suffrage campaigning, but rather Woolf uses this as a point from which to 'explore[s] public duty and private fulfilment, questioning whether the latter can be achieved through the former, or whether a balance can be achieved'. *Public and Private Negotiations*, p. 33.

84. *Virginia Woolf: Dramatic Novelist*, p. 85.

85. Virginia Blain has written interestingly on the narrative voice of *Night and Day* arguing that the narrative experimentation Woolf engages in in *To the Lighthouse* also 'mark[s] the much earlier *Night and Day*; here it reaches a point where "omniscient" almost ceases to be a useful definition of the narrator's function'. 'Narrative Voice and the Female Perspective in Virginia Woolf's Early Novels', p. 127.

86. In her discussion of Virginia Woolf's early novels, Suzanne Raitt has noted that the voice 'that Woolf tried out in *Night and Day* was deliberately not quite her own'. While Raitt links this to Woolf's still precarious mental state while writing suggesting, 'her own [was] too tenuous and too dangerous', I would add that using this rather conventional and conservative narrative voice allows Woolf to invoke and critique certain political and social values represented by this narrator. 'Virginia Woolf's Early Novels: Finding a Voice', in Sellers (ed.), *The Cambridge Companion to Virginia Woolf*, 2nd edn, pp. 29–48 (p. 38).

87. In her introduction to *Night and Day*, Julia Briggs describes the protracted process of writing *Night and Day* which was interrupted at several stages by Woolf's serious mental breakdowns (*ND* xiv).

88. 'Suffrage and Virginia Woolf', 129.
89. London, The Women's Library (LSE), Records of the Fawcett Society and its Predecessors, Correspondence with Other Societies, National Council for Adult Suffrage, 1917–18, 2LSW/E/13/16. Sybil Oldfield has touched on Leonard Woolf's participation in the NCAS campaign for adult suffrage. She writes: 'Margaret Llewelyn Davies had been active in promoting Adult Suffrage for many years going back to before she and Leonard Woolf had even met, and it comes as no surprise that Leonard should join her in campaigning steadfastly on this issue also'. 'Margaret Llewelyn Davies and Leonard Woolf', in Wayne K. Chapman and Janet M. Manson (ed.), *Women in the Milieu of Leonard and Virginia Woolf* (New York: Pace University Press, 1998), pp. 3–32 (pp. 17–18).
90. National Council for Adult Suffrage, 1917–18, 2LSW/E/13/16.
91. For a fuller account of the formation of the NCAS, see Vellacott's *Pacifists, Patriots and the Vote*, p. 140.
92. London, TUC Library, Gertrude Tuckwell Papers, Press Cuttings, *The Yorkshire Post*, 16 August 1916, 604 II/106, Box 25, Reel 12.
93. Gertrude Tuckwell Papers, Press Cuttings, *The Yorkshire Post*, 16 August 1916, 604 II/106, Box 25, Reel 12.
94. Gertrude Tuckwell Papers, Press Cuttings, *The Yorkshire Post*, 16 August 1916, 604 II/106, Box 25, Reel 12.
95. London, TUC Library, Gertrude Tuckwell Papers, Press Clippings, *The Christian Commonwealth*, 11 February 1917, 681/4, Box 37, Reel 17.
96. *Virginia Woolf and Bloomsbury: A Centenary Celebration*, ed. Jane Marcus (Basingstoke: Macmillan, 1987), pp. 242–52 (p. 242).
97. *The Artist, Society & Sexuality in Virginia Woolf's Novels*, p. 37.
98. Park has written on the very different treatment that Rose Pargiter, Woolf's suffragette character in *The Years*, receives in comparison to Mary Datchet, arguing that this disparity in 'authorial sympathy' provides a 'snapshot overview of Woolf's outlook'. 'Suffrage and Woolf', 127.
99. Although in the published version of *The Years* it is only Rose's attendance that suggests this is a meeting of a suffrage society, Anna Snaith's recent edition of the novel refers to a holograph draft in which this is 'clearly a meeting of the WSPU' (*The Years*, ed. Anna Snaith (Cambridge: Cambridge University Press, 2012), p. 465). Kitty's insistence to Eleanor after the meeting, 'force is always wrong' (*TY* 132) is given more context in the manuscript version of the novel: 'The question before the meeting which was whether [...] to join the militant branch of the suffrage movement or not' (*The Years*, ed. Snaith, p. 778).

100. A description of the Holborn building in which the meeting takes place included in drafts of the novel recalls the description of Mary Datchet's office in *Night and Day*: 'There were a great many names on the door, for the house had been cut up into flats and offices. Some were the names of societies; others were the names of private people' (*The Years*, ed. Snaith, p. 631).
101. These political young men that aggravate North appear to be modelled on the 1930s poets whose activist poetry Woolf critiques in 'The Leaning Tower' (*E6* 259–83).
102. *The Years*, ed. Snaith, p. 630.

Chapter 3

Virginia Woolf and the Women's Co-operative Guild, 1913–31

Introduction

Another lapse in this book, I must confess; but if I do it against my humour I shall begin to loathe it; so the one chance of life it has is to submit to lapses uncomplainingly. I remember though that we walked, printed, & Margaret came to tea [...] This time we were whelmed in the Coop. revolution; the characters of Mr. King & Mr. May, & possibilities. I get an occasional swing of the tail which reminds me of the incredibly insignificant position I have in this important world. I get a little depressed, a little anxious to find fault – a question of not being in the right atmosphere [...] But of course her niceness & valiancy always conquer me in spite of injured vanity. (D1 65)

Written in October 1917 while she was struggling to write *Night and Day*, this diary entry reveals Virginia Woolf's fractious relationship both to the Women's Co-operative Guild and its president Margaret Llewelyn Davies. Here Woolf positions the cerebral world of her novel writing in antithetical tension with the public world of Llewelyn Davies's political activism. As with the tension Woolf cultivated between her reviewing and her voluntary teaching at Morley College, this binary registers more than straightforward antagonism. While her reference to being 'whelmed in the Coop. revolution' sounds sarcastically dismissive, this is tempered by Woolf's feelings of inadequacy – the 'swinge' in her tail. The self-awareness of Woolf's admission that she was 'a little anxious to find fault' casts this entry as a mournful self-recrimination rather than as a biting critique of

Llewelyn Davies or the WCG. Woolf's final recognition that in spite of her 'injured vanity' she continues to admire Llewelyn Davies's 'valiancy' hints at the complicated mixture of personal loyalty and indebtedness, genuine respect but also immutable difference, which characterised Woolf's feelings towards the WCG.

Llewelyn Davies was the daughter of the Reverend John Llewelyn Davies, the Christian Socialist clergyman who had instructed Leslie Stephen at Cambridge (*PA* 6). The two men remained friends while their children forged friendships among themselves; Theodore Llewelyn Davies, Margaret's brother, was at Cambridge with Thoby Stephen and was a fairly regular visitor to Gordon Square. While Virginia Stephen must certainly have come across Llewelyn Davies during these years, it was only later in 1909, when introduced to each other by Janet Case, that she recorded her impressions of 'Miss Davies' in a sketch in her diary entitled 'Hampstead':

> I imagine that she might be stern and even bigoted; but that she is also fervent to uphold her lofty views, and has a mind like one of those flint coloured gems upon which the heads of Roman emperors are cut, indelibly. (*PA* 420)

Even early on in their friendship, Woolf's feelings about Llewelyn Davies are marked by competing emotions. Woolf's suspicion that Llewelyn Davies might be 'stern and even bigoted' echoes her misgivings about the dogmatism of other women involved in the public sphere or social reform, notably Mary Sheepshanks.[1] However, that Woolf was captivated by the dexterity and vigour of Llewelyn Davies's mind is clear from her recourse to classical allusion in this description.

Margaret Llewelyn Davies came from a family of prominent social reformers; her father was involved in the founding of the Working Men's Colleges, while her aunt, Emily Davies, was a woman suffragist, campaigner for women's access to the universities and co-founder of Girton College, Cambridge. In contrast to many of her middle-class female peers who dedicated themselves to philanthropic pursuits, such as rent-collecting in Settlement houses or volunteering for the Charity Organisation Society, as Woolf's cousin Marny Vaughan did, upon leaving university Llewelyn Davies 'firmly refused any impulse towards philanthropic work', desiring instead to dedicate her time to a working-class movement.[2] In 1886 she became secretary of the Marylebone branch of the Guild. There her enthusiasm and significant organisational skills secured her swift ascendency and she was elected as general secretary in 1889 and led the Guild until her retirement in 1921. Historians of the WCG agree that it was Llewelyn Davies's rigorous but inclusive leadership style and her commitment to addressing wider social and political issues that transformed the Guild from merely an auxiliary arm of the Co-operative Movement, concerned with harnessing the 'basket power' of its female members to benefit consumers and labourers alike, into an active, self-governing body campaigning on a range of issues impacting on working-class women, significantly divorce law reform, care of maternity and adult suffrage.[3]

Gillian Scott has noted that when the WCG was founded in 1883, 'its leaders were at best ambivalent towards feminism'.[4] In his history of the WCG, G. D. H. Cole describes how the Guild emerged out of 'a modest appeal' written by Mrs Acland to the 'Women's Corner' in the *Co-operative News*.[5] The following appeal was also reproduced in the handbook for the WCG's inaugural congress:

> In this matter of co-operation [...] why should not we women do more than we do? Surely without departing from our own sphere, and without trying to undertake work which can be better done by men, there is more for us women to do than simply to spend money [...] To come and 'buy' is all we can be *asked* to do: but cannot we go further ourselves? Why should not we have our meetings, our readings, our discussions?[6]

Receiving many supportive responses to her article Mrs Acland wasted no time and, as Cole notes, 'at the annual Co-operative Congress in June, 1883, the Women's League for the Spread of Co-operation was formally launched with a membership of fifty and a subscription of 6d. a year'.[7] The role drawn up for this Women's League was designed to 'avoid shocking male susceptibilities', in keeping with Mrs Acland's appeal to a distinctive women's 'sphere' and a gendered division of labour in her article.[8] This would change under Llewelyn Davies's leadership. As Cole suggests: 'She was by no means content that the Guild should act merely as an auxiliary agency for Co-operative propaganda.'[9]

The central role Mrs Acland envisioned for the branch meeting as a serious occasion for 'our readings, our discussions' – a transformation of the typical associations of a mothers' meeting with domestic gossip – remained integral to the Guild. Woolf writes admiringly of one such meeting in 1915 in her diary: 'Mr Hobson spoke – It was very good – The women impressive as usual – because they seem to feel, & to have such a sense of responsibility' (*D1* 12). The Woolfs attended the Guild annual congress in Newcastle in 1913 at Llewelyn Davies's invitation and Leonard Woolf became increasingly involved in Guild activities, making a research and lecturing tour of northern industrial towns in 1913, giving a lecture series to the Guildswomen and receiving a commission to write a book on co-operation and the future of industry in 1917.[10] For her part, Virginia Woolf spent much of the first half of 1914 reading Co-operative Movement manuals and making what she describes in a letter to Leonard Woolf as 'futile notes' (*L1* 44); however, her most sustained and significant activity within the WCG would begin in the autumn of 1916.

The Richmond branch, 1916–23

Perhaps inspired by a mixture of her reading, the impressive spectacle of the meetings she had attended and, of course, Llewelyn Davies's persuasion, Woolf became actively involved in the Guild's Richmond branch in 1916.[11] Monthly meetings were held at Hogarth House and it was apparently Woolf's role to supply speakers.[12] She clearly took this task seriously as it seems, in addition to the speakers supplied by the Guild, Woolf organised for friends and relatives to provide topical papers, including Ray Strachey on the suffrage (*D1* 155) and Adrian Stephen on pacifism (*L2* 261). However, a curt letter to Llewelyn Davies in June 1923 shows that Woolf was keenly aware of the need to maintain the social and political identity of these meetings and was fearful of allowing them to become too much the preserve of celebrity speakers:

> In the first place, can you help me to a speaker for the Guild on Tuesday 2nd[3rd] July? I make no apologies for bothering you. It is all your fault. Never should I have undertaken this appalling business if it hadn't been for you – I want a speech on the Strike. We have had

nothing but brilliancy and charm the last 3 months – Morgan Forster on India, Bob Trevelyan on China, Mary Sheepshanks on Peru: now we must attend to the horrid facts. (*L3* 53)

While it is important to recognise the element of banter behind Woolf's sharp tone and her childish accusation – 'It is all your fault' – there is true exasperation in Woolf's reference to the Richmond branch as 'this appalling business'. That Woolf was still organising speakers for the branch in 1923 certainly reveals her commitment to the branch and to the Co-operative Movement; however, the note of annoyance we find in the quote above creeps into other references to her Guild activities in these years, which often lack the enthusiasm and sympathy of her 1915 account of a Guild meeting. Woolf is frequently amused by the Guildswomen's failure to participate or ask questions 'unless talk drifted near food' in which case they became animated (*D1* 112, *L2* 138). These references also reveal the important way in which social class mediated Woolf's view of her fellow Richmond Guildswomen. Their preoccupation with food is one instance of this, but a more explicit example is Woolf's baffled response to the members' outrage at a talk on venereal disease in January 1917: 'It is queer though, that that class shouldn't discuss these questions openly, considering how much more they are affected by them than we are' (*L2* 139).

By returning Woolf's diary entry (where she appears to sneer at the Guildswomen's narrow interest in food) to its historical context, we find this discussion of food is in fact more politicised than it might initially appear: 'She wanted a bread shop. They all got bread late in the day: for a time they all spoke at once – stories of their own ill treatment & of their neighbours' (*D1* 112). The Guildswoman's suggestion of starting a bread shop and the other members' subsequent consumer complaints represent the bread and butter concerns of the WCG and its members. This record of a Richmond branch meeting is fascinating for several reasons with regard to Woolf's involvement with the WCG. It confirms that she was involved at a grassroots level and was exposed to the most fundamental of the Guildswomen's demands. While it is arguable that her impatience with these stories of 'ill-treatment' registers her distance from the average Guildswoman, supporting her later protestations of 'aesthetic sympathy' in her 'Introductory Letter', the end of this diary entry challenges this conclusion and shows that Woolf's interests were rather closer to those of the Guildswomen than she cares to admit. As Woolf moves from her discussion of Tuesday's meeting to record her doings on Wednesday we find she herself is consumed with the availability of food:

> The bakers windows now provide almost nothing but little plates of dull biscuits; selections of plain cake; & little buns without any plums. If you see a plum, it is invariably a decoy plum; there are no others. This transformation scene has been stealing on imperceptibly; last year we were still allowed iced cakes? Its unthinkable! (*D1* 112)

This desultory look at the baker's window is very funny considering that only a few lines earlier Woolf was complaining about the Guildswomen's inability to talk about anything other than food – bread in particular. Woolf's memories of last year's iced cakes and her indication that some food is now not 'allowed' also records the introduction of rationing in the last years of the First World War, as German U-boat campaigns to sink ships carrying food to Britain gained momentum. In light of the pressure of rationing, the Guildswomen's desire for a bread shop can be read as a timely and dynamic response rather than simply harping on an old grievance. In fact, Woolf herself writes enthusiastically to Llewelyn Davies as early as May 1917 sounding far from cynical or distant: 'We are trying to set up a Bread Shop here; we held a committee to decide about it, at which we all told stories about our house-hold difficulties' (*L2* 152).

According to the minutes of the executive committee of the Workers' National Commttee in March 1917, working-class people were being hit hardest by flour shortages 'as they live almost entirely on bread' and could not afford substitute foods. This committee suggested that 'under these circumstances, the best method seems to be to meet the need of the working people by providing cooked food for them in a municipal kitchen at a price which covers the cost of food preparation and management'.[13] Local newspaper the *Richmond Herald* shows evidence of particular food shortages in Richmond, with references throughout March 1917 to a 'rush on food shops' and a 'scarcity of food affecting Richmond'.[14] This newspaper also charts the calls for and the subsequent formation of a 'Women's

Local Government Association', presided over by Lady Yoxall, to organise communal kitchens and 'advise housewives on questions of economy and how best to conserve the food supply'.[15]

Woolf's letter to Llewelyn Davies concerning the WCG bread shop also mentions the establishment of Lady Yoxall's municipal kitchen. It seems to have inspired little enthusiasm among the Guildswomen: 'Mrs Langston is helping the ladies of Richmond to found a Communal Kitchen. She says "What can you expect of ladies? They don't know anything" [...] Anyhow, according to Mrs. Langston they're going to make a mess of it' (*L2* 152). The *Richmond Herald*'s characterisation of the 'Women's Local Government Association' as a 'committee of ladies' who could hand out advice to housewives brings to mind the misguided attempt by middle-class visitors to instil the 'gospel of porridge' into the working-class women of Lambeth, recorded by Maud Pember Reeves in her report for the Fabian Women's Group in 1913.[16] Likewise, Mrs Langston's scornful rhetorical question – "What can you expect of ladies?" – suggests that the municipal kitchen possessed the taint of class patronage, in contrast to the grassroots bread shop project.

It is tempting to read Woolf's involvement in the formation of a Richmond WCG bread shop as evidence of her solidarity with working-class women and their concerns. It certainly shows that her participation with the Guild went beyond that of a beneficent hostess willing to pull in favours from celebrity friends and that she was willing, even eager, to 'attend to the horrid facts' of bread shortages and strikes. Her account of Mrs Langston's denigration of Lady Yoxall and the other 'ladies' has something of the satisfaction of one allowed in on a joke, just as her own mocking reference to the 'ladies of Richmond' gestures to an 'us' and 'them' divide. It is, however, worth considering how far this alliance is undermined by Woolf's private enthusiasm for the municipal kitchen and her reasons for this. In a letter to Vanessa Bell in April 1917 she writes:

Nelly gave notice our last day at Asheham – as I expected. Neither she nor Lotty feel they can face 6 weeks there in the summer; so I'm speculating on a complete change – one servant, and meals from the communal kitchen, which is going to be started, near us I hope. What do you think? (*L2* 150)

That Woolf saw the municipal kitchen as a means of fulfilling her dream of a life without servants is clear from this letter. And although not reprehensible, Woolf's reflections on 'subsistence' living with only one servant bring into sharp relief the very real material differences between her life and those of the Richmond Guildswomen, who could only 'get their bread late in the day', and should caution us from imagining that an easy kind of solidarity existed between Woolf and the Guildswomen.

It is clear then that Woolf's class impacted on her interactions with the WCG. It is also true that her personal disputes with Llewelyn Davies, which often touched on the sensitive issue of her fiction writing, coloured her attitudes towards this organisation. As I have suggested, Woolf often felt her writing was insignificant in comparison to the public and political work undertaken by Llewelyn Davies, something that hurt her pride and often piqued her temper. There is no doubt that this was exacerbated by Llewelyn Davies's critical reception of *Night and Day*, which Woolf records rather feverishly in her diary:

> Tentatively she began it – how Janet & she felt that perhaps – they might be wrong, but still in their view – in short my article on Charlotte Bronte was so much more to their liking than my novels. Something in my feeling for human beings – some narrowness – some lack of emotion. (*D1* 313)

To imply to Woolf that she lacked proper human emotion after she had been voluntarily running the Richmond branch for almost three years appears insensitive on Llewelyn Davies's part, and Woolf half-enunciates this hurt in a conciliatory letter to Llewelyn Davies after their disagreement: 'We are imperfect human beings, but that's no obstacle to friendship, (on my side) in fact rather an incentive. You'll never like my books, but then shall I ever understand your Guild? Probably not' (*L2* 399).

Taking my cue from Woolf's provocative question in this letter, I now turn to consider the ways in which the only piece of writing that Woolf produced in association with the Guild, her 'Introductory Letter' to a collection of Guildswomen's writing compiled by Llewelyn Davies, articulates her complicated relationship to the WCG, while at the same time attempting to bridge the gulf that

Woolf constructs in this letter between her 'books' and Llewelyn Davies's 'Guild'.

Virginia Woolf's 1931 'Introductory Letter'

Virginia Woolf's response to her friend, and retired president of the WCG, Llewelyn Davies's request for a preface to a collection of autobiographical pieces written by Guildswomen was not auspicious: 'I'm rather doubtful about doing a preface – I'm too much of a picturesque amateur – and I daresay none would be needed' (*L4* 65). Despite her long-term interest in the Guildswomen's writing, which she wrote enthusiastically about to Llewelyn Davies in 1920 (*L2* 435), Woolf's reluctance here was true of all her references to the preface. She remained uneasy about it being used in the published book, which was entitled *Life As We Have Known It*, right up until the point of publication in 1931: 'I have had my doubts from the first. Then, if you feel that it won't do, we suggest that we should send the papers to Barbara Stephen [...] and ask her to write an introduction' (*L4* 213).

Woolf's preface takes the form of a letter 'addressed not to the public' but to Llewelyn Davies herself (*IL* xvii). Although this decision has been identified as an example of Woolf's snobbish superiority, in the context of her self-characterisation as an 'amateur' it may also be read as a means by which to avoid the assumption of expertise.[17] The letter is divided into two temporal halves. The first is dominated by an account of a 1913 meeting of the WCG congress in Newcastle that Woolf had attended. The depiction of the congress in the letter is one re-constructed after a gap of seventeen years. This backward-looking quality, that of a scene struggling to be remembered and remembered accurately, is emphasised by the barrage of questions the narrator asks herself: 'meanwhile what was it all about? What was the meaning of it?' (*IL* xx). The first half of the letter charts not only the narrator's struggle to remember the congress but also to engage with its political message: 'All these questions [...] leave me, in my own blood and bones, untouched' (*IL* xx–xxi). It concludes with an altercation between the narrator and Llewelyn Davies, during which the latter offers up the autobiographical sketches sent to her by the Guildswomen believing they might challenge the narrator's feelings of alienation: 'It might be that we should find these papers interesting; that if we read them the women would cease to be symbols and would become instead individuals' (*IL* xxxi). The second half of the letter stages the present-day narrator's receipt and reading of the letters and the ways in which they indeed do challenge the conclusions she made at the 1913 congress.

The 'Introductory Letter' has been both lauded as one of Woolf's 'most sustained and impassioned pieces of radical writing'[18] and held up as an example par excellence of her deeply ingrained class prejudice.[19] In fact, the text cleverly stymies any straightforward reading, especially regarding Woolf's politics, through its literariness, in particular its experimentation with narrative voice. The introduction's epistolary form may explain a critical reluctance to recognise the preface's literary qualities in common with Woolf's other essays of the period and instead focus solely on its political implications. Woolf's description of herself as a 'picturesque amateur' in her letter to Llewelyn Davies is not just an example of self-deprecating humour, but also obliquely anticiates her particular aesthetic approach in the preface.

The existence of two different drafts of the introduction and Woolf's revision of her first version in fraught collaboration with Llewelyn Davies has been the focus of some critical interest. Naomi Black focuses on the differences between the first version of the letter, published in the *Yale Review* in 1930, and the adapted version, which appeared in the Hogarth Press collection of the Guild pieces in 1931. These include the use of fictional names in the first version, which are not used in the second, and a stronger emphasis on the physical appearance of the Guildswomen in the first version, which is slightly toned down in the second. She rightly suggests that the 'collaboration between Virginia Woolf and the leaders of the guild was not a entirely easy one'.[20] Black recognises Woolf's anxiety as a 'benevolent spectator' and the text's concerns regarding altruism and suggests that while in the letter these issues go unresolved, in '*Three Guineas* the solution will be spelled out'.[21]

Jane Marcus shares Black's interest in the publication history of the 'Introductory Letter' but focuses in detail on what she considers the controversy of the preface's posthumous publication in Woolf's collected essays. According to Marcus, in deciding to publish the unrevised *Yale Review* version of the preface in his edited version of his wife's collected essays, Leonard Woolf 'was acting politically' and exposing a desire to undermine Virginia Woolf's credentials as a political thinker.[22] Marcus insists that 'with the help of Margaret Llewelyn Davies and the working women writers themselves' Woolf was able to 'clarify her opinions about the relation of class to art' in her later draft.[23] This characterisation of the revisionary process as a sororally supportive one overlooks the strained tone of Woolf's letters to Llewelyn Davies, concerning her suggested revisions and those of the collection's authors. A letter from Llewelyn Davies to Dorothea Ponsonby dated 2 March refers to the collection, but shows its editor dejected about the project:

> We have been getting through the material for the little book of memories by my coopve women themselves [...] I am not very pleased or happy about it. I doubt if it wd. be felt at all interesting & people really dont care about women's lives.[24]

Her doleful suggestion that 'people dont really care about women's lives' represents an important point of connection between her thinking and Woolf's on the 'obscurity' of women's lives, perhaps accounting for Llewelyn Davies's determination to have an introduction written by Woolf. While it may have been Woolf's literary credentials and specific feminist preoccupations that represented her appeal as a preface writer, it is unlikely that Llewelyn Davies expected Woolf to use the introduction to explore vexed questions of cross-class identification and as an opportunity to experiment with narrative voice.[25]

*   *   *

The first page of the 'Introductory Letter' acts itself as an introduction to the 'preface' that follows. This initial meta-narrative interest in the nature of the text in progress and the manner in which it playfully eschews regular literary definitions should from the start indicate that this text cannot be read straightforwardly. Woolf ruminates on the book of autobiographical pieces before her: 'What quality has it? What ideas does it suggest?' (*IL* xvii). With these elevated questions still lingering, the narrative shifts to the letter proper and so too does the tone: 'You have forgotten (I wrote) a hot June morning in Newcastle in the year 1913, or at least you will not remember what I remember, because you were otherwise engaged' (*IL* xviii). The note of accusation in the narrative voice is in marked contrast to that of the pre-preface, however the parenthetical qualification of '(I wrote)' far from taking ownership of this tone, in fact creates a distance between the writing Woolf and the speaking Woolf of the passage. This playful use of parentheses recurs throughout the letter and is used both to maintain the elusiveness of the narrative 'I' and to expose the constructedness of the text. It also imaginatively links the 'Introductory Letter' and Woolf's earlier essay *A Room of One's Own*, where parentheses are also used by Woolf to resist being identified with the 'I' of the text: 'Here then was I (call me Mary Beton, Mary Seton, Mary Carmichael or by any name you please – it is not a matter of any importance)' (*AROO* 4). This passage in the 'Introductory Letter' is laden with clever qualifications and licences. While a note of warning can be heard in the phrases 'you will not remember what I remember', implying that Llewelyn Davies might not like what Woolf remembers, I instead read this passage as foregrounding the subjectivity of memory, and hinting at the possibility that the writing Woolf of 1931 will be deliberately remembering differently for literary effect.

The next time we encounter the speaker of the letter she is part of a collective: 'we, many hundreds of us, scraped and shuffled and filled the entire body of some vast municipal building' (*IL* xviii). A few pages later in the letter, Woolf re-positions the narrative voice so that it speaks for 'your [Llewelyn Davies's] guests, who had come from London and elsewhere, not to take part, but to listen' (*IL* xx). The reader should not straightforwardly link the first mention of the 'many hundreds' with the 'guests' – clearly coded as middle-class there and later explicitly feminised (*IL* xxiii, xxvii). The letter reveals that the speaker is seated among the delegates themselves and the first plural evoked by the speaker includes these working-class Guildswomen: 'A bell struck; a figure rose; a woman took her way from among us; she mounted a platform' (*IL* xviii). However, by the end of the second half the letter's voice speaks categorically from the position of an uneasy 'middle-class visitor' (*IL* xxxi), and appears to speak for many: 'Let us explain what we mean, we said' (*IL* xxviii). That the 'us' here refers to middle-class 'Ladies' is clear and I do not suggest the initial formulation of 'us' that includes the delegates equates to an easy identification. Instead, I want to emphasise the way in which the instability of the speaker's plural may check the desire to make uncomplicated conclusions about who 'we' is in the letter.[26]

Reference to other records of the 1913 WCG congress helps to establish the actual details of attendance at the event and further complicates the already problematic issue of narrative voice in Woolf's preface. Leonard Woolf gives a lengthy description of the 1913 conference in his autobiography. Although, intriguingly, he does not mention that his wife accompanied him there, his account usefully confirms that he was present at the conference, which begins to call into question the account of an audience of 'hundreds' of middle-class, female observers that Virginia Woolf describes in the letter.[27] Leonard Woolf is unapologetic about his position as a class-bound observer but is impressed by the Guildswomen, who he describes as an 'unofficial parliament of 650 working-class women', and their 'extraordinary native, intuitive understanding of [...] their own problems'.[28]

A report Leonard Woolf wrote of the 1916 WCG congress for *Jus Suffragii*, the organ of the International Suffrage Movement, offers an interesting precedent for the speaker's uneasy identification and the mixed perspective we find in the opening description of the congress in Virginia Woolf's 'Introductory Letter'.[29] This account provides a description of congress proceedings with which to compare those of the 'Introductory Letter':

> One speaker after another stepped out from her place on the floor, and, turning her back upon the President and platform, addressed her fellow-Guildswomen in a speech which was limited to a few minutes by the clock. If one happened to be a member of the middle classes with a seat on the platform, there was something in this little proceeding symbolical of the whole Congress [...] Working-women were addressing working-women about the questions that interest them, and not to have shared their experiences seemed for the first time perhaps to set a woman, or even a man, apart in a way that was curiously humiliating. (*E5* 632)

Leonard Woolf's account of the steady stream of speakers, one 'after another' mounting the platform and presenting a 'speech which was limited to a few minutes by the clock', anticipates Virginia Woolf's description of the Guildswomen taking their turns to speak 'for precisely five minutes' (*IL* xviii) before returning to their seats in the belly of the hall. What is more significant is Leonard Woolf's attempt to enunciate what Woolf would later describe as 'the contradictory and complex feelings which beset the middle-class visitor' (*IL* xxxi) at a WCG congress. Leonard Woolf's suggestion that a middle-class visitor 'with a seat on the platform' might react to the speeches, not with the rather placid but slightly patronising feelings of respect and admiration he describes in his autobiography, but feel instead, set 'apart in a way that was curiously humiliating' is echoed in the speaker's admission that they are 'irretrievably cut off from the actors' (*IL* xxi) and later their exchange with Llewelyn Davies: 'We had been humiliated' (*IL* xxvii).[30]

Leonard Woolf's 1916 account in *Jus Suffragii* also sets out the details of the seating arrangements at the congress. Now that we know where these middle-class visitors sat and that they sat separately from the congress delegates, by turning to the authorised account of the 1913 congress in Newcastle in the WCG annual report we may be able to establish just who they were in 1913. Before detailing the resolutions passed, the annual report states there were 'a total of 617 delegates from 302 branches', as well as delegations from the Women's Labour League, the National Men's Guild and the Co-operative Union.[31] The proceedings as they are recorded in the annual report reveal a highly organised congress, replete with votes and resolutions. It offers a welcome alternative to both Leonard Woolf's slightly patronising but well meaning portrait of an 'unofficial parliament' and Virginia Woolf's militarised regiment of delegates (*IL* xviii). Consulting this record alongside Virginia Woolf's 'Introductory Letter' encourages us not to lose sight of the issues that were debated at the congress or the fact that it was an event at which the delegates were at the heart. Both Leonard and Virginia Woolf were automatically removed from the congress proceedings, as they were not just emotionally but technically observers, since neither could participate in any votes or resolutions. At the close of the Guild account of the 1913 annual congress we are given a glimpse of who the 'guests' the 'Introductory Letter' speaks for might actually have been. After listing 'the various bodies represented' there is another more modest list: 'The visitors present included Mr and Mrs L. S. Woolf, Miss

G. Bergstrom (Sweden), Sir Thomas Oliver (Newcastle) and Miss Pease (Newcastle)'.[32] This motley crew of observers hardly resembles the hoard of fractious middle-class ladies that Woolf's remembered account implies. And while perhaps the writer of the report used their discretion when deciding whom to include in this section, there seems little logic in their choices if they were selective.

Leonard Woolf only rose to the attention of 'the Webbs, sitting in the centre of their Fabian spider-web' because of an article he wrote about the conference later in June 1913 and, although his novel *The Wise Virgins* was published that year, he hardly would have counted as a celebrity attendant.[33] Virginia Woolf, likewise, was not yet a notable enough author for her name to be recognisable. Sir Thomas Oliver, the distinguished doctor, was a pioneer of industrial hygiene and aligned with many of the Guild's causes, so his inclusion is less remarkable. Miss G. Bergstrom may perhaps have been visiting as a foreign observer from a Guild in her native Sweden – we can see from accounts of previous congresses that this occasionally happened.[34] Miss Pease may have been a relation of the Quaker and co-founder of the Fabians, Edward R. Pease, who lived and worked for a time in Newcastle. The visitors, aside from the Woolfs, all appear to have had strong connections and sympathies with the Guild, a stark contrast to the collective reticence Woolf constructs for her visitors in her preface (*IL* xx).

Consulting the WCG annual reports provides evidence about who attended the congress in June 1913 and in doing so establishes the degree to which Woolf's memories of the conference do not merely deviate from those of Margaret Llewelyn Davies and the Guild in minor ways, but instead represent a creative re-remembering of the whole event. A reading of Woolf's account that emphasises its fictionality is supported by one of her own unpublished sketches also written in 1930 and aptly titled 'Inaccurate Memories'.[35] The story begins with general reflections on the difficulty of writing remembered scenes accurately and, in fact, the desirability of this inevitable inaccuracy. It then focuses in on the story of a young boy in his ancestral Scottish home playing with a telescope and how he eventually encounters real 'life' in the form of an embracing couple spied through the instrument.[36] It is the reflective introduction with its assertion that 'some words or scenes have a peculiar power to go on living and possibly growing and so very likely changing in the mind long after the context in which they were found has been forgotten' that provides a most instructive crib for reading the 'Introductory Letter'.[37] Woolf's theory of particular scenes, 'wandering about in the mind' where they 'arouse associations and so form a new group of ideas' offers a way into thinking about the impact that Woolf's confinement in a nursing home almost immediately after the Guild conference and the suicide attempt and long period of convalescence that followed in 1913 and early 1914 may have had on her memories of the conference.

Memory and mental illness: Virginia Woolf's 'Introductory Letter' and *On Being Ill*

While Woolf's letters and diaries usually provide an index of events and opinions, references to the WCG conference of June 1913 are rare. Indeed, correspondence during the summer of 1913 is uncharacteristically sparse and this can perhaps be read as a portent of the traumatic events that defined this period of Woolf's life. In a letter written in May 1913 to Katherine Cox, Woolf describes Leonard Woolf's self-educative tour of northern Co-operative societies as follows: 'Leonard has undertaken to lecture and write and listen to people preaching in obscure but enlightened northern towns' (*L2* 26–7). A few days later she mentions the conference in a letter to Violet Dickinson: 'then [...] to New Castle on Tyne, to join the Cooperative Women. It seems impossible to foretell where life will take one' (*L2* 28). There are then few letters charting the rest of June and July. In Leonard Woolf's autobiography he details how Virginia Woolf became particularly unwell at the beginning of July: 'The symptoms of headache increased, she could not sleep, she would hardly eat anything.'[38] He also describes how Woolf attended a Fabian conference with him in Keswick on 22 July but was not well and spent most of the trip in her hotel room. On returning from the conference the Woolfs visited Virginia's long-term physician George Savage who 'said she must go at once to a nursing home in Twickenham and stay there for some weeks remaining in bed'.[39] Leonard Woolf's autobiography and Quentin Bell's biography of his aunt both describe the events following Woolf's rest-cure in Twickenham, and how upon returning from a trip to Somerset she overdosed on veronal and had to spend months recovering, first at her half-brother George Duckworth's country house Dalingridge Place in Sussex and after that at Asheham, for the most part under the watchful care of up to four private nurses.[40]

Woolf's periods of mental illness have been the subject of much critical attention and disagreement and I enter into this area with care.[41] My reason for providing this biographical detail and for flagging up the fraught character of 1913 is that armed with this information we may find something rather different in the ruminating tone of the first page of Woolf's preface and its suddenly poignant questions: 'What old arguments and memories does it rouse in me?' (*IL* xvii). Woolf's admission that 'all of this had nothing to do with an introduction or a preface, but brought you to mind and certain pictures from the past' (*IL* xvii) encourages a reading of the letter that recognises that in remembering the WCG conference of June 1913 Woolf must perhaps also interrogate the 'madness' and confinement that followed it and the way in which these more harrowing 'pictures from the past' are written into her 'Introductory Letter'.

Virginia Woolf was admitted to Burley Park nursing home in Twickenham on 25 July 1913 and stayed there until 11 August. She was familiar with Burley and its owner, Miss Jean Thomas, as she had been sent there for a spell two years before in the summer of 1910. While her accounts of her time there do not paint a picture of a penal or overtly cruel institution, the 'rest-cure' Woolf was treated with ran along the traditional lines conceived by American neurologist Silas Weir Mitchell.[42] Woolf complains in letters from her 1910 and 1913 stays about mandatory inactivity and an enforced, enlarged diet.[43]

In light of this, the feelings of incapacitation and inactivity that characterise the 'Introductory Letter' take on an enhanced meaning. The speaker of the 'Introductory Letter' complains that all of the campaigning done by the WCG is undermined by the fact that none of the women delegates present has the vote: 'The mind might be active; the mind might be aggressive; but the mind was without a body; it had no legs or arms with which to enforce its will' (*IL* xxi). Here Woolf's grotesquely amputated version of the traditional body politic metaphor not only illustrates the Guildswomen's stunted political agency without the power of the suffrage, but also encodes the frustration and helplessness she experienced as a result of the enforced inactivity of her rest-cure and rural convalescences in 1913. By associating the conditions of votelessness and enforced mental health treatment, Woolf identifies and condemns the pervasiveness of women's oppression.

Later in the letter the speaker categorically denies this commensurateness of experience or this level of identification between 'ladies' and the delegates at the congress. She insists that only once it is possible to meet 'not as masters or mistresses or customers with a counter between us, but over a wash-tub or in the parlour casually and congenially as fellow-beings' would 'friendship and sympathy [...] supervene' (*IL* xxix). Although it is true that this stubborn dwelling on difference appears to represent a stronger impulse in the letter than the poignant allegiance we find in Woolf's mind/body metaphor, it is precisely the fleeting but striking quality of the language here that successfully disrupts the prevailing dogmatism of the narrative voice and makes it such a haunting internal challenge.

Woolf's experiences of incarceration and mental health treatment did not always result in the kind of political allegiance or identification with the Guildswomen that can be located in the passage above. Woolf's portrayal of the Guildswomen's enhanced physicality and ungainly size may also be linked to her experiences of mental health treatment. Her persistent focus on the Guildswomen's physical appearance is challenging and uncomfortable for Woolf's supporters. It was also a major concern for Llewelyn Davies, as Woolf's letters to her bear out. Woolf's amazement that the Guildswomen 'cant be told that they weigh on an average 12 stone' and other flippant remarks, such as: 'I'm amused by the importance attached to the size of the Guilders. Vanity seems to be the same in all classes' (*L4* 228), mean these letters can be read as expressions of a particularly nasty assault on the bodies of working-class women.

This fixation may represent a link with the enforced weight gain Woolf underwent as part of her treatment. In his biography of Woolf, Bell describes how her eating habits were the subject of fraught arguments and much anxiety during the Woolfs' trip to Somerset: 'She became convinced her body was in some way monstrous [...] the only course was to refuse to eat'.[44] This reluctance to eat characterised all of Woolf's periods of mental illness and was targeted by the rest-cure's prescription of a 'milk diet of up to four or five pints daily'.[45] Woolf's letters from this period often mention her weight gain and, even when her tone is cheerful, Woolf's anxiety about her size is discernable. She describes herself as 'some gigantic sow' (*L2* 35) in a letter to Leonard Woolf in December 1913 and later in 1915, taking up their correspondence again after over a year of recurring illness, Woolf writes to Lytton Strachey: 'I am really all right again, and weigh 12 stone! – three more than I've ever had' (*L2* 67). This last quotation is especially interesting in terms of Woolf's apparently playful comment about the Guildswomen's average weight. It seems obvious that Woolf's settling at twelve stone is no arbitrary choice, but represents a significant way in which Woolf imaginatively links her experience of the 1913 congress with her experience of mental illness. That Woolf attributes her own 1915 weight, achieved after years of enforced feeding, to the Guildswomen suggests another form of complicated identification between Woolf and the Guildswomen.

It is also possible to read Woolf's preoccupation with the physical appearance of the Guildswomen in the 'Introductory Letter' as bound up with her memories of the nurses at Burley Park and the private nurses with whom she lived for six months. In a letter to Leonard Woolf, Woolf writes 'I've not been very good I'm afraid – but I do think it will be better when we're together. Here its all so unreal' (*L2* 33). If we are to judge by Leonard Woolf's account of the 'stages' of her 'manic-depressive insanity', Virginia Woolf's admission that she has 'not been very good' could refer to hostility or opposition to her nurses.[46] And there certainly is something 'unreal' and nightmarish in Woolf's presentation of the 'marksmen'-like (*IL* xix) Guildswomen. This is particularly true of the following passage:

> They plunged their arms in hot water and scrubbed the clothes themselves. In consequence their bodies were thick-set and muscular, their hands were large, and they had slow emphatic gestures [...] They touched nothing lightly. They gripped papers and pencils as if they were brooms. Their faces were firm and heavily folded and lined with deep lines. It seemed as if their muscles were always taut and on the stretch. (*IL* xxiv)

This description feels out of place in the preface and there is nothing of the pithy glibness that elsewhere characterises the narrative voice

(*IL* xxiii, xxviii). The Guildswomen appear genuinely unsettling. The emphasis on their 'slow emphatic gestures' and looming largeness means that they appear to be groggily observed by one reclining in bed, rather than a member of a seated audience. The quality of the language in this passage also registers anxiety. Take, for instance, the repetition of 'lines' in the description of the women's faces: 'heavily folded and lined with deep lines'. More disturbing still is the repeated trope of the Guildswomen's huge arms 'plunged' into hot water and then later 'in the wash-tub again' (*IL* xxv). It is not too much of a stretch to see this motif as recalling, not necessarily from experience but rather from some terrified fantasy, the water-based treatments experienced by hysterics in Victorian insane asylums and administered by caretakers and nurses.[47]

* * *

The unreal, almost hallucinatory, quality of this passage disrupts what is otherwise an argumentative, conversational text. It is stylistically much closer to Woolf's visionary essay *On Being Ill* published by the Hogarth Press just a year before *Life As We Have Known It*.[48] Woolf regarded *On Being Ill* as 'one of [her] best' pieces of work and was deeply disappointed by T. S. Eliot's lack of enthusiasm on receiving it for publication in *The Criterion* (*D3* 49). The essay opens with a consideration of the neglect of illness as a theme in literature. Woolf suggests that the reason for this may be human beings' belief in the primacy of the mind, represented by literature's conspiracy to ignore the body, showing instead how 'the mind has civilised the universe' (*E5* 195). Woolf reflects on the difficulty of inscribing the unreality of illness into literature:

> 'I am in bed with influenza' – but what does that convey of the great experience; how the world has changed its shape; the tools of business grown remote [...] and friends have changed, some putting on a strange beauty, others deformed to the squatness of toads, while the whole landscape of life lies remote and fair, like the shore seen from a ship far out at sea [...] (*E5* 197)

Woolf's description of the altered perception and perspective experienced by the invalid is interesting in terms of the presentation of the congress and the delegates in the passage above from the 'Introductory Letter'. The Guildswomen's gigantic proportions and the speaker's dreadful fascination with their 'slow' and 'emphatic' movement can be convincingly read as recording the world of the 'recumbent' (*E5* 198), one that has 'changed its shape' (*E5* 197) as a result of their ill health. The speaker's feeling of separateness throughout the letter's first half, 'of being irretrievably cut off from the actors', and their acute awareness of the 'hollowness in the sound' (*IL* xxi) of their clapping and stamping, also registers the eschewed sense of perception and personal embodiment Woolf constructs in *On Being Ill*.

The Hogarth Press edition of *On Being Ill* was a special edition and all 250 copies were typeset and signed by Woolf herself. A diary entry from 16 June 1930 reveals Woolf fretful at an interruption by Ethel Smyth while she was 'methodically devoting my morning to finishing the last page of type setting: On Being Ill' (*D3* 306). In a subsequent entry Woolf exaggerates the number of copies that she has signed, saying 600 when the total was 250 (*D3* 315). In this same entry, Woolf muses on her past illnesses: 'It suddenly comes over me how I used to hook a piece of paper to me out of the nurse's eye in other illnesses – what a tremendous desire to write I had' (*D3* 315). This represents a striking example of the way in which Woolf's personal history of mental illness and, in particular, her interactions with her nurses preyed on her mind during the summer of 1930.

During these same summer months, Woolf was working with some difficulty on her piece on the WCG. She records in her diary on Sunday 18 May that '[w]ith great plodding I have managed to write about the Women's Guild' (*D3* 304), and a letter to her sister in June shows she was still occupied with the task (*L4* 175). That the re-publication of *On Being Ill* overlapped with Woolf's drafting and re-drafting of her preface is tellingly evidenced by the mingling of concerns and conversation that exists between these texts. What I have read as the letter's subtextual concern with Woolf's 1913 breakdown certainly also exists in her concurrent literary commitment to publishing a revealing and personal essay on illness.

And we need not rely entirely upon the dates of letters and diary entries, for the texts themselves, in particular through their shared preoccupation with sympathy, reveal this companion quality. In *On*

Being Ill Woolf emphasises the 'childish outspokenness in illness' (*E5* 198) and the recognition of the limits of sympathy that accompany this. The essay sternly insists that while the pressure to sympathise – 'to communicate, to civilize, to share, to cultivate the desert [...] to work together by night' – overwhelms the healthy, '[i]n illness this make-believe ceases' (*E5* 198). Arguably the 'Introductory Letter' posits a similar argument through its critique of the 'altruistic' and 'fictitious' (*IL* xxi, xxviii) sympathy of middle-class political observers. The way in which 'the vast effort of sympathy [...] is uneasily shuffled off for another time' (*E5* 197) in *On Being Ill* is surely recalled in the account of 'a weight of discomfort [...] settling and shifting itself uneasily from side to side in your visitors' minds' (*IL* xx) during the delegates' speeches in the 'Introductory Letter'.

Woolf's association of feelings of altruistic sympathy with physical symptoms in the 'Introductory Letter' does not simply obliquely reference her state of ill health in 1913: 'It was aesthetic sympathy, the sympathy of the eye and of the imagination, not of the heart and of the nerves; and such sympathy is always physically uncomfortable' (*IL* xxviii). Woolf's attempt to distinguish between the right and wrong types of sympathy – between the imaginary and the guttural – reveals a concern with the limits of sympathy and a wider anxiety about the aptness and accuracy of the term itself. This 'physical' discomfort can be read as mirroring the effect of the ill-fitting terminology of sympathy in the 'Introductory Letter'. Throughout the essay, Woolf flags up the term's insufficiency, dramatising its etymology and casting around for an alternative that can express the reality of the alliance or identification she experiences, while also accommodating that to which she aspires.

This critique of sympathy is at its most striking and historicised when the letter's narrator plays the 'childish game' of 'let's pretend' in an attempt to generate a real understanding of the Guildswomen's lives and concerns (*IL* xxii). In her study of Adam Smith's eighteenth-century work of moral philosophy *The Theory of Moral Sentiments*, Fonna Forman-Barzilai describes his theory of sympathy:

> The only way a spectator can generate fellow-feeling for the agent, according to Smith, is imaginatively to project herself into the agent's world and to ask herself whether she would be motivated by his circumstances to feel and act as he does.[49]

The central role of the imagination to Smith's theory and the way in which the sympathiser is constructed explicitly as a spectator add new significance to the speaker's game in the 'Introductory Letter':[50]

> 'Let's pretend,' one said to oneself, *looking at the speaker*, 'that I am Mrs. Giles of Durham City.' *A woman of the name had just turned to address us.* 'I am the wife of a miner. He comes home thick with grime [...] Then he must have his supper. But there is only a copper. My range is crowded with saucepans [...] All my crocks are covered with dust again. Why in the Lord's name have I not hot water and electric light laid on when middle-class women ...' So up I jump and demand passionately 'labour saving appliances and housing reform' [...] But after all the imagination is largely the child of the flesh. One could not be Mrs. Giles of Durham because one's body had never stood at the wash-tub. (*IL* xxii–xxiii; italics are my own)

It is necessary to quote from this section at length in order to reveal the degree to which this episode may be read as enacting and challenging Smith's model of sympathy. The speaker's attempt to sympathise with 'Mrs. Giles' by imagining herself in this woman's position strongly echo Smith's form of imaginative sympathy. As is clear from the italicised sections, an accompanying awareness of the synonymity of the positions of sympathiser and spectator in this 'conjuring trick', also gestures to the way in which this episode appears to engage with a dominant theory of sympathy. However, despite carefully following a Smithian model, the speaker describes the attempt as a failure, feeling the gulf between her experience and that of the Guildswomen too wide to breach. This conclusion appears to represent an implicit criticism of Smith's model where 'a complete "unison" of sentiment between different people differently situated is impossible' and, Forman-Barzilai suggests, unproblematic.[51] Woolf's dramatising and subsequent rejection of Smith's paradigm of sympathy in this passage is significant, not only because it situates the 'Introductory Letter' within debates about the nature of sympathy, but also because it indicates a break with established thought and a desire to engender a new terminology.

Again, we are reminded of the conceptual overlap with the letter's companion piece, *On Being Ill*, and in particular that essay's assertion of the need for a 'brand new' language with which to speak and write about illness. The description in *On Being Ill* of the invalid 'forced to coin words himself' (*E5* 196) anticipates both Woolf's project in the 'Introductory Letter' and the convoluted and evolutionary history of the meaning of sympathy. The latter has been the subject of much critical interest, in particular the way in which the coining of 'empathy' in the English language in the early twentieth century altered the presiding eighteenth-century definitions of sympathy established by Adam Smith and David Hume.[52]

In a 1913 collection of essays, Vernon Lee coins the word 'empathy' from the German word *Einfühlung,* meaning 'feeling into'.[53] Defining it purely in terms of a person's reception of and response to a work of art, Lee explains that 'Empathy is, together with mere Sensation, probably the chief factor of preference [...] in aesthetic contemplation'.[54] While she recognises the links between the concepts of empathy and sympathy, Lee states that understanding empathy purely 'based on its analogy with *sympathy*' would be to miss the newer term's particular application to aesthetics.[55] Critic Suzanne Keen has noted that early in the twentieth century the term 'empathy' in fact adopted much of what was once meant by 'sympathy' and that both terms belong to the same linguistic 'family tree'.[56] In spite of this, Brigid Lowe has suggested these terms are 'often opposed to one another, with "empathy" comprehending feeling with another person from their point of view, the feeling of their feelings, and "sympathy" indicating a feeling for them from a distinct, outside, or at least still separate, perspective'.[57]

Woolf's terminological unease with sympathy in the 'Introductory Letter' may be read in the context of the emergence of the new term 'empathy'. Having tested Adam Smith's traditional model of imaginary sympathy and found this wanting, could it be that the sympathy 'of the heart and of the nerves' (*IL* xxviii) Woolf's speaker angles for is best described by the newer term empathy? That the speaker's eventual understanding of the Guildswomen only comes through reading their autobiographies and appreciating the moving 'accuracy and clarity' (*IL* xxxx) of their writing recalls Lee's model of 'aesthetic empathy'.[58]

A similar strategy can be located in *On Being Ill*. Here the solipsistic 'recumbent' that dominates the main part of the essay with its complaints is transformed into a captivated narrator of their sickbed reading. The essay self-reflexively dramatises the atmospheric change as the narrator experiences it in the book by Augustus Hare they are reading: 'So Hare, too, takes his time; the charm steals upon us imperceptibly' (*E5* 203). In the re-telling of the story of Lady Waterford that closes the essay, the invalid speaker recedes into the background. The poignancy of the closing image of the mid-Victorian velvet curtain 'crushed together where she had grasped it in her agony' (*E5* 204) presents a challenge to the essay's earlier conclusions about sympathy, just as the simple poetry of the Guildswomen's biographical accounts move the speaker at the end of the 'Introductory Letter', ameliorating her previous sense of detachment and alienation.[59]

However, in the 'Introductory Letter' this apparent commitment to the notion of empathy and its championing of the power of the arts is scuppered by two doubting threads that run insistently through the letter's second half. First, while the speaker is impressed and moved by the Guildswomen's autobiographies, she repeatedly reminds the reader that, lacking 'detachment and imaginative breadth', they do not constitute literature (*IL* xxxix) and that they are 'only fragments' (*IL* xxxxi). These criticisms and their reasonable tone are not consistent with the empathy of 'aesthetic contemplation' Lee modelled in the same year as the WCG conference Woolf remembers.[60]

The second way in which the letter's conclusion resists an easy enactment of empathy is through the following powerful caveat: 'But that the pages here printed should mean all this to those who cannot supplement the written word with the memory of faces and the sound of voices is perhaps unlikely' (*IL* xxxix). The incongruously formal tone of this address represents an authorial intervention on Woolf's part in a text which otherwise playfully avoids a straightforward narrative voice. It is an attempt to refocus attention on the 1913 congress in Newcastle and to emphasise the real importance of her attendance and participation there, in spite of the gripes about 'boredom and despair' (*IL* xxii). Woolf suggests that neither Smith's sympathy nor Lee's empathy recognises the vital role of action, here signalled by 'the memory of faces and the sound of voices' (*IL* xxxix), in securing the kind of identification she seeks. This condition, with its allusions to mutual action, then, encourages us to return to a passage earlier in the letter and reconsider the language used there:

Thus if it were possible to meet them [the Guildswomen] not as masters or mistresses or customers with a counter between us, but over the wash-tub or in the parlour casually and congenially as fellow-beings with the same wishes and ends in view, a great liberation would follow, and perhaps friendship and sympathy would supervene. (*IL* xxix)

The fellowship imagined in the passage does not reproduce the notions of sympathy or empathy in contemporary currency. It instead forges a new ideal of identification galvanised with the language of political solidarity. The description of a group united by 'the same wishes and ends in view' anticipates our modern definition of solidarity as 'the state or quality of being perfectly united or at one in some respect, esp. in interests, sympathies, or aspirations',[61] while the portent of 'a great liberation' to follow evokes the etymological roots of the word, which is based on the French and entered the English language in 1848 in order to convey the nature of the revolution of that year in France and across Europe.

* * *

I want to return to the question of Woolf's characterisation of the Guildswomen in her preface, in particular the ways in which their social class is coded in the letter. What I have read as Woolf's imaginative association of the Guildswomen with her nurses is certainly founded on what she considers their shared class identity. In the 'Introductory Letter', Woolf repeatedly imagines the Guildswomen not in the context of the conference but engaged in housework, watching pans on a stove and holding brooms (*IL* xxiv).[62] In her letters to Leonard Woolf from Asheham, where she was recuperating with the help of four nurses, she reveals that she has been helping them with housework: 'We have been cleaning the drawing room. Its really rather fun, and makes a wonderful difference, even in the smell of the air [...] lots of odd jobs have been done' (*L2* 35). Although here Woolf seems delighted to participate in 'odd jobs' it is clear in a later letter to Violet Dickinson that, while she was merely holidaying in the world of housework to pass the time of her convalescence, the nurses' association with this menial, class-bound work is ingrained: 'We're trying hard to find a houseparlour maid. It will be such a mercy to get rid of nurses and all this ridiculous nonsense' (*L2* 39).

Historical studies of mental health care provision in this period, especially their detailing of staff requirements and duties, give us additional insight into the likely social position of Woolf's nurses at Burley Park and the private nurses subsequently hired by Leonard Woolf to care for her at Dalingridge and Asheham. In their study *The Politics of Madness,* Joseph Melling and Bill Forsythe detail the 'ethos of treatment, care and management' at Exminster public asylum when it was under the guiding hand of mental health care reformer Dr John Charles Bucknill.[63] In their discussion of asylum staff, Melling and Forsythe are clear that the terms 'attendant' and 'nurse' were used interchangeably. That no medical training or experience was required of the men and women who occupied these roles is evidenced by the near parity of their wages with those of agricultural workers or domestic servants.[64] Bucknill himself is quoted as describing the workload of attendants as 'a "very onerous and tiring" one and [...] females often departed for the lighter burden of domestic employment'.[65]

This observation, along with Peter Nolan's job description of a mid-Victorian attendant as 'cleaning, bed-making, dressing patients, serving meals, and supervising patients in the airing courts and at work in the farms and in the gardens', establish that the position of attendant/nurse correlated closely to that of a domestic servant, not only in terms of pay but also duties.[66] Thus, Woolf's talk of 'getting rid' of her nurses and replacing them with a new 'houseparlour maid' can be put down to not only her own mental association of the roles and the class of their holders, but their actual parity in institutions. Household chores were also used as part of a particularly gendered course of treatment for women in Exminster and other public institutions like it. Melling and Forsythe describe how '[w]omen who were "suffering from low spirits or delusions" were placed in [...] [private cottage] accommodation and engaged in household work under the supervision of an asylum attendant'.[67] When viewed in this context, Woolf's rather incongruous report that she had been 'cleaning the drawing room' makes more sense; perhaps her nurses believed this wholesome housework would bring her out of herself and lift her spirits.[68]

While Burley Park, with its lawns, ponds and upper-class clientele, was in many ways different to the Victorian public asylum, in terms of its staff and their duties Burley and other private nursing homes and asylums of its ilk remained similar to these earlier institutions. As a history of Burley Park does not exist, we must rely on accounts of alternative but comparable institutions; for example, Ticehurst in Sussex. Although Ticehurst differs from Burley in that it was a medically licensed asylum rather than a 'nursing home', by catering for exclusively upper-class patients, both provided an alternative to the socially stigmatising public asylum. As we see in Charlotte MacKenzie's history of Ticehurst, the distinguished social class of its patients also influenced what Ticehurst sought in its attendants. Like Bucknill, the Newington family, who ran Ticehurst for four generations, were keen to hire male attendants from 'the services' but for markedly different reasons. While Bucknill wanted heavy-armed, disciplined attendants to ensure order in the asylum, the Newingtons preferred men who had previously 'been officers' servants or mess-waiters, because, in addition to having acquired a sense of discipline and duty, they start with the great advantage of knowing how to speak to gentlemen'.[69]

MacKenzie's portrait of Ticehurst in the Edwardian period shows an institution in which class distinction was enshrined and an attendant's awareness of their social inferiority was part of their job description; attendants were viewed 'primarily as "body servants" or "valets" whose moral influence was exercised by treating patients with the deference their social standing commanded in ordinary life'.[70] It was thus essential that Ticehurst and other private institutions like it attracted a higher quality of attendant and they did this with substantially higher wages than public asylums, along with perks such as longer holidays.[71] In spite of these benefits, it is clear from the continued correlation between attendants and domestic servants, which Mackenzie points out, and the deferential behaviour expected of them that these attendants came almost entirely from the local working-classes.[72]

The little information we can glean about Burley and its staff from Woolf's letters reveal similarities with Ticehurst. In a letter from 1910 to her sister, Woolf complains of the suffocating religiosity of Burley and comments of Miss Jean Thomas: 'Apparently she is well off, and takes patients more or less as a spiritual work'

(*L1* 431). The deep religious conviction of Miss Bradbury, Woolf's nurse, and the instructive tone of her discussion as Woolf records it in her letter are consistent with the 'morally wholesome atmosphere' that attendants were expected to create at Ticehurst.[73] Likewise, Woolf's comment that 'Miss T. is charming, and Miss Bradbury is a good woman, but you cant conceive how I want intelligent conversation' (*L1* 431) is telling in terms of class. While Miss Thomas is 'charming', just like the 'ladies' Woolf conjures in her 'Introductory Letter' to contrast with the 'sculpturesque', solid Guildswomen (*IL* xxviii), Miss Bradbury, her nurse, is a 'good woman', a phrase that, in turn, recalls the vigour of the working-class delegates at the congress.

It is perhaps not surprising that Woolf's memories of her nurses and of the delegates at the WCG conference should be conflated, as both groups held similar class associations and attributes for her. What remains intriguing, however, is the way Woolf is able, at once, to gesture to the stifling of political agency experienced by all women, as we saw in the earlier discussion of her amputation metaphor, while still exposing her own ingrained class prejudice. The following section will consider how Woolf's narrative stratgies in the 'Introductory Letter' make this balance possible.

Class and voice: reading the 'Cook Sketch' and the 'Introductory Letter'

This chapter has already gestured to the artful idiosyncrasies of the narrative voice in 'Introductory Letter' and this closing discussion will probe these questions further by comparing the complex interactions of class and voice in this introduction with those of an unpublished, unfinished sketch, drafted by Woolf just two months after the publication of *Life As We Have Known It* and written entirely in the voice of a domestic cook.

Written in October 1931, the 'Cook Sketch' covers three pages of a little-known 1931 manuscript notebook, which is for the most part dedicated to a draft of Woolf's 1932 essay 'A Letter to a Young Poet'.[74] Written in a loose and looping hand and breaking off mid-sentence, Woolf characterises the sketch as a 'random rollicking' writing exercise in her diary and a bit of light relief after the 'grind'

(*D4* 48) of writing *The Waves*. The cook's narrative has an impressive scope, taking in contemporary political issues, most significantly the impact of the economic crisis, while also recounting her experiences of working in domestic service. At times in this sketch Woolf appears to be snobbishly satirising her working-class cook; for instance, through her taste for trivia concerning her 'betters' – Princess Mary's grocery shopping and Ramsay MacDonald's showering habits ('waking at 5 they say with a [shower bath] thrown at him'). While at others she demonstrates an interest in the details of her character's inner life; for instance, when the view of Hampstead steeple reminds her of 'one of those places I've been to when I was a girl with my first baby: Tommy Atkins, the [baker's] son at Aldershot'.

It is also clear that Woolf drew on her experiences of WCG activism when drafting this sketch. This is most obvious in the cook's discussion of food availability and her anxiety concerning price rises: 'the girls in the shops say "Prices wont stay down after this [quarter]. Of course they've the old stock on hand now. But if the Budget rises, [they'll] rise too. Prices follow suit.' It is significant that food prices here are situated firmly in the political context of the economic depression and the Budget – note the capital B. This appears to re-work the concerns regarding bread shortages that Woolf encountered in 1917 and that gave rise to the Richmond bread shop idea. For the Richmond Guildswomen in 1917 food was a political issue that inspired grassroots activism and Woolf's cook's careful record of weights, cuts of meat and prices expresses the same concern. Woolf also modelled her cook's biography on details from the Guildswomen's memoirs and there is considerable imaginative and thematic overlap between the 'Introductory Letter' and the 'Cook Sketch'. Woolf's account of the politicised character of the Guildswomen at the 1913 congress and her suggestion that 'The minds of working women were humming and their imaginations were awake' (*IL* xxxvi) anticipates her characterisation of her cook who complains, in one of the most striking passages of the 'Cook Sketch', 'what the government is for if its not to protect us working classes I don't know'.

Elsewhere I have pointed out the intertexual dialogue that exists between the 'Introductory Letter' and the 'Cook Sketch' and speculated on how the highly politicised debate over Woolf's class politics in the 'Introductory Letter' 'might be mediated by our knowledge that shortly after the publication of *Life As We Have Known It* [...] Woolf was writing her own mock-autobiographical sketch of a working woman'.[75] In returning to this set of questions here, I am keen to explore the ways in which Woolf uses these texts to collectively probe the, for her, consistently problematic issue of cross-class identification. The anxious game of 'let's pretend' and the inadequacy of the speaker's powers of imagination take on additional meaning when read alongside Woolf's experiment with voice in the 'Cook Sketch'. Likewise, the class ventriloquism we encounter in the 'Cook Sketch' might encourage us to reassess the stability of the speaking 'I' of the 'Introductory Letter' and permit us to wonder whether some of the performativity that characterises Woolf's sketch is also present in her introduction.

Virginia Woolf's anxiety regarding writing working-class voices and her failure to include working-class characters in her fiction are well noted and make the discovery of the 'Cook Sketch' all the more significant.[76] In her book, *Mrs Woolf and the Servants,* Alison Light has argued that 'the figure of the servant and of the working woman haunts Woolf's experiments in literary modernism and sets a limit to what she can achieve'.[77] I touched on this interesting question of haunting in my discussion of *The Voyage Out* in chapter 1 and showed that Woolf is rather more critical of her society's expectations of a spectre-like quality in their servants than Light's remark allows. The idea that Woolf's treatment of working-class characters 'sets a limit' on her achievements in modernism overlooks the ways in which politics and aesthetics interact in Woolf's writing. Woolf's interrogation of class and voice in the 'Cook Sketch' is a crucial example of this.

I have argued in a previous piece about the 'Cook Sketch'[78] that it may be read as a specific reaction to, or revivivication of, the working-class voices that were expunged from early drafts of *The Waves*. There are also ways in which the sketch extends the argument Woolf begins with herself in the 'Introductory Letter' about her abilities as a writer. The terms of this debate are set out most clearly in the game of 'let's pretend' that the speaker attempts to play. This game is not just about Woolf's resistance to altruism as I have suggested; it also concerns the power and limits of the writer's imagination. The speaker concludes:

> But after all the imagination is largely the child of the flesh. One could not be Mrs. Giles of Durham because one's body had never stood at the wash-tub; one's hands had never wrung and scrubbed and chopped up whatever the meat may be that makes a miner's supper. (*IL* xxiii)

The speaker here seems resigned to their imaginative limits and, more to the point, unconcerned about them. This blasè tone is reinforced when she suggests, a few lines later: 'Something was always creeping in from a world that was not their world and making the picture false and the game too much of a game to be worth playing' (*IL* xxiii). It is difficult to take this conclusion seriously as Woolf's final word on the matter if reading the 'Introductory Letter' alongside the 'Cook Sketch'. That Woolf was still experimenting with writing in the voice of a class that was not her own renders problematic the dogmatic tone of the quotation above. The speaker's sniffy reference to 'whatever the meat may be that makes a miner's supper' appears disingenuous read alongside the 'Cook Sketch', which reveals Woolf's scrupulous knowledge of various cuts of meat and understanding of wider issues in domestic economy. The sketch includes references to bacon, mutton, haunches and a 'bullock's liver' and Woolf's cook worries throughout about price rises and the malpractice of shop-keepers:

> And the tricks they play, if ones not watching: the innards & the neck cant weigh all that: not two pounds 3 {oz} ounces which is what they charge us for: & then the backs come so high – its wicked in these days of want; when every penny counts.

It is not only the detailed familiarity of the 'Cook Sketch' with a working-class social reality that renders strange the speaker of the letter's insistence that such things are beyond her imaginative scope. Precisely the kinds of imaginative play the sketch demonstrates do this too. Most strikingly, the way in which Woolf imagines herself into the political position of a working woman, having her cook reflect on the impact of the budget on food prices – 'But if the Budget rises, [they'll] rise too. Prices follow suit' – and criticise Ramsay MacDonald for his disloyalty to working people – 'I saw Mr Macdonald once myself – a disappointment he was too. Neither one thing nor the other' – is at odds with the speaker of the letter's failure to identify with the specifically political demands for 'labour saving appliances and housing reform' (*IL* xxii) made by Guildswomen.

I am interested in how we can account for such a prominent performance of the failure of imagination in the 'Introductory Letter' and how it might bear on our reading of voice in this essay. The narrator's willed lack of imagination here communicates a complicated point about Woolf's class politics and there is much at stake in the breakdown of the speaker's imagination that concludes the game of 'let's pretend'.

To be sure it registers Woolf's anxiety about class and her status as a writer; these potently combine later in the essay when the speaker defensively insists: 'no working man or woman works harder or is in closer touch with reality than a painter with his brush or a writer with his pen' (*IL* xxix). However, the speaker's language in this passage and the disinterested resignation of their tone also gestures to the degree of performance at work in the 'Introductory Letter'. The almost comic complacency with which the speaker explains why her imaginative trick must fail is a good example:

> The picture therefore was always letting in irrelevancies. One sat in an armchair or read a book. One saw landscapes, perhaps Greece or Italy, where Mrs. Giles or Mrs. Edwards must have seen slag heaps and rows upon rows of slate-roofed houses. (*IL* xxiii)

The careless parenthiatical use of commas to enclose 'perhaps Greece or Italy' are pitted against the extravagant contrasts in this passage and result in the speaker seeming more than a little foolish. The repeated use of the (very Woolfian) pronoun 'one' contributes to the negative characterisation of the speaker. We are reminded of some of the assumptions behind Woolf's most famous use of the impersonal pronoun in *A Room of One's Own*. And yet in this passage Woolf appears aware of the problems asscociated with this usage and to be deliberately mobilising this as part of a satire directed against her speaker and, crucially, the class of women she claims to speak for.

Recognising the degree to which the speaker of the letter is a constructed character, and one whose voice cannot be straightforwardly identified with Woolf's own, is necessary in order to understand the subtle class politics at work in the letter. In her 1992 essay on Virginia Woolf and class, which is also among the first serious considerations of the 'Introductory Letter', Mary M. Childers cautions against a 'crafty reading' that focuses on the letter's narrative strategies in order to 'argue that in this preface Woolf is not presenting herself so much as her understanding of the political location of middle-class women'.[79] I sympathise with Childers' urgent desire for us not to let Woolf off the hook by dwelling on aesthetic questions, but, as Anna Snaith has pointed out, it is not as easy to separate out Woolf's narrative concerns and her politics as Childers suggests.[80] It is also true that the discovery of the 'Cook Sketch' provides a transformed reading context for the 'Introductory Letter' and goes some way to support the case I make for the neglected literary qualities of the letter. Read alongside the 'Cook Sketch', the 'Introductory Letter' can be read as a companion experiment with voice and class, in which Woolf constructs a complacent middle-class speaker who is answered, a matter of months later, by the cook.

Much has been written on the subject of narrative voice in Woolf's essays, in particular the way in which Woolf evades being easily identified with the 'I' of these texts.[81] Mark Hussey has noted that the 'spectator' of the 'Introductory Letter' represents a 'subject' speaking from a 'specified standpoint' rather than Woolf herself.[82] More recently, Alice Wood has persuasively argued that adopting the 'perspective of an uninformed middle-class narrator' allowed Woolf to 'foster identification from a middle-class reader', at whom the collection was largely aimed.[83] However, I believe the voice we encounter in the 'Introductory Letter' is also edged with satire. The narrative voice of the first half of the letter is one of a put-upon and reluctant rather than a 'benevolent observer'. The seemingly snooty observation that the book for which she has been asked to write a preface 'is not a book' (*IL* xvii), and the decision to address the letter to Llewelyn Davies and not to the public lend weight to Childers' reading of class in the essay. However, this initial chilly reserve and the portrait of a churlish and defensive middle-class observer that follows are deliberately built up in the first half of the preface so they may be probed and deflated in the second half. If, as I argue, the voice of Woolf's middle-class 'visitor' cannot be straightforwardly designated as Woolf's own but is instead constructed and even caricatured we need to think differently about what has been described as Woolf's class prejudice in this preface.

The speaker's peculiar and, again, defensive reponse to the Guild-women's campaigning is an example that might benefit from this kind of rethinking: '[i]f every reform they demand was granted this very instant it would not touch one hair of my comfortable capitalistic head' (*IL* xxi). The tone of this passage is ironic. The childish use of 'this very instant' and then 'one hair of her comfortable capitalistic head' knowingly parodies the subtle combination of complacency and defensiveness that typify middle-class responses to working-class demands. By contrast, Childers reads this claim as evidence of Woolf's failure to recognise the ways in which middle-class women depend upon the labour of working-class women in a capitalist society. Childers points to the speaker's lines about laundry, in which she argues Woolf represses the 'knowledge that there is a power relation between women employers and their women servants'.[84] I would argue that the absence of the servant who is told 'that cover must go to the wash, or those sheets need changing' (*IL* xxiv) is made deliberately conspicuous in this passage in another instance of Woolf sending up her narrator. And the servant who remains silent in the 'Introductory Letter' is given a voice, albeit in a complicated way, in the 'Cook Sketch'. The cook reports the labour-intensive laundering the mother of a menial worker in a 'bacon factory' must do to get his clothes clean: 'his mother had to {?} stand his socks in vinegar to get out the brine'.

My intention here is not to present the 'Cook Sketch' as an escape route for Woolf. For one thing, the 'Cook Sketch' was not written for publication, so cannot represent an answer to the 'Introductory Letter' or, more specifically, its privileged narrator. Instead, I would argue that the coalescence of concerns we can see in these texts – of which the conspicuous absence of the servant's voice in the letter and its prominence in the 'Cook Sketch' is but one example – gestures to the affinity between them. They probe the same anxieties concerning voice and using similar stratgies of ventriloquism to do so. In the 'Cook Sketch' Woolf attempts to speak with a voice that was not her own and consistently evaded her writerly skill elsewhere, while in the 'Introductory Letter' Woolf speaks a caricatured version of her own upper-middle-class voice.

Bathetic parody is employed throughout the letter is order to flag up Woolf's anxieties concerning cross-class identification, but also to simultaneously critically undercut middle-class assumptions. As we have seen, it is particularly clear during the narrator's failed game of 'let's pretend'. If the speaker's nonchalant references to the sublime landscapes of Greece and Italy are rendered ridiculous, so too is her absurd observation that the Guildswomen cannot 'order, over the telephone, a cheap but quite adequate seat at the Opera' (*IL* xxiii). The same parenthetical structure operates here, separating off 'over the phone' as though the speaker were being offhand when really they are really showing off.

When recounting their experiences of the conference to Margaret Llewelyn Davies, the narrator's immediate response, '[w]e had been humiliated and enraged' (*IL* xxvii), is telling. It betrays the frustration that informs the first half of the remembered account, which continues to emerge in the narrator's churlish repetition of now familiar tropes: 'we pay our bills with cheques' (*IL* xxx) and with physical jolts of annoyance: 'But, we said, and here perhaps fiddled with a paper knife, or poked the fire impatiently by way of expressing our discontent, what is the use of it all?' (*IL* xxx). The 'perhaps' interjected in this line is important in terms of the letter's narrative voice. Here, more clearly than anywhere else in the preface, we get the sense of two voices: one speaking from 1913 and the other speaking from the present day and gently mocking her snobbish early incarnation. The 'perhaps' indicates the pressure of recording a remembered incident, but it also registers a knowingness and even a condescension on the part of the narrator.

What follows is the crucial moment of the letter – Llewelyn Davies's introduction of the letters from the Guildswomen. Although the narrator only receives them after much delay, the effect of reading them is meant to appear transformative and instructive. The shift in the narrator in the second half of the letter is distinct. Instead of one preoccupied with her difference and detachment she becomes the Guild's historian and its champion: 'Thus in a year or two they were to demand peace and disarmament and the spread of Co-operative principles, not only among the working people of Great Britain, but among the nations of the world' (*IL* xxxviii).

And the letter concludes with a powerful snub to the self-important narrator of the first half in the form of Miss Kidd's devastating testimony. When the narrator first encounters Miss Kidd only a few pages earlier she whimsically caricatures her as a 'watch-dog' with a 'gloom which seemed to issue from her dress' (*IL* xxvi). The letter concludes with Miss Kidd's account of being raped by her employer and becoming a mother at eighteen, after which the narrator is obliged to recant her portrait of Miss Kidd and give up her assumption of literary authority: 'Whether that is literature or not literature I do not presume to say' (*IL* xxxxi). In this way the women of the Guild are certainly given the last word and the narrator is sharply reprimanded.

Revealing the instability and thoroughly constructed character of the narrative voice of the 'Introductory Letter' provides evidence that Woolf is not merely reproducing class prejudice but performing and probing it. Read alongside the 'Cook Sketch' as part of a wider project concerning class and voice, we can see the ways in which Woolf's aesthetic decisions in this essay are deeply implicated in the social and political questions it explores. As I have suggested, Woolf's attempts to avoid being too easily identified with the narrator of her letter represent an important link with her literary practice in *A Room of One's Own,* pointing to this essay's significant relationship to Woolf's body of creative non-fiction. Woolf's letter to Margaret Llewelyn Davies asking for permission to have the preface printed in the *Yale Review* usefully establishes the literary and semi-fictional quality of her work:

> Meanwhile an American editor, to whom I had promised an article, has read it [the first draft of the 'Introductory Letter']; and wants to publish it in September as an article – or rather as fiction. What I want to know is whether you would object to me doing this […] The Americans, the editor said, are completely in the dark about co-operation and Guilds and it would be read as literature simply. (*L4* 191)

It is clear that Woolf's primary objective in this letter is pragmatic; she is at once keen to reassure Llewelyn Davies of the harmlessness of allowing the preface to be published without her revisions in America and to honour an outstanding commission for the *Yale*

Review. However, her suggestion that the piece could be read as 'literature simply' encourages us to consider the literary qualities of the preface, including its playful narrative voice. This literariness allowed Woolf to reflect on private experience at the same time as exploring her political allegiances, to challenge altruism while attempting to forge a new language of political solidarity and in this way her 'Introductory Letter' is not so far from her works of fiction as has been suggested.

Notes

1. Hermione Lee has described the 'mixed-feelings' Woolf felt towards the 'public-spirited women' of her acquaintance: 'All Mary Sheepshanks's pacifist, suffragist, left-wing women friends – Molly Hamilton, Lillian Harris, Margaret Llewelyn Davies – brought out the same reaction.' *Virginia Woolf*, p. 222.
2. Gillian Scott, *Feminism and the Politics of Working Women: The Women's Co-operative Guild, 1880s to the Second World War* (London: University College London Press, 1998), p. 44. In her history of the WCG, Llewelyn Davies is explicit about the distinction between the involvement of middle-class volunteers within the Guild and their involvement in purely philanthropic ventures: 'Connected with the Guild, as Editors of the "Women's Corner," as Organising Secretaries, and as occasional Branch Presidents or Secretaries, have been a few women who have had time – "that commodity much needed by working women" – at their disposal, and whose sympathies attracted them to a working-class organisation rather than to philanthropic work. But those who join the Guild take their place on an equality with all, standing for election with the rest, and winning their way if the members wish it. They must identity themselves with working-class interests, and come as interpreters of the needs and wishes of the workers. The Guild does not seek outsiders of "position" to preside over its functions or direct its councils.' *The Women's Co-operative Guild, 1883–1904* (Kirkby: Women's Co-operative Guild, 1904), p. 150.
3. See G. D. H. Cole, *A Century of Co-operation* (Manchester: Co-operative Union, 1944), p. 218 and Gillian Scott, 'Working-Class Feminism? The Women's Co-operative Guild, 1880s–1914', in Eileen Janes Yeo (ed.), *Mary Wollstonecraft and 200 Years of Feminism* (London: Rivers Oram, 1997), pp. 134–44 (p. 140).

4. 'Working-Class Feminism? The Women's Co-operative Guild, 1880s–1914', p. 140.
5. *A Century of Co-operation*, p. 216.
6. Hull, Hull History Centre, Papers of the Women's Co-operative Guild, *Women's Co-operative Guild Congress Handbook, 1894*, U DCW/3/1, p. 10.
7. *A Century of Co-operation*, p. 216.
8. *A Century of Co-operation*, p. 216.
9. *A Century of Co-operation*, p. 218.
10. For the details of Leonard Woolf's increasing involvement with the Guild in 1913 and 1914, see *Beginning Again*, pp. 101–9. For the complicated publication history of his book *Co-operation and the Future of Industry*, see *D1* 71–2, n.8.
11. Although the first mention of a Richmond branch meeting appears in a letter to Llewelyn Davies in January 1917 (*L2* 138), the tone suggests that this was not the first one to have been held at Hogarth House or the first Woolf had presided over. During 1915 and 1916 Woolf experienced a recurrence of the mental illness she had suffered with in 1910 and 1913, and Llewelyn Davies was a source of constant support to Leonard Woolf during this difficult time. Oldfield, 'Margaret Llewelyn Davies and Leonard Woolf', p. 8. It is then also possible that Llewelyn Davies encouraged Virginia Woolf's involvement with the Guild in the years following this particularly traumatic breakdown as a distraction.
12. There is some vagueness about what position Woolf occupied within her branch. For example, while in a letter to Roger Fry in May 1919 Woolf refers to 'the Branch of the W.C.G. of which, till lately, I was president' (*L2* 356), Quentin Bell instead suggests his aunt acted as 'secretary' for the branch. *Virginia Woolf*, vol. 2, p. 3. Naomi Black's description of Woolf's involvement is as follows: 'For several years Virginia organized meetings and speakers for the Richmond branch of the WCG; in 1919 she noted that she had been "till lately" the president of a guild branch, and in 1923 she was still seeking speakers for guild meetings and reported having been doing so for four years.' *Virginia Woolf as Feminist*, p. 39. By referring to the official WCG manual circulated to branches throughout the country, we can see that while presiding over meetings certainly was the work of the president, undertaking correspondence was that of the secretary. Hull, Hull History Centre, Papers of the Women's Co-operative Guild, *How to Start and Work a Branch, with Model Branch Rules*, 1895, U DCW/4/20. Woolf seems then to have been performing a hybrid role within her branch.

13. Hull, Hull History Centre, Papers of the Women's Co-operative Guild, Minutes of the Executive Committee of the Workers' National Committee, 1 March 1917, U DCW/7/10, p. 4.
14. *Richmond Herald*, 10 March 1917, p. 6, and 17 March 1917, p. 8.
15. *Richmond Herald*, 17 March 1917, p. 8, and 21 April 1917, p. 7.
16. *Round About a Pound a Week* (1913) (London: Persephone Books, 2008), p. 49.
17. Childers, 'Virginia Woolf on the Outside Looking Down', 66.
18. Kate Flint, 'Reading Uncommonly: Virginia Woolf and the Practice of Reading', *The Yearbook of English Studies*, 26 (1996), 187–98 (p. 190).
19. Light, *Mrs Woolf and the Servants* (London: Penguin, 2007), pp. 204–5.
20. Black, *Virginia Woolf as Feminist*, p. 120.
21. *Virginia Woolf as Feminist*, p. 118.
22. 'No More Horses', 281.
23. 'No More Horses', 280–1.
24. Linchmere, Shulbrede Priory, Papers of Dorothea and Arthur Ponsonby, Margaret Llewelyn Davies to Dorothea Ponsonby, 2 March [n.y.].
25. Recent readings of the 'Introductory Letter' have been attentive to the way in which class is figured in the essay and to the implications of the text's uneasiness and historical contingency. Jessica Berman has recognised that far from writing off 'the problem of solidarity', Woolf's essay attempts to work through these questions (*Modernist Fiction*, p. 118). Rachel Bowlby has explored the problematic way in which community is constructed in the letter ('Meet me in St. Louis: Virginia Woolf and Community', in Jeanette McVicker and Laura Davis (eds), *Virginia Woolf & Communities: Selected Papers from the Eighth Annual Conference on Virginia Woolf* (New York: Pace University Press, 1999), pp. 147–60), while Ben Clarke has suggested 'the complex ways in which the politics of class and gender intersect and modify one another' in the essay ('"But the Barrier is Impassable": Virginia Woolf and Class', in Anna Burrells, Steve Ellis, Deborah Parsons and Kathryn Simpson (eds), *Woolfian Boundaries: Selected Papers from the Sixteenth Annual International Conference on Virginia Woolf* (Clemson, SC: Clemson University Digital Press, 2007), pp. 36–42 (p. 41)). Elena Gualtieri's essay on the 'Introductory Letter' stresses the significance of the text's dual historical context and reads Woolf's essay in the context of her economic position. Gualtieri also makes a strong case for *Life As We Have Known It* having a distinctive influence on Woolf's later work, particularly *Three Guineas* ('Woolf, Economics, and Class Politics: Learning to Count', in Bryony Randall and Jane Goldman (eds), *Virginia Woolf in Context* (Cambridge: Cambridge University Press, 2012), pp. 183–92). Alice Wood has also drawn attention to the ways in which the letter promotes

'scrutiny of middle-class anxieties about social inequality and difference' ('Facing *Life as We Have Known It*: Virginia Woolf and the Women's Co-operative Guild', *Literature and History*, 23 (2014), 18–34 (p. 31)).
26. The shifting character of the 'we' in the letter is even more obvious in the context of Catherine Webb's account of the 1913 Congress in her history of the Guild. There she describes the seating arrangements at the event: 'Although the sessions were presided over by Mrs. Wimhurst, reinforced by a bell, a vice-president, central committee, council members, a standing orders committee, officers, and (not least) Miss Llewelyn Davies, the Guild's honoured general secretary, and all the due platform of visitors, "foreign" delegates and distinguished representatives from "other forces" it was the delegates on the floor of the hall who kept the discussions at the high level of excellence.' *The Woman with the Basket: The History of the Women's Co-operative Guild 1883–1927* (Manchester: Co-operative Wholesale Society's Printing Works, 1927), p. 150.
27. *Beginning Again*, pp. 106–7.
28. *Beginning Again*, p. 106.
29. Originally published on 1 September in *Jus Suffragii*, this article has been reproduced as an appendix to Woolf's essays from 1929 to 1932 (*E5* 631–4).
30. Sybil Oldfield describes how Margaret Llewelyn Davies mistakenly attributed this article to Virginia rather than Leonard Woolf when she pasted it into one of her Guild scrapbooks. 'Margaret Llewelyn Davies and Leonard Woolf', p. 30. There are strong similarities between the report and the 'Introductory Letter'; particularly in the ways they describe the disenfranchisement of the Guildswomen and the way in which their votelessness hinders their political agenda. Leonard Woolf writes: 'But when one left the Hall, and read the newspaper placards with their latest news from the trenches, and looked upon the immense pile of the Houses of Parliament, one realised with a shock that all this force of women's experience and brain power was being allowed to waste itself upon the air [...] Without votes they are without a weapon by which they can ensure that they shall be listened to and their knowledge made use of' (*E5* 633–4). This is echoed in 'Introductory Letter: 'It would pass out of the open window and become part of the clamour of the lorries and the striving of the hooves on the cobbles of Newcastle beneath' (*IL* xxi). With these similarities in mind, Llewelyn Davies's mistake seems less remarkable. Although her scrapbook may pre-date the 'Introductory Letter', this misattribution still usefully reveals the kindred quality of these pieces. Interestingly, this *Jus Suffragii* article does not feature in

the bibliography of Leonard Woolf (Leila Luedeking and Michael Edmonds, *Leonard Woolf: A Bibliography* (Winchester: St Paul's Bibliographies, 1992)), leaving the possibility open that Margaret Llewelyn Davies's attribution of the article to Virginia Woolf may have had some truth in it. Michèle Barrett's recent article on the substantial research undertaken by Virginia Woolf for her husband's 1920 book *Empire and Commerce in Africa* has foregrounded the question of the Woolfs' working collaborations, and it may be that this article falls into this category. 'Virginia Woolf's Research for *Empire and Commerce in Africa* (Leonard Woolf, 1920)', *Woolf Studies Annual*, 19 (2013), 83–122.

31. London, LSE, *Women's Co-operative Guild Thirty-first Annual Report, May, 1913–May, 1914*, COLL MISC 0657, p. 40.
32. LSE, *Women's Co-operative Guild Thirty-first Annual Report, May, 1913–May, 1914*, COLL MISC 0657, p. 40.
33. *Beginning Again*, p. 114.
34. LSE, *Women's Co-operative Guild Thirty-first Annual Report, May, 1913–May, 1914*, COLL MISC 0657, p. 39.
35. Falmer, University of Sussex Special Collections at The Keep, Monks House Papers (MHP), Unpublished Complete Stories and Sketches by Virginia Woolf, Incongruous/inaccurate Memories (Sir Henry Taylor), 1930, SxMs18/2/B/B.9/K.
36. MHP, Incongruous/inaccurate Memories (Sir Henry Taylor), 1930, SxMs18/2/B/B.9/K, p. 5. A version of this anecdote also appears in Woolf's short story 'The Searchlight' (*CSF* 269–72).
37. MHP, Incongruous/inaccurate Memories (Sir Henry Taylor), 1930, SxMs18/2/B/B.9/K, p. 1.
38. Woolf, *Beginning Again*, p. 150.
39. *Beginning Again*, p. 150.
40. *Beginning Again*, pp. 149–67; *Virginia Woolf: A Biography*, vol. 2 (London: Hogarth Press, 1972), pp. 12–18.
41. Stephen Trombley has attempted to overturn what he considers to be the 'lay assumption[s]' made about Woolf's mental illness. *'All That Summer She Was Mad': Virginia Woolf and her Doctors* (London: Junction Books, 1981), p. 9. In a similar vein, Roger Poole has been critical of the use of words like 'insanity' and 'madness' by Quentin Bell and Leonard Woolf to describe Woolf's illness. *The Unknown Virginia Woolf* (Cambridge: Cambridge University Press, 1978), p.1. While Poole and Trombley have tried to present a more sympathetic understanding of Woolf's mental condition informed by medical developments, Thomas Szasz suggests that both Woolfs 'used the concept of madness and the profession of psychiatry to manage and

manipulate their own and each other's lives'. *'My Madness Saved Me': The Madness and Marriage of Virginia Woolf* (London: Transaction, 2006), p. 13. In an interdisciplinary study of Virginia Woolf, Thomas Caramagno 'reexamine[s] her madness and her fiction in the light of recent discoveries about the biological basis of manic-depressive illness' in an effort to lift 'from Woolf's shoulders the derogatory weight of responsibility for her illness' and challenge Freudian readings of her condition. *The Flight of the Mind: Virginia Woolf's Art and Manic-Depressive Illness* (Berkeley: University of California Press, 1992), pp. 1–2. In her biography of Woolf, Hermione Lee treats Woolf's 'madness' in depth, suggesting 'she was a sane woman who had an illness', drawing attention to the physical symptoms that accompanied her psychological ones. While Lee stresses the peril of reading Woolf's 'fiction only as therapy' or her 'illness as a gift', she does indicate the way in which Woolf was able to 'create an original language of her own, in fiction and in autobiographical writing, which could explain her illness to her and give it value'. *Virginia Woolf*, pp. 175–200.
42. Elaine Showalter describes the origins and procedures of the 'rest-cure' in *The Female Malady: Women, Madness and English Culture* (London: Virago, 1987), pp. 138–40.
43. In 1910 Virginia complains in a letter to Vanessa Bell: 'Then there is all the eating and drinking and being shut up in the dark' (*L1* 430). To Leonard she writes: 'You've been working all day and I've been doing nothing [...] Nothing has happened' (*L2* 34).
44. *Virginia Woolf*, vol. 2, p. 15.
45. Lee, *Virginia Woolf*, p. 183.
46. *Beginning Again*, p. 161.
47. Showalter, *The Female Malady*, pp. 137–8.
48. *On Being Ill* was first published in 1926 by T. S. Eliot in his *New Criterion* and later reprinted by the Hogarth Press in 1930. For the essay's full publishing history see Hermione Lee's introduction to this essay (*OBI* xi–xxxii).
49. *Adam Smith and the Circles of Sympathy: Cosmopolitanism and Moral Theory* (Cambridge: Cambridge University Press, 2010), p. 65.
50. For a fuller discussion of the significance of spectatorship to Adam Smith's theory of sympathy and its implications in readings of 'scenes of sympathy' in Victorian novels, see Audrey Jaffe, *Scenes of Sympathy: Identity and Representation in Victorian Fiction* (Ithaca, NY: Cornell University Press, 2000).
51. *Adam Smith and the Circles of Sympathy*, p. 67.

52. For elaborations of Adam Smith's and David Hume's philosophies of sympathy and further consideration of their interpolation in twentieth-century literature, see Sophie Ratcliffe, *On Sympathy* (Oxford: Oxford University Press, 2008) pp. 6–11.
53. Lee also expounded this theory of 'aesthetic empathy' in her essay 'Gospels of Anarchy' earlier in 1908. For more on this see Christa Zorn, *Vernon Lee: Aesthetics, History, and the Victorian Female Intellectual* (Athens, OH: Ohio University Press, 2003), pp. xxv–vi.
54. *The Beautiful: An Introduction to Psychological Aesthetics* (Cambridge: Cambridge University Press, 1913), pp. 67–8.
55. *The Beautiful*, p. 67.
56. *Empathy and the Novel* (Oxford: Oxford University Press, 2007), p. 41.
57. *Victorian Fiction and the Insights of Sympathy* (New York: Anthem Press, 2007), p. 9.
58. Zorn, *Vernon Lee*, p. xxv.
59. Hermione Lee has explored the way in which the invalid's efforts to create this new language are recalled in this final poignant vignette that closes the essay. She suggests that the crushed curtain represents 'a startling echo of the sick person who, earlier in the essay, has to take his pain in one hand and "a lump of pure sound" in the other and "crushed them together" to produce a "brand new word"' (*OBI* xxii).
60. *The Beautiful*, p. 68.
61. 'solidarity, n.', *OED Online*, June 2013, Oxford University Press, http://0-www.oed.com.catalogue.ulrls.lon.ac.uk/view/Entry/184237?redirectedFrom=solidarity [accessed 31 March 2015; requires membership].
62. Elena Gualtieri has noted this tendency in the letter and suggests 'the bodies of working women are seen by Woolf as entirely and completely defined by their position in the social division of labour'. *Sketching the Past: Virginia Woolf's Essays* (Basingstoke: Macmillan, 2000), p. 79. Jessica Berman similarly notes how in the letter 'capitalist patriarchal society' marks the bodies of women: 'Doing the washing up becomes an activity inscribed upon the bodies of the working-class women that not only marks them as different but that also makes them subject to their flesh.' *Modernist Fiction*, p. 119.
63. *The Politics of Madness: The State, Insanity and Society in England, 1845–1914* (London: Routledge, 2006), p. 46.
64. 'In 1903 the Head male Attendant earned £124 per year while the Head Nurse received only £71. Their subordinates fared much worse; with male night attendants earning £36 to £45 a year and females £25–£27

[...] This indicates that attendants earned no more than the substantial number of agricultural labourers whom they supervised as patients'. Melling and Forsythe, *The Politics of Madness*, p. 57.
65. Melling and Forsythe, *The Politics of Madness*, p. 57.
66. 'Mental Health Nursing in Great Britain', in Hugh Freeman and German E. Berrios (eds), *150 Years of British Psychiatry, Volume II: The Aftermath* (London: Athlone Press, 1996), pp. 171–92 (p. 177).
67. *The Politics of Madness*, p. 52.
68. Louie Mayer, the Woolfs' cook, describes how on the morning of the day of Virginia Woolf's suicide, Leonard Woolf had encouraged her to help Mayer with cleaning his study as just such a form of therapy: 'He had been talking to her in her bedroom during the morning because it seemed to be one of her bad days again, and he must have suggested that she might like to do something, perhaps help with the housework.' *Recollections of Virginia Woolf by Her Contemporaries*, ed. Joan Russell Noble (London: Peter Owen, 1972), p. 160.
69. Charlotte MacKenzie, *Psychiatry for the Rich: A History of Ticehurst Private Asylum* (London: Routledge, 1992), p. 181.
70. *Psychiatry for the Rich*, p. 181.
71. *Psychiatry for the Rich*, p. 144.
72. *Psychiatry for the Rich*, p. 144.
73. *Psychiatry for the Rich*, p. 180.
74. A full transcription of the 'Cook Sketch' is included as an appendix to this book and all quotations come from this version.
75. Clara Jones, 'Virginia Woolf's 1931 "Cook Sketch"', *Woolf Studies Annual*, 20 (2014), 1–25 (p. 12).
76. See Beer, *The Common Ground*, pp. 89–90 and Finn Fordham, *I do, I undo, I redo: The Textual Genesis of Modernist Selves in Hopkins, Yeats, Conrad, Forster, Joyce and Woolf* (Oxford: Oxford University Press, 2010), p. 257.
77. Light, p. xviii.
78. 'Virginia Woolf's 1931 "Cook Sketch"', 1–25.
79. 'Virginia Woolf on the Outside Looking Down', 67.
80. *Virginia Woolf: Public and Private Negotiations*, p. 116.
81. See Elaine Showalter's discussion of impersonality and the narrative 'I' of *A Room of One's Own* in 'Virginia Woolf and the Flight into Androgyny', in *A Literature of Their Own: British Novelists from Brontë to Lessing* (London: Virago, 1978), pp. 263–97. Also see Lisa Low's 'Refusing to Hit Back: Virginia Woolf and the Impersonality Question', in Rosenberg and Dubino (eds), *Virginia Woolf and the Essay*, pp. 257–73, for a critical response to Showalter's position.

82. 'Mrs Thatcher and Mrs Woolf', *Modern Fiction Studies*, 50 (2004), 8–30 (p. 21). Childers is also perceptive on the ironic and performative strategies at play in the 'Introductory Letter'; however, she doubts that they perform a valid formal service other than allowing Woolf to wriggle out of wholehearted support of the WCG: 'A performative strategy may serve to register complexity, but it may also register complicity or simple evasiveness.' 'Virginia Woolf on the Outside Looking Down', 64.
83. 'Facing *Life as We Have Known It*', pp. 26 and 27.
84. 'Virginia Woolf on the Outside Looking Down', 67.

Chapter 4

Virginia Woolf and the Rodmell Women's Institute, 1940–1

Introduction

> Then the [W.I.] plays rehearsed here yesterday. My contribution to the war is the sacrifice of pleasure: I'm bored: bored and appalled by the readymade commonplaceness of these plays: which they cant act unless we help. I mean, the minds so cheap, compared with ours, like a bad novel – thats my contribution – to have my mind smeared by the village & WEA mind; & to endure it, & the simper. (*D5* 288)

Virginia Woolf's May 1940 diary entry detailing her involvement in the production of two village plays by the Rodmell Women's Institute shows her at her most vitriolic and visceral, but also desperate. And yet, in spite of the violence of her private commentary on this activity, Woolf's membership and active participation in the Rodmell WI has received little sustained scholarly attention and rarely appears in the roll call of her political and social activisms.[1] This final instance of Woolf's social participation frustrates any scholarly attempt to map a progressive or necessarily coherent narrative of Woolf's activism. In recent accounts of Woolf's politics, the 1930s have tended to dominate[2] and it is easy to see why Woolf's more humdrum activities with the WI – collecting membership money or organising talks in the village hall – have been overshadowed by the ideological and historical urgency of her anti-fascist work in this period. Not only does the apparently centrist, though allegedly right-leaning, bias of the WI fail to conform with the otherwise left-wing agendas of the other groups Woolf was associated with, but, as the above quotation illustrates, her association with the WI was also riven with ambivalence, just as her previous instances of political and social participation had been.

Further attention to this diary entry reveals the real urgency of Woolf's involvement with the WI and its implications for our understanding of her political and literary practice in the last years of her life. At first reading it appears to be the snobbish tirade of an exasperated Woolf furious at once again being made to 'join', having comforted herself after the publication of *Three Guineas* in 1938 – her contribution to society as she saw it – with the mantra: 'No longer famous, no longer on a pedestal; no longer hawked in by societies: on my own, for ever' (*D5* 136–7). However, there is more to this private tantrum than simply disappointment at once again being hauled into the world of participation. In this passage we find Woolf's increasing anxiety about the war explosively combined with her abiding class prejudice and all focused, with disproportionate violence, on the apparently innocuous body of the WI. Woolf's scathing evocation of the war effort reveals her trademark distaste for the jingoism that accompanies national crises.[3] That Woolf identifies the WI plays with precisely this kind of crass, performative patriotism is clear in her final reference to the 'simper[ing]' she is forced to endure.

This passage also illustrates some of Woolf's most problematic attitudes towards social class. Her horror at the 'readymade commonplaceness' of the WI plays and her comparison with 'a bad novel' call upon the distinctive new language of mass consumerism and represent some of the most unpleasant remarks in her private writing.

While the bulk of Woolf's rage here is directed against the WI and their plays, her inclusion of the Workers' Educational Association at the end of this diatribe is worth noting. Melba Cuddy-Keane reads this outburst as evidence of Woolf's residual frustration at the lacklustre response of the WEA audience to the talk (later published as 'The Leaning Tower') that she had given earlier in April.[4] Woolf's coupling of two such ideologically disparate groups here – the culturally and politically conservative WI and the left-wing WEA – is odd, given her familiarity with their social and political projects. Reference to the manuscript of Woolf's diary entry shows some hesitation and a deleted capital 'W' before she writes 'WEA mind', which might suggest she wrote WEA by accident, confusing the acronyms in her furious haste.[5]

A more interesting account of this coupling of the WI and WEA may be found in the way in which Woolf's class snobbery is intimately bound up with a critique of working-class literary/cultural productions. By linking these organisations in the final line of this passage, Woolf appears to contextualise her contempt for the 'ready-made' plays produced by the working-class members of the Rodmell WI in the educative project of the WEA, which provided adult education to working-class men and women.

As with many of Woolf's most vituperative diary entries, she is at pains to qualify her vitriol against the WI:

> But this is to be qualified – only theres Miss Griffiths [Hogarth Press clerk] coming for the weekend – all simper & qualification. So, if Margaret Ll. Davies says, how insolent we middleclass women are, I argue, why cant the workers then reject us? Whats wrong is the conventionality – not the coarseness. So that its all lulled & dulled. The very opposite of 'common' or working class. (*D5* 288–9)

Rather than qualifying her outburst, this passage only serves to expose Woolf's complicated class politics further while also revealing the symbolic position the WI had come to occupy for her in these arguments. Here Woolf reprises her debate with Margaret Llewelyn Davies over her draft of the 'Introductory Letter', re-stating her impatience with what she considered the misguided aping of middle-class manners by the working class.[6] Woolf longs for what she imagines to be an authentic, 'common' working-class character – one not 'lulled & dulled' by the influence of bourgeois values. This improbable desire for a radicalised working class who will 'reject' her rather than deferentially accept her 'help', as in the first passage, can be usefully understood in terms of what Hermione Lee has recognised as Woolf's acute resentment at being 'identified with the middle-class gentry' who occupied the 'better houses' in the village and who frequently organised voluntary groups and societies, such as the WI.[7] A 1941 letter to Lady Simon illustrates this well. Woolf writes proudly, but a little disingenuously: 'We live in the heart of the lower village world, to whom Leonard lectures on potatoes and politics. The gentry dont call' (*L6* 464).

In spite of all her impatience with her fellow members, elsewhere in her letters and diaries Woolf seems proud of her involvement with the WI. This appreciation is registered in a letter to Margaret Llewelyn Davies in April 1940: 'I'm becoming, you'll be amused to hear, an active member of the Womens Institute, who've just asked me to write a play for the villagers to act. And to produce it myself. I should like to if I could' (*L6* 391).

Woolf's clear pride in being asked to write a play for 'the villagers to act' and her pointed use of the word 'active' here, signalling an embracing of the language of participation, are undercut by her *own* rather superior amusement at her 'active' involvement. In this way Woolf's account of her participation in the Rodmell WI is conditioned by the same competing impulses of desire for inclusion and ironic detachment that marked her involvement with Morley College and the WCG. There is something wistful in Woolf's final admission – 'I should like to if I could' – that hints at a self-conscious recognition of this competition.

This chapter explores how Woolf's complicated and often emotionally charged responses to the Rodmell WI encourage a reconsideration of the political and literary significance of this late activity. A more nuanced understanding of the WI's ideology – in which democracy, domesticity, ruralism and class conciliation were potently combined to construct an ideal of English womanhood – might make sense of the ambivalent quality of Woolf's allegiance and provide a new context in which to read her late fiction and non-fiction, which is itself so preoccupied with the intersections of class, gender and culture.

The Rodmell Women's Institute

In a February 1941 letter to Virginia Woolf, Elizabeth Bowen illustrates the Women's Institutes' powerful hold over the English imagination after just twenty-six years in existence: 'As a matter of fact I do very much miss W.I.s: since I came to live in London I feel I don't live in England at all.'[8] Established in 1915, the Women's Institute Movement was a Canadian import brought over by Mrs Alfred Watt with the purpose of 'stimulating interest in the agricultural industry' while 'providing centres for educational and social intercourse' for women in rural communities.[9] At its inception, the WI operated under the auspices of the Agricultural Organisation Society and its work raising agricultural awareness among rural women was considered 'a branch of A.O.S. work' and a crucial contribution to the war effort.[10]

By 1918 the WI had gained independence and its own national federation with branches across the country.[11] As a result of its emergence during a period of national crisis, the WI was founded along deeply patriotic and nationalist lines, which in turn became central to the movement's identity. This agenda is clear in the WI's motto 'For Home and Country', which provided the title for its monthly organ *Home and Country,* and in the movement's emphasis on rural women as almost spiritual custodians of a particular and authentic kind of Englishness. Historian of the WI Maggie Andrews has argued that:

> The association of ruralism and rural women with Englishness and their role as the guardians of a tradition, of a way of life, was by the 1940s ingrained. Although neither tradition nor Englishness were fixed concepts, these rural women saw themselves as the essence of English womanhood, indeed, it was embedded in their identity.[12]

What we encounter in Bowen's letter to Woolf is, then, a potent expression of the WI's ideology, in particular its cultivation of a certain model of Englishness that is synonymous with the countryside.[13] The combination of ruralism and patriotism at the heart of WI principles provides an additional and revealing context for Woolf's violent outburst against the Rodmell WI. In 1938 Virginia Woolf had made an uncompromising, anti-nationalist statement of feminist nomadism central to her argument in *Three Guineas:* '[a]s a woman, I have no country. As a woman I want no country. As a woman my country is the whole world' (*TG* 234). To find herself, just two years later, a relied-upon member of a deeply patriotic group, which appeared to champion a version of femininity closely bound up with domesticity, must have been more than a little alarming. The National Federation of Women's Institutes (NFWI) did not represent the realisation of the 'society of outsiders' that Woolf imagined in *Three Guineas* and it is hard to believe that this disjuncture did not occur to or indeed grate on Woolf.

Historians of the WI and its early leaders are keen to stress its democratic character and the break with tradition this marked. Maggie Andrews explains that the set membership fee of two shillings 'was considered a significantly democratic move', because it made membership available to women of all classes and 'wealthier women could not pay more than this and consequently acquire an unreasonable level of influence within the Institute'.[14] Contemporary institutional histories of the movement also make much of the egalitarian character of the WI and the upset this caused in some still semi-feudal villages.[15] In spite of the WI's commitment to democratic principles and its efforts to appeal to all rural women, Catriona Beaumont notes that class hierarchies were reflected in the WI's institutional formation as 'the majority of branch officials and national leaders were drawn from the middle classes'.[16] It is likely that this class stratification is what has led left-wing and Marxist historians of inter-war England to see the WI as a bastion of middle-class conservatism, rather than as the figure of progressive democracy that it clearly identified itself as.[17]

The Rodmell WI is a case in point, with the local middle classes occupying prominent positions on the branch's executive. In her reminiscences of Virginia Woolf, Diana Gardner, her neighbour in Rodmell, recalls Woolf's growing involvement with the WI and makes some very telling remarks about the makeup of the group.[18] Gardner, in an interesting parallel to Woolf, describes how 'as part of [her] war-work' she acted as secretary to the Rodmell WI under the presidency of the 'very determined, socially-minded' Mrs Chavasse, who, having moved to Sussex from a comfortable life in the Midlands, 'decided to give the village and the Women's Institute her generous time'.[19] It is unclear whether Gardner means this drily or not, but she makes it clear that Mrs Chavasse, with her 'white hair immaculate, [...] expensive and striking clothes and real jewellery', and the 'rich imported pastries' and 'real lace tablecloths' that she introduced to the WI meetings, belonged to the upper echelons of Rodmell society.[20] Gardner's description of the members' happy acceptance of Mrs Chavasse's new regime emphasises the class stratification of the Rodmell WI:

> Naturally, the members, in that rather sad, draughty village hall, painted dark green and brown and approached quite often through nettles, were impressed and many were grateful, for the majority were the wives of farm labourers; only a few were not and these were the wives of farm bailiffs, of the blacksmith, the daughter of the man who had been the miller and one or two 'educated' women, but not many.[21]

This passage is interesting not just because of the detailed sense of the class makeup of the Rodmell WI we ascertain from it, but also for the suggestive language Gardner uses. Her list of the WI members, which finishes with the complicated line 'the daughter of the man who had been the miller and one or two "educated" women, but not many', with its pointed use of 'daughter' and 'educated', includes an anagrammatic gesture to Woolf's *Three Guineas,* which she wrote as an 'educated man's daughter' (*TG* 129). As a committed reader of Woolf's writing – she mentions *Three Guineas* on the page following the quotation above – it is unlikely the powerful significance of these words would have evaded Gardner.

The argument of *Three Guineas* becomes increasingly implicated in Gardner's account of the Rodmell WI when she describes local objections to the 'new look WI' under Mrs Chavasse's leadership and Woolf's initial reluctance to join the group. While she recalls the working-class majority of members appreciated Mrs Chavasse's innovations, Gardner remembers a 'woman journalist who rented a cottage for a time' asking: 'Why was the Rodmell Women's Institute not run by the women of the village themselves rather than by the educated or leisured ones?'[22] Gardner explains that the 'the village women' were often too tired or busy to run the WI and had little of the necessary organisational skills.[23] It was a criticism that Gardner encountered again when she asked Woolf if she would join the Rodmell branch: 'Virginia Woolf at first demurred: she was not entirely in sympathy with the Women's Institute; it was run always by middle-class women and not by the village women themselves'.[24]

Woolf's criticism of the class formation of the WI is consistent with her view expressed in *Three Guineas* that for working-class women to obtain political determination they must organise themselves and with her resistance in that text to speaking for anyone but the daughters of educated men (*TG* 310). It also casts her impatience in her May 1940 diary in particularly classed terms: 'they cant act unless we help'.

* * *

The first mention of the WI we encounter is in Woolf's April 1940 letter to Llewelyn Davies, where she boasts she is becoming 'an active member of the Womens Institute' (*L6* 391). We find both enthusiasm and a satirical impulse in this letter. While Woolf's parenthetical inclusion – 'you'll be amused to hear' – needs to be read in the context of her fractious friendship with Llewelyn Davies, it also registers the mocking, sideways look she would continue to adopt throughout her involvement with the WI. The letter continues in a similarly playful vein:

> Oh dear how full of doings villages are – and of violent quarrels and of incessant intrigues. The hatred of the parsons wife [Mrs Ebbs] passes belief. We're thought red hot revolutionaries because the Labour party meets in our dining room. (*L6* 391)

For Woolf the WI had clearly not yet assumed the powerful significance it held for Elizabeth Bowen and was instead associated with what she characterises as the incessant 'doings' of the village. This passage also gives the distinct impression that Woolf was seduced by the details of village life; her fascination with its in-fighting, in particular the hatred directed at Mrs Ebbs the former president of the WI, undercuts her imperious tone. Likewise, Woolf's suggestion that she and Leonard are considered 'red hot revolutionaries' does not represent simply a flaunting of her left-wing credentials to Llewelyn Davies. While Woolf is clearly proud of being identified as an agitating and progressive force in the village, this reference to Labour Party meetings, which were held at Monk's House during the same period, in the same letter that she remarks on her activity with the

WI, reveals an awareness and perhaps even an anxiety about these parallel activities and their possible incompatibility.

Hermione Lee has written persuasively on Woolf's competing feelings of interest and wariness towards life in Rodmell and described how the coming of the Second World War made her reticence towards village life difficult to maintain.[25] In spite of her initial interest in the WI and her swift ascendance to its upper echelons – she concludes a letter to Vita Sackville-West in April writing, importantly: 'I must stop and take tea with Mrs Chavasse, the dr's widow, in order to discuss the village plays' (*L6* 395) – Woolf continued to associate it privately with the demands of village life she would rather shirk. In a letter to Ethel Smyth on 17 May 1940 she writes: 'Its a good thing to have books to believe in – and any number of little drudgeries: food to order: a village play to rehearse; and old Mrs West and her idiot boy – they took an hour this afternoon' (*L6* 399).

The impatience we encounter in this letter, as ever, only presents one side of Woolf's increasingly complicated relationship with the Rodmell WI. Just over a week later she wrote almost breathlessly to her niece, Judith Stephen: 'I can't give you all the gossip of Rodmell, because it would need a ream. We're acting village plays; written by the gardener's wife, and the chauffeur's wife; and acted by the other villagers' (*L6* 400). Rather than taciturn outsider, in this letter Woolf presents herself as at the heart of things and in command of all the village gossip going. Similarly, the deictic inclusivity of her wording – 'We're acting village plays' – could not be further from the despairing and put-upon voice Woolf used just ten days earlier when she complained of being 'bored and appalled' by the WI and its plays.

This apparently light-hearted and enthusiastic letter shares some of the curious contradictions of her letter to Llewelyn Davies. The egalitarian gesture implicit in her use of the plural subject 'we' is undermined first by her loaded references to the village playwrights as 'the gardener's wife, and the chauffeur's wife' and then by her suggestion that the plays will be 'acted by the other villagers'. Woolf denies both women their names and highlights their social status by placing them squarely within the role of employee. Similarly, by saying the plays will be performed by the 'other villagers', Woolf appears to go back on her initial statement – 'We're acting village plays' – and creates a distance between herself and this activity. This small passage shows Woolf simultaneously inside and outside the WI fold; she moves from being, literally, an actor in village life to being a removed observer.

The ambiguity of this passage is also problematic for the more practical reason that it makes it difficult to identify exactly what Woolf's role within the production of the plays was. That Woolf met with Mrs Chavasse 'to discuss the village plays' gives little away, apart from perhaps suggesting that the otherwise independent-minded WI president had decided in this instance to call upon Woolf's perceived superior knowledge of the arts. Given that this meeting occurred on 28 April, prior to any references to rehearsals, we might infer it was a meeting to decide on which plays were to be performed. It is likely, then, that when Woolf writes 'we're acting village plays' she means something quite different. Perhaps here 'acting' stands in as shorthand for all activity surrounding the plays. It is also possible that Woolf is again implying something more existential when she writes this, hinting at the need for performance in her participation with the WI, what she describes as 'simpering' elsewhere. Later in this chapter I will spend more time exploring Woolf's involvement with the WI plays but for now it is worth noting that beyond the WI-authored plays, which were performed in August 1940 (*L6* 418), Woolf refers to 'rehearsers' in a letter to Angelica Bell at the end of August (*L6* 422);[26] to a village play performed at a fête in September (*L6* 430); and we know from local newspapers that another WI play was performed in November 1940.[27]

Woolf also put on her own performance of a sort in the form of her autobiographical talk given on 23 July[28] on the Dreadnought Hoax, which she describes as follows:

> For 11 days I've been contracting in the glare of different faces. It ended yesterday with the W.I.: my talk – it was talked – about the Dreadnought. A simple, on the whole natural, friendly occasion. Cups of tea; biscuits; & Mrs Chavasse, in a tight dress, presiding: out of respect for me, it was a Book tea. Miss Gardner had 3 Gs. pinned to her frock; Mrs Tompsett 3 weeks: & someone else a silver spoon. (*D5* 303)

This diary entry represents a pleasing instance of Woolf caught out, surprised by what a nice time she has had in the company of the Rodmell WI. She seems comforted by what is understated about the event; she takes pleasure in the everyday 'cups of tea; biscuits' when she might have found them humdrum. Although her mention of 'Mrs Chavasse, in a tight dress' represents a lapse, this is mitigated by her pleasure in it being 'a Book tea' in her honour.

A letter the following day to Ethel Smyth also registers this new warmth towards the WI and the degree to which the enthusiastic reception of her talk pleased her: 'I spoke to the Women's Institute yesterday about the Dreadnought hoax. And it made them laugh. Dont you think this proves, beyond a doubt, that I have a heart?' (*L6* 407). As well as recording the high point of Woolf's participation with the Rodmell WI, Woolf's account of her talk remains dogged with feelings of insecurity and ambivalence. Her apparently flippant question to Ethel arguably reveals her real concern with the implications of her involvement with the WI, although her conclusions are ambiguous. Through her insistence that by giving her talk she has proven 'beyond a doubt' that she has a heart, Woolf seems to link her work with the WI with a charitable activity, not unlike the philanthropic activities her sister Stella Duckworth performed in the late 1890s.

Woolf's emphasis on having made the women laugh invites us to read this passage and Woolf's take on her activity a little differently. For Woolf the women's laughter and enjoyment of her paper, the simplicity and friendliness of the occasion, represents a bridging of the vast gulf that she felt separated her from the Guildswomen of the 1913 WCG conference in her 'Introductory Letter'. Much of Woolf's private writing about the WI, and this passage in particular, should be read in the context of her long-standing preoccupation with questions of cross-class identification and solidarity. The way she describes the event of the hoax talk stands in clear opposition to Woolf's sterile experience of the 1913 WCG conference, and the way in which she embraces this as a badge proving her 'heart' is a departure from the purely 'aesthetic sympathy' she is capable of there. While it may be tempting to read Woolf's warmth as a sign of her increasing capacity for cross-class identification, we must set her ease at the WI meeting in the context of the WI's well-established project of class conciliation. It is perhaps then not a surprise that Woolf felt the WI meeting was 'natural, friendly and simple', because these were tenets written into the very constitution of the WI.

Woolf's talk on the Dreadnought Hoax and much-begrudged but dedicated participation in the WI plays must also have made an impression on the WI members, or at least Mrs Chavasse, who, Diana Gardner tells us, was keen 'to make use of all the talent that could be found locally',[29] as in November 1940 Woolf was asked to stand for the WI committee. Her account of this episode marks a return to her caustic view of the WI:

> Early in the morning Annie came, asked me to stand for W.I. cttee. 'No' I cried too violently. The poor dont understand humour. I repented; went round later & found her in the sunny parlour with all the sisters [?] artificial carnations, & said I would. For I could see, by the pleasure she felt when I offered to nominate her, that she takes this infernal dull bore seriously: its an excitement [...] If one lives in a village, one had better snatch its offerings. (*D5* 335)

This passage is frustrating and amusing for several reasons. Perhaps the most obvious is Woolf's pseudo-anthropological aside – '[t]he poor dont understand humour' – that is rendered particularly puzzling when we consider that only a few months earlier Annie Thompsett and the rest of the predominantly working-class members of the WI had laughed heartily at Woolf's Dreadnought Hoax talk. Like the quote that introduced this chapter this passage is marked with the language of duty. Woolf 'repents' after declining Annie's offer of nomination, not only by accepting but also by offering to nominate her in return. Woolf's urbane dismissal of the WI elections as an 'infernal dull bore' and her patronising concession that for Annie it must be 'an excitement' are undermined by her grudging afterthought that '[i]f one lives in a village, one had better snatch its offerings'. The subject position here is ambiguous. The use of 'one' maintains a rather superior distance between Woolf and the village, while the greediness of 'snatch' reveals an eagerness to be involved and, crucially, included. In the language of this passage we find Woolf again curiously oscillating between the position of insider and outsider.

The *East Sussex News* report of the Rodmell WI committee elections shows that Woolf was successfully elected:

> The Ballot for the committee of 1941 was taken and resulted in the election of the following: Mrs Chavasse, president; Mrs Dean, vice-president; Mrs Bleach, Miss Gardner, Mrs Penfold, Mrs Richardson, Mrs Smith and Mrs Woolf. The report of the year's activities was read by the secretary and the financial statement by the treasurer [...] An attractive display of handcraft by members, including some excellent specimens of bookbinding was inspected with interest.[30]

Whether it was out of deference to Woolf's superior social position in the village and in keeping with the WI's apparently unshakeable and unspoken tradition that committees were made up of middle-class women, or because Woolf had proven her commitment to the group through her work on the plays and her talk, she was nominated as treasurer and her first job was to read out the year's financial statement. A December letter to Ethel Smyth shows Woolf less than enthusiastic about her newly acquired role: 'Boredom and distraction and fights with matter, have been hag riding me this fortnight [...] the Women's Institute elect me Treasurer. And I have to collect 30 sixpences and pay Mrs Freeth 2/3 for hire of hall' (L6 449–50).

While Woolf had little interest in her responsibilities as treasurer, this is not to say she didn't take her position on the WI committee seriously. In the months that followed her election Woolf fashioned herself a role similar to the one she occupied for so many years in the Richmond branch of the WCG, that of social secretary or fixer. She took to this alternative capacity with great energy, calling upon friends and family to present talks and slides to the Rodmell WI. Just a few days after her election Woolf wrote excitedly to Vita Sackville-West: 'Its true I've been made treasurer of the Women's Institute [Rodmell]: also I want to ask you about lantern slides of Persia; and will you come and talk' (L6 448). Woolf's touching self-importance here and her misleading claim to be the treasurer of the entire 'Women's Institute' reveal an alternative version of her involvement in which she appears active and committed. In a December letter to Sackville-West, Woolf shows a capacity to wheedle and flatter in order to secure a speaker:

> You cant think how they beamed and boomed over you. They've all heard you on the wireless. Miss Gardner our secretary has The Land

by heart. The one passion they all share is for Persia. What about slides? […] But details can wait. Only tell me you'll come; and accept my – oh accumulated blessings. (*L6* 451)

Woolf did not just perform the relatively simple task of asking friends to speak; she also took responsibility for the format of these talks and organised lantern slides for both Sackville-West's talk on Persia and Angelica Bell's talk on 'Modern Drama'[31] (*L6* 452):

The slide arrived safe. But Miss Gardner […] says we must get a Lantern. The Epi-dia-scope (Greek for looking through and over, I think) wont take slides only photographs. But you haven't photographs, I suppose? Anyhow its easy to come by the Lantern. As for the Epi-dia-scope, I've run mad hunting one down in Lewes for Angelica's lecture on The Stage tomorrow. (*L6* 462)

I quote at length to emphasise the technical dimension of Woolf's role and to reveal the degree to which she was willing to be involved in what is always the less glamorous, more technical side of organising events. Woolf's willingness to involve her friends and family with the groups with which she was active is, along with her powerful ambivalence towards all this activity, one of the few lines of continuity we can trace throughout her activism. She persuaded Adrian Stephen to teach Greek at Morley College and Vanessa to donate paintings to the college, while she invited the likes of E. M. Forster and Robert Trevelyan to speak to the WCG. This apparently abundant willingness to draw others in and capitalise on her friendships for the 'good' of these political and social groups is not only at odds with Woolf's ambivalence towards her own activity, but also with what is often considered the highly individualist and elitist character of Bloomsbury sociability.[32] An account of Woolf's political and social participation might caution us from accepting this portrait too wholeheartedly.

Woolf, then, assumed a number of roles during the course of her involvement with the WI and it is fair to observe that she felt most at ease in her familiar (and self-appointed) role of events organiser. Despite the WI's emphasis on its democratic character and its desire to push an agenda of class conciliation rather than agitation, for Woolf the WI seems to have become precisely the focus of her anxieties and hopes about class in this period. It is clear that Woolf saw the Rodmell WI as very much a microcosm of the village and, in keeping with the aspirations and key tenets of the WI, she was aware and sometimes critical of their representing a certain brand of Englishness to which the village was integral. This is most evident in her scathing association of the WI plays with the 'village mind' in her May 1940 letter. While this example illustrates Woolf's distaste for the WI and its 'villagism', which here she associates with a lack of imagination and parochialism, elsewhere she conforms to a more patriotic and conventional view of the WI women:

> Here we lead a disjointed jumping life. I had a niece staying here; another in a cottage. They collected friends in the air force and so on. We had a fête: also a village play. The sirens sounded in the middle. All the mothers sat stolid. I also admired that very much. (*L6* 430)

Woolf's portrait of 'the mothers' sitting 'stolid' while air-raid sirens howl, calls upon the national characteristic of English stiff upper-lip and is marked by a certain nostalgic attachment to such traditions. Even this apparently benign passage includes a lingering feeling of detachment. Woolf's restrained observation – 'I also admired that very much' – registers respect, but there is also something in its observational tone that speaks of her feeling of outsidership.

This combination of alienation and longing recurs throughout Woolf's diaries in this period and is something that she probes repeatedly and often painfully:

> When I think of Monks House when we took it [...] & how I hated the village – which now has become familiar & even friendly – arent I on the Cttee of the WI – dont I go to a meeting on Monday? (*D5* 341)

This November 1940 entry, written just prior to her election as treasurer, again reveals the synonymity of village and WI in Woolf's mind. And while here Woolf seems to be tracing her changing relationship with the village and her new feelings of ease and familiarity, her final questions, ringing with insecurity, challenge this narrative and again bring the WI to the foreground of Woolf's conflicting emotions about village life.

Virginia Woolf's Dreadnought Hoax talk

In 1910, along with hoax ringleader Horace Cole, her brother Adrian Stephen, Duncan Grant, Anthony Buxton and Guy Ridley, Virginia Stephen took the train to Weymouth disguised as an Abyssinian Prince and was given a tour of what was then Britain's premier battleship, the Dreadnought, by a number of high-ranking naval officials, including Admiral Sir William May and her own first cousin Willy Fisher, who was Commander of the Dreadnought. Although the pranksters completed their tour and returned to London without detection, when Cole leaked the hoax to the *Daily Mirror* it fast became something of a *cause célèbre*, prompting questions in the House of Commons about the security of the nation's naval vessels (*E6* 572). Although Virginia Stephen escaped any punishment, Adrian Stephen had to endure an interview with the First Lord of the Admiralty, while, according to Woolf's talk, Duncan Grant was kidnapped by Willy Fisher and three Naval Officers and then caned (or, rather, ceremonially tapped with a cane) on Hampstead Heath (*E6* 574–5).

Scholars recognise the political significance of Virginia Stephen's participation in the Dreadnought Hoax of 1910, identifying in this audacious act early evidence of the anti-patriarchal and anti-imperialist politics that she would later articulate in her polemic writing.[33] That scholars agree this was an explosive act of political dissent and critique make it significant that Woolf should have called upon this episode thirty years later as a subject for her talk to the Rodmell WI. Georgia Johnston's discovery of the missing pages of Woolf's draft of the talk in the WI archive held at The Women's Library at the LSE[34] invites a consideration of how the context of a WI meeting might have influenced Woolf's decisions in this talk. Johnston rightly states that in her talk Woolf was 'presenting an inherently political act' and I want to probe further the ways in which this talk represented Woolf entering into a critical dialogue with the WI and its nationalist ideology.[35]

At the outset Woolf's speech gives little sign of being of a radical or destabilising character. It is written with Woolf's idiosyncratic humour and is a mixture of slapstick and self-parody. The determinedly light-hearted tone of the speech may also be read as a concessionary response to the WI's most prized rule, 'that nothing which "might cause friction or lead to serious differences" should be discussed' at a WI meeting.[36] And yet, through a more detailed engagement with the narrative quirks and the network of subtextual allusions that run through the talk it becomes clear that its humorous tone belies its serious implications, not least Woolf's efforts not to appease WI conventions but to question them.

Woolf's opening is a good example of the way in which she combines cosy familiarity with the threat of subordination:

> I wonder if any of you happened to listen in last April fools day when some one gave an account of what he called the greatest hoax in history? I listened in; because I happen[ed] to be concerned in that particular hoax. I took part in it. Well, my version of that hoax was rather different from the wireless version. I thought it might amuse you if I told you the true story – if I told you what really happened. The story is the story of how a party of six wild young people went on board the *Dreadnought* as the Emp[eror] of Abyssinia and his suite. (E6 561)

The tone of Woolf's opening question is easy and conversational, while her repeated use of the newly coined phrase 'listen in' evokes a cosy setting and crucially gestures to the shared domestic experience of all the women present in her audience. This central positioning of the wireless domesticates Woolf's opening and is in keeping with what we have seen was the WI's central concern with women's role in their homes. It also reveals Woolf's understanding of the particular significance of 'listening in' to rural women and the way in which the advent of the wireless transformed what were formerly often isolated and quiet lives.[37] Having cultivated this comfortable atmosphere, Woolf undermines it by revealing that she plans to deviate from the sanctioned wireless version of the hoax and tell her own 'version'. The way in which Woolf lingers over this turn in her introduction – 'if I told you the true story – if I told you what really happened' – renders her revelation that her story will be that of 'six wild young people' all the more dramatic and potentially at odds with the WI's desire for uncontroversial talks.

Woolf's apparent flouting of WI conventions does not end here. Her account of the Dreadnought Hoax features cross-dressing, the ceaseless mockery of national and imperial institutions, including the admiralty and navy, and concludes with the 'ceremonial' caning of Duncan Grant on Hampstead Heath – an episode loaded with homoerotic allusion. As the talk was delivered on 23 July 1940 in the midst of the Second World War and given that Woolf believed the Rodmell WI to be centrally implicated in the contemporary patriotic and nationalist culture of jargon and false sentiment, we may perhaps read her flagrant contempt for the machinery of war as a coded criticism of WI ideology. The most potent example of this comes after Woolf's account of the hoax itself when she is describing the fallout for her brother and Duncan Grant:

> But we heard afterwards that one result of our visit had been that the regulations were tightened up; and that rules were made about telegrams that make it almost impossible now to repeat the joke. <I am glad to think that I too have been of help to my country> (E6 573)

The ironic allusion to the WI's motto 'For Home and Country' in the final line must surely not have been missed by the women present in the audience that day. Diana Gardner – who, expecting a 'Book Tea' and 'a kind of competition when everyone wore a badge on which was written her favourite book',[38] was wearing a pin with *Three Guineas* on it (D5 303) – presumably perceived the criticism implied in Woolf's mock-patriotic claim. The pointed inclusion of 'too' in this sentence seems a clear invitation to read Woolf's joke at the expense of the WI and of the women present, many of who were likely to be involved in war work. Such a reading of the talk as, in part, sending up the values of the WI perhaps also casts new light on the rather strange decision at *Home and Country* not to publish the talk once they had traced it in 1955.[39]

That Woolf's flamboyant talk on the Dreadnought Hoax was laced with satire and that she took this opportunity to poke fun at her WI hosts should come as no surprise given her well-known dislike of formal lectures and the playful precedent we find in the stabbing of the Angel in the House in 'Professions for Women'. However, Woolf's decision to eschew the expected talk on books for something more subversive was not driven simply by a desire to shock her WI audience. Such an appraisal not only underestimates

Woolf's attachment to the WI – the complex mixture of frustration and tenderness she felt for her fellow members – but also overlooks the clear element of complicity in her audience, which we can find in their laughter, stressed by Woolf in her letter to Smyth. By returning to the image of Miss Gardner with '3 Gs. pinned to her frock' (*D5* 303) we find a clue as to what Woolf might really have been doing in this tricky talk. Woolf is not simply making gags to satisfy her own rebellious instincts; she is also restating many of the key arguments relating to feminism, pacifism and class that dominated her 1938 polemic *Three Guineas* and the talk she had given just two months earlier to the Brighton WEA, later published as 'The Leaning Tower'.

The way in which a critique of male wealth and education is artfully integrated into Woolf's speech represents a clear link with her other late essays. Early in her talk when she is describing the character and pranks of Horace Cole, she says, by way of pointed explanation: 'He couldn't take up any profession. And fortunately for himself he had a good deal of money' (*E6* 562). Something in her use of 'himself' rather than 'him' makes this reference to Cole's wealth more emphatic, implying its exclusivity. A similar effect is created later when Woolf describes her brother's and Coles's experiences at Cambridge:

> Horace turned up in his rooms one day and said, Hullo Stephen, what are you doing with all those books? Reading for my exam. said my brother. Oh nonsense said Horace. Lets do something amusing. Well, my brother was only too happy to throw away his books. And so they amused themselves. (*E6* 562)

The reader/audience here senses Woolf's frustration that her own sacrifices to what she termed 'Arthur's education fund' in *Three Guineas* have bought her brother the freedom to ignore his studies and pursue amusement. Woolf implies that the education received by Cambridge undergraduates is not simply academic, but, as she suggests in 'The Leaning Tower', social as well (*E6* 266). The last clipped observation in this passage reinforces the exclusivity of this enjoyment and by its pointed use of 'they' unites Woolf and her audience of WI women in a silent, female 'us'. Jane Marcus has observed a similar rhetorical procedure at work in *A Room of One's Own*, which was based on a series of talks given to audiences at the women's colleges Newnham and Girton in Cambridge. In her compelling reading of *A Room* as lesbian seduction, Marcus observes: 'The conspiracy she sets up with her audience is of women in league together against authority.'[40] Such a conspiratorial dimension also characterises Woolf's Dreadnought talk, in which she adopts a similarly light-hearted and charming tone in order to forge this bond with her audience.

Woven into Woolf's account of her madcap adventure is also an identifiable thread of pacifism, linking it theoretically and imaginatively to *Three Guineas*. Initially this appears to be part of the play of the speech; for instance, when she says: 'In those days the young officers had a gay time. They were always up to some lark' (*E6* 563). The coming of the First World War hangs heavily over Woolf's portrait of carefree and, crucially, young soldiers in 1910. When Woolf introduces the war explicitly it represents a moment of poignancy that disrupts the jolliness of the talk:

> The same young officer who had met us at the station took us back to the pier. His name was Peter Willoughby; and I am sorry to say that he was killed very soon afterwards at the battle of Jutland. There he sat beside Horace Cole pointing out objects of interest. He had perfect manners. (*E6* 570)

Introducing the death of a 'young' and charming officer into the talk would not only have recalled the terrifying casualties of the First World War but would have reminded every woman in the audience of the current hostilities too. This powerful pacifist strain in the talk emerges again, unexpectedly, in Duncan Grant's refusal to fight his naval abductors on Hampstead Heath: 'Duncan Grant stood there like a lamb. It was useless to fight [...] And this rather upset them' (*E6* 574). Woolf parodies masculine aggression and makes the same link between arcane tradition and patriarchal power as she does in *Three Guineas* when she claims that 'two ceremonial taps' had avenged the 'honour of the navy' (*E6* 575).

In her talk Woolf embraces the opportunity of an all-women audience and puts into practice what she had theorised in *Three Guineas*; she attempts to communicate the need for women to be opposed to war. However, as we know from Diana Gardner's account of the social makeup of the Rodmell WI, Woolf was not delivering her message to the kind of audience she was writing for in *Three Guineas*. The fact that Woolf was speaking to a more diverse audience than the rather rigid one she formulated in *Three Guineas* suggests that this WI talk was an instance in which her social practice was more ambitious than her written theory. By camouflaging her didacticism with raucous, for the most part inclusive, humour, Woolf secures the WI women's collusion in this critique through their laughter.

The conspiratorial character of this laughter is arguably borne out by one of the letters that is housed in the same folder as the speech in The Women's Library. It is a letter from Mrs Minnie Decur of the Forge House, Rodmell, written in 1955 in response to a notice in *Home and Country* requesting details of which WI Woolf had been involved with.

> Dear Madame,
> In reply to your letter in the current number of 'Home & Country' Rodmell East Sussex was the name of the WI at which the late Virginia Woolf gave her never to be forgotten talk. She came to live in Rodmell in 1919, but did not join us until well into the war, when she was elected Treasurer, we asked her to give us a 'Talk' on 'Books', but she said she had decided to tell us about a Hoax in which she had once taken part. It really was one of the most amusing talks we have ever had in our WI. We were very nearly helpless with laughter. I only wish I could give you the story in detail [...] Our WI began in 1919 & I joined at once so I can assure you this is quite a correct account.[41]

There are a number of striking details in this account. In the first instance, Mrs Decur's touting of Woolf's speech as 'her never to be forgotten talk' is certainly not a categorically positive remark and begs the obvious question, why was the talk so unforgettable?, to which we are not supplied a satisfactory answer. The ambiguity of this statement is suggestive and sets the tone for the rest of the letter.

Also telling is Mrs Decur's inclusion of the fact that Woolf 'came to live in Rodmell in 1919, but did not join us until well into the war'. This apparently neutral remark is edged with criticism. Unlike Mrs Decur who, we discover later in her letter, 'joined at once' when the Rodmell WI was established in 1919, Woolf, the implication is, could not bring herself to join until '*well into* the war' [italics my own]. It is significant that Mrs Decur's account makes the connection between Woolf's joining the WI and the deepening of war, not only because in this it is consistent with Woolf's own identification of her involvement with the WI as her 'contribution to the war', but also because it suggests that this was clear to other members too.

This brings us to perhaps the most significant detail in the letter. Mrs Decur recalls that Woolf was asked to do one thing – 'give [...] a "Talk" on "Books"' – but instead she did quite another – 'but she said she had decided to tell us about a Hoax in which she had once taken part'. Minnie Decur's playful use of punctuation in this passage almost seems to register an awareness of the maverick nature of Woolf's talk. But after this dramatic, heavily punctuated account of the lead-up to the talk, the original reader of this letter must have been frustrated by the absence of any details of the talk itself. Instead Mrs Decur retreats into hilarity: 'It really was one of the most amusing talks we have ever had in our WI. We were very nearly helpless with laughter.' After all this rather knowing laughter her apology for not being able to provide any details of the talk itself strikes the reader as a little disingenuous. While she may simply have forgotten the details of the talk she does not mention this, saying: 'I only wish I could give you the story in detail.' The ambiguity with which the letter opens re-emerges here in the women's laughter and Mrs Decur's evasion of detail. Even her brisk statement of her WI credentials at the end of this passage, rather than assuring us that 'this is quite a correct account', leaves the distinct impression that something has been left out.

The way in which the event was recorded in the *East Sussex News* lays a similar emphasis on the humour of the speech and reveals some more details of the arrangement of the evening:

> The monthly meeting was held in the Village Hall on Tuesday. The president (Mrs. Chavasse) occupied the chair. Members joined in singing 'Jerusalem.' Mrs Virginia Woolf, the authoress, who is a member of the Institute, gave an amusing description of a visit to the 'Dreadnought,' which was really a famous hoax. Mrs Withers Green, who has been a most efficient secretary for seven months, is leaving the village, and a hearty vote of thanks was accorded her on the proposition of the president. Miss Gardner has been elected secretary for the remainder of the year. A book title competition and games brought a very pleasant evening to a conclusion.[42]

The phrasing of this account seems part of a calculated attempt to play down the possibly subversive character of the talk by 'the authoress' by positioning the words 'Dreadnought' and 'hoax' at different ends of the sentence. There is also something striking and extremely funny in the way in which the group singing of 'Jerusalem' and Virginia Woolf's 'amusing description' of her anti-imperialist hoax are juxtaposed in this account, seeming to highlight the tension in the evening's order of ceremony.[43]

Virginia Woolf and the village drama movement

Woolf's talk on the Dreadnought Hoax, with its flamboyant mixture of slapstick, suspense and thematic emphasis on performance, helpfully foregrounds issues that are central to this section, which reads Woolf's involvement with WI drama in the broader context of the emergence of the inter-war village drama movement. It is clear from an outline of Woolf's involvement with the Rodmell WI that her participation focused on the group's theatrical exploits. While it is difficult to establish what her actual role was in preparing these plays we can, however, be sure that she was a member of the audience that watched them. While we unfortunately have none of the Rodmell WI records from the period that Woolf was a member, her own private accounts of these plays, read in conjunction with local newspaper reports, provide important details about what sort of plays these were and who performed in them and thus allow us to reflect on how Rodmell WI drama fitted into the wider narrative of village drama at that moment.

In recent years a new body of scholarship has emerged focusing on Woolf's relationship to the theatre. These studies variously consider Woolf's engagement with contemporary drama in her fiction and non-fiction, her participation in Bloomsbury theatricals, her sole work of drama *Freshwater* and her own status as a theatre-goer.[44] Steven D. Putzel argues that 'drama, theatre and performance formed a continuous subtext in Virginia Woolf's art and in her life',[45] highlighting her involvement in the Play Reading Society set up by Clive Bell in 1907 and her frequent dramatic collaborations with her Bell nephews and niece at Charleston.[46]

Virginia Woolf's involvement with the WI plays closely coincided with a development in literary modernism's relationship with the theatre, with both high and late modernist figures, including E. M. Forster, T. S. Eliot, W. H. Auden, Stephen Spender and Christopher Isherwood, writing for the stage. Woolf's responses to this dramatic work ranged from being moved by Stephen Spender's 1938 verse-play *Trial of a Judge*, produced at the socialist Unity Theatre (*D5* 131), to being 'selfishly relieved' at the poor reception of T. S. Eliot's *The Family Reunion* in 1939 (*D5* 210). In 1938 Leonard Woolf was also writing a play and Woolf records on 31 March 1938: 'L. writing his play – the one he's brewed these 10 years & more' (*D5* 133). However, Leonard's play, 'The Hotel' – a blackly comic commentary on 'the horrors of the twilight age of Europe' – struggled to find a theatre to take it on, despite interest from the Group Theatre and the Co-operative Society Theatre (*L6* 343).

During the late 1930s Woolf's niece, Angelica Bell, studied acting at the London Studio Theatre and appeared in several productions that were eagerly attended by her aunt. Woolf went as far as to ask Vita Sackville-West, on Angelica's behalf, whether she would act as a guarantor for her and other members of the acting troupe, the London Village Players, who toured plays around the countryside (*L6* 322). And in a 1938 letter to Saxon Sydney-Turner, Woolf refers to a possible collaboration with Michel St Denis, drama theorist and founder of the London Studio Theatre, on a 'highly stylized version' (*L6* 238) of Homer's *Odyssey*. It is perhaps surprising then, particularly in the context of the modernist turn to the stage and the emergence of the politicised drama of Auden and Spender, that Woolf's most sustained theatrical activity during this period should have been helping her local WI to produce locally authored plays on, as we shall see, consummately rural themes.

Lately new work by rural historians has sought to re-emphasise the cultural history of the inter-war countryside, remedying 'the way in which the countryside has been eliminated from our national history, or at best seen as nothing more than the location of the agricultural industry'.[47] This has led to a reconsideration of the cultural contributions of voluntary groups such as the WI and a growing interest in the proliferation of amateur theatre groups and village theatricals throughout rural England in this period. In his work on village theatre, Mick Wallis focuses on Mary Kelly, pioneer and key theorist of the village drama movement and founder of the Village Drama Society in 1919.[48] After working as a VAD during the First World War, Kelly established the Kelly Players in her home village of Kelly in Devon (named after her family). She was eager to capitalise on what she believed were the significant social upheavals of the war and to create a group that would include all villagers, regardless of class.[49] As is evident in her theoretical writing on village theatre, Kelly firmly believed that 'the countryman' had a unique dramatic instinct due to his close relationship with nature and what Kelly considered his dramatic inheritance. While recognising that the advent of the Kelly Players represented a continuity with certain pre-war paternalistic patterns, Wallis also argues that this new dramatic group 'signalled a modest commitment to democratic change'.[50]

The success of the Kelly Players inspired Mary Kelly to create the Village Drama Society (VDS) in 1919 in order 'to encourage similar experimentation in other villages, beginning with an appeal through the Church newspapers'.[51] In her retrospective review of the VDS and the inter-war revival of village drama, Kelly records that the largest and most positive response to her appeal came from the NFWI.[52] Wallis also notes that 'the rapid growth of the VDS was facilitated by the network of Women's Institutes, which provided a ready-made infrastructure for meetings'.[53] Kelly writes gratefully of the support the VDS received from the WI and insists that a 'close friendship existed between the Village Drama Society and the National Federation of Women's Institutes'.[54] Kelly often wrote on matters of drama and performance pseudonymously for *Home and Country* and she acted as a judge and respondent at a WI drama festival.[55] It was not simply for their role in the spread of village drama across the country that Kelly admired the WI; she believed that by 'insisting on social equality within its borders' the 'Women's Institutes have revolutionized women's life in the country'.[56]

In spite of her respect for the NFWI, Kelly had some reservations about their prominence and activity within the village drama movement. For instance, Kelly appears ambivalent about the number of all-women productions produced by the WI, which is perhaps no surprise given her particular and sometimes nostalgic attachment to the figure of the instinctively dramatic, labouring country*man*. Kelly critically suggests that 'the W.I. shut their doors on their menfolk, and kept the drama to their own members' and that, because of this, 'village drama came to be almost synonymous with W.I. drama; unfortunately too, for this reason, the men came to consider the drama as a pastime "only fit for women and children"'.[57] Kelly is also reticent on the subject of the increasing demand for all-women plays that WI drama groups created, suggesting that 'where a market is certain, a lot of rubbish will inevitably be brought to it'.[58] And while insisting that such plays will 'always be limited, for there are very few "all-women emotions"', she interestingly recognises that 'it is true that there is a side to women's life where she walks alone, and that side deserves expression as well as any other aspect of life'.[59]

In her account of inter-war village drama, Caitlin Adams pays specific attention to the tensions that existed in the movement, locating these in the very founding imperatives of the movement:

> In rural areas, amateur players and the reformers who sought to help them looked to drama to fulfil two, possibly contradictory, imperatives: first, to strengthen a sense of community, and second, to bring villagers into contact with a wider movement in literature and art. Drama in the village was never just about presenting plays: it was always an arena for contestation over communal history and collective identity.[60]

This desire to revive interest in 'communal history' and restore 'collective identity' in the villages through drama, which inspired Mary Kelly and the work of the VDS, may account for the WI's enthusiasm for village drama, as it was a body that championed villagism and local history.[61] The preoccupation with 'virtues such as simplicity, directness and sincerity [...] as the hallmarks of rural authenticity'[62] and the promotion of these qualities as central to village productions by the VDS are consistent with the WI's self-identification as a custodian of an authentic rural English identity. Equally, the WI's protectiveness of its rural character was reflected in a 'deep anxiety that villagers, if left to themselves, might choose to represent urbane or "sophisticated" values on stage – and that in doing so could dilute rural virtues'.[63]

Drama performed by the WI seems to have ranged 'from Shakespeare to new plays in dialect'.[64] However, as WI drama societies were often all-women groups with little money for staging, they were 'largely responsible for the demand for "cottage" or "kitchen" plays which took place around the family hearth (though the post office was an overused alternative)'.[65] This influx of domestic, one-act plays for village societies were, primarily, written by women, and the records of the East Sussex Federation confirm this preference for these one-act dramas.[66]

In spite of the popularity of this emerging genre with WI drama societies throughout the country, the controversy surrounding all-women casts remained a hotly debated issue. Adams suggests the proliferation of single-sex acting societies was also a source of anxiety for the NFWI leadership:

> There were repeated attempts at county federation councils to pass resolutions against women-only WI drama groups. Many observers (some of them women) inside and outside the WI insisted that single-sex drama societies could not attain the high standard of which village productions ought to be capable.[67]

This reaction to all-women drama societies, such as the one Woolf was involved with, reveals the real local significance of these drama groups and the kinds of debates they inspired. Clearly it was one thing for a women-only organisation like the WI to exist in villages across the country – although this itself caused controversy in some areas in the WI's early years – but somehow it was quite another for all-women acting groups to emerge. Concerns over dramatic standards appear to be a cover for more profound anxieties about community cohesion and about women's roles in society, thus neatly illustrating Adams's observation that the activities of village drama societies and their preoccupation with staging local identity 'could not help but highlight anxieties about class and gender, and modernity'.[68] Such internal wrangling over the nature and function of village drama and the WI's central but at times contentious role within this should encourage us to approach Woolf's involvement with the WI plays with a sensitivity to these issues.

* * *

A March 1934 article in the *Sussex Express* entitled 'Amateur Drama Revival Influence of the Women's Institute' usefully illustrates the character the revival of village drama took in East Sussex and the prominent role performed by the East Sussex Federation of Women's Institutes (ESFWI) in promoting this renewed interest in drama.[69] The article addresses what it describes as 'the remarkable revival in East Sussex of interest in amateur theatricals' and pays tribute to the ESFWI's role in this renaissance:

> The East Sussex Federation have done as much, if not more, than any other federation in this respect. They have always been in the van of the movement, introducing innovations with the object of still further popularising the drama, innovations which have been copied all over the country.[70]

This article not only evidences the popularity of village drama in East Sussex, but also the ESFWI's commitment to this activity and the seriousness with which it was approached. Later in the article, the ESFWI's support of drama in its branches takes on a rather steely edge when the secretary of the Federation is quoted as saying:

> There was a lot to be done, and a lot was being done to get people to want to act something better than what is known as a sketch, and to get them to realise there was far more pleasure to be derived from doing better plays.[71]

The rigorousness of this approach to WI drama is borne out by the records of the East Sussex Federation. Numerous references to demonstrations, schools and competitions appear under the drama subheading in the Federation's monthly letters to its branches throughout the 1930s.[72] In April 1937 the monthly letter advertises an imminent 'Producers' School at the King Charles Hall, Tunbridge Wells', which was to be directed by none other than Virginia Woolf's cousin Virginia Isham. Woolf had previously made supplications to Vita Sackville-West on Isham's behalf – similar to those she made for her niece – asking whether Isham could put on a play in the grounds of Sissinghurst (*L5* 205). As well as providing expert instruction at various events, in 1938 the Federation alerted its members to the provision of 'advisory visits' by the Sussex Rural Community

Council to 'enable any producer who desires it to obtain an additional "outside" opinion, given by an expert, upon the production and/or presentation of a particular play being rehearsed by the Society in question'.[73]

Stressing the business-like and serious approach taken by the East Sussex Federation to its branch's dramatic exploits provides an important regional context for Woolf's involvement with the Rodmell group. That Woolf's cousin played a prominent role in the organisation of East Sussex WI drama, and given what I have suggested was her own position as Mrs Chavasse's consultant on Rodmell WI plays, we may infer that Woolf would have been familiar with the protocols of WI drama and perhaps the various political considerations involved in staging village theatre.

As I have already noted, Woolf's involvement with the Rodmell WI drama group began in April 1940 when she was approached by Mrs Chavasse and was asked to write and produce a play for 'the villagers to act'. While Woolf demurred from writing a play herself, she was involved in the production and staging of two plays written by WI members, Alice Carter and Ida Smith. The letters and diary entries already quoted reveal Woolf's impatience with and near-contempt for these productions. However, the way in which these plays were reported in local newspapers situate them, and Woolf's involvement in their production from late April until their performance in August 1940, in the context of the renaissance of village theatre in East Sussex. The scant but telling plot details and the cast lists provided invite a reconsideration of Woolf's almost guttural antagonism towards them.

The plays that Virginia Woolf wrote about in her May 1940 letter to her niece, Judith Stephen, were performed after three months of rehearsals at a WI meeting on 20 August.[74] The *East Sussex News* dated 23 August 1940 gives the following report of the meeting at which the plays were performed:

> The Women's Institute met at the Village Hall. There was a large attendance of members and friends, who had the pleasure of listening to an inspiring address by Lady Reading on the many and varied activities of the Women's Voluntary Services [...] Then followed two original one-act plays written by members of the institute – 'Fond Relations' by Alice Carter; and 'Fake Alarm' [sic] by Ida Smith. They

were well acted and hearty applause and calls for the authors brought the first part of the meeting to a close.[75]

Caitlin Adams has observed that 'some theatre groups admitted men and performed for the whole village, while others produced plays only for fellow members of the WI and their children'.[76] While women and children performed these plays, the performances seem to have been open to the whole village, with 'a large attendance of members and friends'. The wider context of the meeting is also worth considering. Lady Reading founded the Women's Voluntary Service (WVS) at the outbreak of war in order to enlist and organise women in rural areas to educate and prepare their communities for the coming air raids and bomb attacks. Allowing Lady Reading to come and speak on the subject of the WVS and their wartime activities was not strictly in keeping with the WI's policy of non-sectarianism.[77] Given Woolf's own recent sniping references to 'jargon from my first aid practice and the Women's Institute' (*L6* 409) and her explosive row with Leonard when he wanted to join the Local Defence Volunteers in Rodmell (*D5* 284), we can imagine that Lady Reading's 'inspirational address' might have piqued Woolf's temper.

A report in the *Sussex Express* goes into greater detail about the plays themselves:

> The first, 'Fond Relations,' was written by Mrs. Carter, and was a satirical character study of an old man's (presumed dead!) relations. It was performed by Mrs Carter (author and producer), Mrs Penfold, Mrs Percy Thompsett, and Mrs Kennard. The second play, written and produced by Mrs Smith, was an air-raid comedy, 'False Alarm'. The performers were Mrs. Smith, Mrs Richardson, Mrs Penfold and Master David Smith.[78]

'Fond Relations' resembles one of the one-act domestic comedies that were so popular among WI drama groups, while 'False Alarm' falls into the timely genre of 'air-raid comedy'. Being performed directly after Lady Reading's talk on the WVS, which is likely to have included a discussion of air-raid protocol and precautions, must have lent 'False Alarm' a kind of pointed and uneasy comedy. For Woolf, whose own constant and barely suppressed fear of what losing the war would spell for her and Leonard sometimes pierced the calm record of life in Rodmell during the summer of 1940,[79] the 'jargon' of the WVS followed by a light-hearted 'air-raid comedy' must have seemed gruesome. The subject matter of Ida Smith's play perhaps casts Woolf's visceral aversion to the plays in rather a different light. Her dramatic use of the words 'sacrifice' and 'smeared' take on additional, potent meaning when read in the context of the fear of annihilation that loomed spectrally 'behind' her humdrum, voluntary activities in the village.

Woolf's vexed involvement in the production of Ida Smith's and Alice Carter's plays and the classed terms in which she responds to them in her May diary entry and throughout the rehearsals should also be understood in the context of the argument she presented in her talk to the Brighton WEA in April 1940, just a month before her work on the WI plays began. In this talk Woolf gives a historical-materialist account of the relationship between the production of literature and the English class system. She drily observes: 'It cannot be mere chance that this minute class of educated people has produced so much that is good as writing; and that the vast mass of people without education has produced so little that is good' (*E6* 265). The essay concludes with Woolf looking forward to the end of the war and, with it, social transformations – the income tax that will force more middle-class parents to send their children to local elementary schools and the public library that will allow every reader to become a critic of literature and society – which will, in turn, bring about the end of 'old-class literature' (*E6* 275).

Woolf also levels a critique against what she considers the self-indulgence of contemporary political poetry. Her criticism of these poets is interestingly echoed in her frustration with the WI playwrights. Woolf complains that the 'Leaning Tower Poets' produce poems and novels 'full of confusion and of compromise' (*E6* 269), while she is scathing about the 'readymade commonplaceness' of the WI-authored plays. There is certainly a syntactic and imaginative link between Woolf's use of 'compromise' and 'commonplace' here that arguably invites us to read Woolf's irritation with the plays in the context of her wider frustration with the state of the 'class literature' she rails against in 'The Leaning Tower'. A subtext of disappointment runs through what appears to be simply Woolf's snobbish affront at the plays. We can see Woolf struggling to express this in her coda to her attack on the plays: 'Whats wrong is the conventionality – not the coarseness. So that its all lulled & dulled. The very opposite of "common" or working class' (D5 289). Here Woolf seems to share with the leaders of village drama a (problematic) desire to encounter an 'authentic', working-class voice in the WI plays and is disappointed when the WI dramatists echo conventional forms and voices. Woolf's rather romantic anticipation of a classless literature in which 'all the different dialects' will flood the 'clipped and cabined vocabulary' (E6 275) of the middle-class poet, also links 'The Leaning Tower' to contemporary debates concerning the significance and value of local dialects within village drama. Having given this triumphant and prophetic talk only weeks before, it is quite possible that Woolf had hoped that these plays might have signalled the start of the 'stronger [...] more varied literature' (E6 276) she anticipated.

The second Rodmell WI play staged in 1940 took place at the 21st birthday celebrations of the branch, held on 17 December 1940.[80] While it is unclear how far Woolf was involved in the preparations for this production, she was certainly in the audience, as she records attending the celebrations in a letter to Angelica Bell (L6 452). The celebratory tone of Woolf's letter is echoed in the report of the meeting that featured in the *East Sussex News*:

> There was a large attendance of members and friends of the Women's Institute at the 21st birthday celebrations, which took place on Tuesday at the Village Hall. Mrs N. Clowes, M.B.E., of Cooksbridge, was the guest of honour, as it was she who introduced the movement to the village in 1919. A telegram of congratulation was received from Lady Denman (chairman of the National Federation of Women's Institutes). After the singing of 'Jerusalem,' Mrs Clowes gave a cheery talk on 'The beautiful valley in which you live.' She urged the members to see the bright side of things and to look forward to a better and happier future when peace shall reign once more. A short musical programme followed, including two items by the festival choir, and solos by Mrs Penfold, Mrs Smith and Mrs Stacey. Tea, provided by the members, was enjoyed by all present, with a beautiful birthday cake decorated with 21 candles – a gift from the president. The concluding item was a humorous sketch entitled 'Goose Chase' by Mabel Constanduros, cleverly acted by members of the Institute Drama Club, those taking part being Mrs Bleach, Miss Bleach, Mrs

Richardson, Mrs Penfold, Miss Thompsett and Mrs Smith, the last-named being responsible for the production of the play. The players were heartily applauded by a very appreciative audience. Mr Woolf voiced the thanks of husbands of the members who were present, and the singing of the national anthem brought a memorable evening to a conclusion.[81]

In contrast to the plays penned by Ida Smith and Alice Carter, 'Goose Chase' by Mabel Constanduros and Howard Agg was a staple of amateur theatre groups.[82] Like the two plays the group performed in August, 'Goose Chase' is also a one-act domestic comedy for an all-female cast. A conventional farce, 'Goose Chase' follows Great-Aunt Popsy, her niece Lizzie and Lizzie's daughters Jane and Peggy as they hunt around their kitchen for the missing golden beads of another, recently deceased, Great Aunt. After various interruptions from Cowslip – the dairymaid who is described in the stage directions as 'a fat, stupid, untidy-looking girl with a hot face, who keeps wringing her hands in her coarse apron. She speaks with a strong rustic accent' – the women realise the beads must have been hidden in a chair given to the much-disliked Aunt Hannah just in time for said aunt to appear and reveal she has sold the chair and kept the gold for herself.[83]

Although there is nothing in Woolf's letters or diaries to indicate that she performed in this play, the fact that it was Leonard Woolf who 'voiced the thanks of husbands' present could suggest that Woolf's involvement with the group's drama club persisted. The image of Virginia Woolf, treasurer of her local WI, standing to sing the national anthem and listening attentively to a congratulatory telegram from Lady Denman, offers a strikingly conservative alternative to the subversive outsider and the leftist-activist versions of Woolf we find elsewhere, and acts as a useful reminder of the complex and often contradictory quality of Woolf's social and political participation.

Between the Acts (1941)

In her book, *Mrs Woolf and the Servants*, Alison Light implies that the writing of *Between the Acts*, with its central focus of a pageant-play, was for Virginia Woolf an antidote to the stifling boredom of working on the WI plays.[84] Light, with other scholars,[85] is right to point out a connection between Woolf's involvement with the WI plays and her final novel's preoccupation with drama. However, Woolf's engagement with the WI in *Between the Acts* should not be read as a straightforward reaction against its amateur dramatics. It is not simply the centrality of village theatre in *Between the Acts* that reveals the influence of Woolf's activity with the WI. The prominent and discursive themes of Englishness, nostalgia and progress we encounter in Woolf's final novel need to be understood in the context of Woolf's relationship with the Rodmell WI. This discussion suggests the ways in which the novel may also be read as entering into a wider ideological dialogue with the WI, whose dual (and often mutually problematic) founding principles of patriotism and democracy Woolf interrogates in the novel.

Published posthumously in 1941, Woolf's final novel displays a panorama of her writerly skill; the narrative ranges from the brooding and prescient to the playful and extravagant. F. R. Leavis's contemporary accusation that it is a novel that lacks a 'moral interest' or an 'interest in action'[86] has since been roundly challenged by an impressive body of scholarship exploring the novel's dynamic engagement with historical and political questions and the centrality of Woolf's feminism and pacifism to its narrative.[87]

Woolf began drafting *Between the Acts* in April 1938 as a diversion from the laborious task of writing Roger Fry's biography (*D5* 135). She wrote and redrafted several versions of the novel before finishing it in February 1941 (*D5* 356). Woolf did not work steadily on the novel for the whole of this two-and-a-half-year stretch. After an initial burst of activity by December 1938 Woolf had written 120 pages and was positive but rather hazy about the novel's direction (*D5* 193). Mark Hussey notes in his introduction to the novel, that after working 'intermittently' at her book, alongside work on Fry's biography, in the 'autumn of 1939, work on "Pointz Hall" slackened as she concentrated on finishing *Roger Fry* and producing numerous reviews and essays'.[88] Woolf's return to dedicated work on her novel in May 1940 interestingly coincided with the height of her work on the WI plays. Her violent outburst against the plays in her diary entry of 29 May also records her return to work on her novel: 'Began P.H again today, & threshed & threshed till perhaps a little grain can be collected' (*D5* 289). Throughout the summer of 1940 Woolf considered ways to end the novel and by December 1940, the month 'Goose Chase' was performed, Woolf reports in her diary: 'I've been copying my Ms. of P.H., & am word drugged' (*D5* 346).

Between the Acts is set in June 1939 on the day that an annual village pageant is staged in the grounds of the Oliver family's country house, Pointz Hall. While characters are busy preparing for the pageant – sandwich making and stage dressing – as Gillian Beer notes, 'the coming war broods over the whole community' (*BTA* ix). Much of the novel is taken up with the performance and reception of Miss La Trobe's unconventional pageant. As Alice Wood notes, La Trobe eschews the nationalist conventions of pageantry – 'exploring England's cultural and social history with little concern for political events, military victories or defeats'.[89] She tells the story of England's cultural 'development', presenting four pastiches of different literary periods: Jed Esty describes these as 'Elizabethan drama, Restoration comedy, Victorian melodrama, and the present day'.[90]

Given the centrality and spectacle of the village pageant, readings of the novel tend to focus on this performance and what it tells us, variously, about Woolf's conception of literary history, the role of the artist in society and her (often conflicting) ideas about community.[91] In a number of critical accounts of the novel it is also considered a given that Miss La Trobe is an encoded version of Woolf herself and, by extension, that La Trobe's creative experiments mirror those of her creator. Woolf certainly regarded *Between the Acts* as a stylistic departure, and this is made clear in a diary entry early in the drafting process: 'P.H. is to be a series of contrasts. Will it come off? Am I in earnest? Its to end with a play' (*D5* 159). Here Woolf's tone is one of both excitement and apprehension and her self-questioning can be read as anticipating Miss La Trobe's anxiety over the reception of her ambitious pageant (*BTA* 107). On the completion of the first draft of the novel, Woolf's tone remains positive: 'I am a little triumphant about the book. I think its an interesting attempt in a new method' (*D5* 340).

* * *

There are a number of obvious details in Woolf's novel that call attention to her real-life involvement with WI drama. For example, Isa Oliver's musings on her uninvited lunch guest, the irrepressible Mrs Manresa, include a cloaked reference to the educational activities of the WI:

> Often when Ralph Manresa had to stay in town she came down alone; wore an old garden hat; taught the village women *not* how to pickle and preserve; but how to weave frivolous baskets out of coloured straw. Pleasure's what they want, she said. (*BTA* 28)

Although not named, the WI is evoked here through the reference to the dull pursuits of 'pickling and preserving'. However, there is a second, less obvious critique working through this reference that perhaps casts Woolf's feelings towards the group in a more nuanced light. Gillian Beer links Mrs Manresa's deviation from the traditional, domestic occupations of the WI to Woolf's own 'uneasy relations with the local Women's Institute' (*BTA* 135). Mrs Manresa's claim – 'Pleasure's what they want' – reveals a blithe confidence in her own familiarity with the desires of 'the village women' that is as problematic as the jam-making prescribed by the WI. While Isa Oliver views this basket-making as a sign of Mrs Manresa's genuine affection for the countryside, there is a narrative suspicion of Mrs Manresa which is even more pronounced in her subsequent, self-congratulatory identification with 'the servants', who she claims are not so 'grown up' (*BTA* 29) as the Olivers. This portrait of Mrs Manresa and her position as a 'townie' who comes to the countryside for weekends is partly reflective of Woolf's own anxiety about her status in Rodmell and her uneasiness about assuming too substantial a role in the WI, which she believed should be run 'by the village women themselves'.

Another striking gesture to the WI plays appears in Lucy Swithin's account of the previous years' pageants:

> 'One year we had *Gammer Gurton's Needle*'. said Mrs Swithin. 'One year we wrote the play ourselves. The son of our blacksmith – Tony? Tommy? – had the loveliest voice. And Elsie at the Crossways – how she mimicked! Took us all off. Bart; Giles; Old Flimsy – that's me. People are gifted – very. The question is – how to bring it out? (*BTA* 37–8)

Lucy's identification of the 'son of our blacksmith' and her telling stumbling over his forename perhaps self-consciously recalls Woolf's reference to the WI plays being 'written by the gardener's wife, and the chauffeur's wife'. Similarly, in this passage Woolf draws on her own experience of seeing Angelica Bell perform in a touring production of *Gammer Gurton's Needle* in August 1938 put on by the London Village Players (*D5* 162).

In addition to these obvious examples, Lucy's account reinscribes some of the uneasy identification we encountered in Woolf's references to her involvement with the WI in her private writing. For instance, Lucy begins inclusively with the repeated phrase 'one year we', which suggests she is speaking collectively, for the whole village. However, the dynamics of this account change when she comes to describe Elsie's mimicking; the 'us' that previously seemed to include the whole community now refers only to the Olivers: 'Bart; Giles; Old Flimsy'. This constriction of the pronoun not only undermines the deictic tone of the opening but also causes the reader to reconsider the nature of the pageant, which until this point in the novel has been extravagantly characterised as a bucolic and all-embracing occasion – I'm thinking in particular of Woolf's tongue-in-cheek description of breeches-wearing young men and women hanging garlands around the barn (*BTA* 19). The subtly shifting tone of Lucy's speech recalls Woolf's own account of the Rodmell village plays in the letter to Judith Stephen I discussed earlier: 'We're acting village plays; written by the gardener's wife, and the chauffeur's wife; and acted by the other villagers' (*L6* 400).

This shared funnelling structure, which opens up the possibility of a collective identity and simultaneously closes it down, that links these two extracts also reminds us of Woolf's oft-discussed diary entry in which she sets out her ambitions for the novel that would be *Between the Acts*:

> 'I' rejected: 'We' substituted: to whom at the end there shall be an invocation? 'We'... composed of many different things ... we all life, all art, all waifs & strays – a rambling capricious but somehow unified whole – the present state of my mind? (*D5* 135)

Woolf's concern with giving voice to a collective identity in this passage can also be traced through her responses to her activity with the WI, which clearly mediate Lucy's account of past pageants. The influence of the WI is also arguably perceptible in Woolf's preoccupation with the viability of communal art in *Between the Acts*, as expressed in Lucy's final, slightly anxious invocation: 'People are gifted – very. The question is – how to bring it out?'

It is clear, then, that Woolf's experience with the Rodmell WI did not simply suggest subject matter for the novel, but also importantly informed its key themes, in particular its debates about community. Running parallel to questions about staging collective identity posed in the pageant is a subsidiary debate about democracy, in which the principles and practice of the WI are deeply implicated. This takes place in the run-up to the performance and during its various intervals. The episode in which Lucy Swithin joins Mrs Sands, the Olivers' cook, in the kitchen to make sandwiches is a crucial example of this. The scene opens with what may be read as a gesture to the well-established WI rule against any remarks that might cause friction or offence: ' "The sandwiches … " said Mrs. Swithin, coming into the kitchen. She refrained from adding "Sands" to "sandwiches," for Sand and sandwiches clashed. "Never play," her mother used to say, "on people's names" ' (*BTA* 22). As the scene continues, this spirit of conciliation is maintained through the women's collaborative sandwich making: 'Mrs. Sands fetched bread; Mrs. Swithin fetched ham. One cut the bread; the other the ham. It was soothing, it was consolidating, this handwork together' (*BTA* 23).

In spite of its pleasing, nursery rhyme-like symmetry, this is not the democratic scene of class conciliation it may first appear. For instance, it becomes clear that the statement – 'It was soothing, it was consolidating, this handwork together' – though not attributed to either woman, is truer of Mrs Swithin's experience, as for her this work in the kitchen is clearly a yearly novelty in honour of the pageant. By contrast, Mrs Sands must stifle her annoyance at the 'people making work in the kitchen while they had a high old time hanging paper roses in the barn' (*BTA* 23). While this portrait of Mrs Sands the cook as stolid and grudge-bearing is typical of Woolf's view of domestic servants and exposes her own class prejudice, it is worth noting that Mrs Sands's resentment is not directed against Mrs Swithin, at whose insistence the sandwiches are made, but against other working-class characters who have escaped their regular roles and attendant duties for one morning. The misdirection of Mrs Sands's ire and Mrs Swithin's complete immunity to any of this tension reveal Woolf engaging with the dynamics of class and exposing what she considers the false ideas of progress and democracy cherished by the upper-middle classes.

If Mrs Sands embodies the conservative and 'conventional' qualities and values Woolf associated with her fellow WI members, her nephew, Billy, whom she critically describes as 'doing [...] what boys shouldn't; cheeking the master' (*BTA* 23), disrupts the status quo of this domestic scene. With its hint of dissent and even class antagonism, Billy's 'cheek' represents a challenge to the project of class conciliation, or rather 'consolidation', that is played out between Mrs Swithin and Mrs Sands. That a desire to ameliorate class awareness and antagonism accompanied contemporary rhetoric about democracy, in particular within the WI movement, is something that Woolf seems keenly aware of in this scene. This episode concludes with a further critique of Lucy Swithin's complacency and her ingrained sense of entitlement: ' "There!" said Mrs Swithin, surveying the sandwiches, some neat, some not. "I'll take 'em to the barn". As for the lemonade, she assumed, without a flicker of doubt, that Jane the kitchen maid would follow after' (*BTA* 23–4). Any remaining sense that what has occurred was a democratic, co-operative exchange is undermined by Lucy Swithin's instinctive assumption that 'the kitchen maid would follow after' her.

This narrative scepticism regarding social progress along democratic lines is addressed more directly later in the novel during the interval tea of the pageant. This scene opens with another example of Woolf's distinctively classed characterisation of Mrs Sands, the cook. After an extended description of all the animal life – mice, 'countless beetles and insects', 'a stray bitch' and bluebottles (*BTA* 61) – inhabiting the barn, Mrs Sands's entrance is deliberately and harshly at odds with the poetry of this section:

> But Mrs. Sands was approaching. She was pushing her way through the crowd [...] She could see the great open door. But butterflies she never saw; mice were only black pellets in kitchen drawers; moths she bundled in her hands and put out of the window. Bitches suggested only servant girls misbehaving. (*BTA* 62)

The circumscription of Mrs Sands's world-view and, again, her acid reaction to her fellow workers – here the misbehaving servant girls signal a similar insurrectionary impulse to Billy in the sandwich-making episode – register Woolf's complicated and sometimes contradictory attitudes towards domestic workers. Mrs Sands, narrow and unable to see beyond her kitchen, contrasts starkly with the narrator of the 'Cook Sketch' with her dynamic association of ideas and imaginative investments – for instance in her 'brooch shaped like a lyre'. Likewise, the cook's willingness to identify and speak in the interest of 'us working classes' could not be further from Mrs Sands's characterisation of other servants and cheeky Billy.

Underlying this critique of Mrs Sands is the suggestion that such circumscription is part of a larger societal problem. This is reinforced by the description of 'the villagers'' reluctance to enter the barn and claim their tea before one of 'the gentry' has led the way during the interval. In this episode Woolf is critical both of working-class deference and of a middle-class paternalism:

> The villagers still hung back. They must have someone to start the ball rolling. 'Well, I'm dying for my tea!' [Mrs Manresa] said in her public voice; and strode forward. She laid hold of a thick china mug. Mrs. Sands giving precedence, of course, to one of the gentry, filled it at once. David gave her cake. She was the first to drink, the first to bite. The villagers still hung back. 'It's all my eye about democracy,' she concluded. So did Mrs. Parker, taking her mug too. The people looked to them. They led; the rest followed. (*BTA* 63)

Mrs Manresa's adoption of 'her public voice' in this extract holds echoes of Woolf's own interaction with the WI, which she repeatedly characterises as performative and 'simpering'. Again, we find Mrs Sands powerfully positioned in the class dynamics of this episode; she appears as an arbiter of social relations and a preserver of class hierarchy, 'giving precedence, of course, to one of the gentry'. With her trademark sensitivity to the political potency of social rituals, Woolf makes the ceremony of afternoon tea speak the fixity of the class system, leading to Mrs Manresa's frustrated exclamation: 'It's all my eye about democracy'. The register of the passage then imperceptibly shifts from Mrs Manresa's irritation to Mrs Parker's sentimental feudalism: 'The people looked to them. They led; the rest followed.'

This passage indicts Mrs Sands's conservatism, Mrs Manresa's rather tabloid invocation of 'democracy' and Mrs Parker's nostalgic attachment to notions of the gentry's social responsibility, revealing Woolf's profound scepticism regarding questions of progress. This is also clear in Mr Oliver and Lucy Swithin's failure to partake even in the performance of egalitarianism: 'Chairs had been reserved for them. Mrs. Sands had sent them tea. It would have caused more bother than it was worth – asserting the democratic principle; standing in the crowd at the table' (*BTA* 66). During this episode we encounter Woolf's own genuine contempt for the 'democratic principle', the anxiety that Ben Harker notes accompanies her fear of being 'ruled by Nelly'.[92] However, it is also important to recognise the critique Woolf levels against what she identifies as the performance of democracy in this scene – the suggestion being that the 'democratic principle' is something rather different from democratic practice. The narrative disdain for the 'soft' democracy of the interval tea is reflective of Woolf's dissatisfaction with the democratic ethos of the WI.

The Reverend Streatfield's garbled and unsatisfactory interpretation of Miss La Trobe's experimental pageant represents another instance of Woolf critiquing such superficial use of democratic arguments:

> We were shown, unless I mistake, the effort renewed. A few were chosen; the many passed in the background. That surely we were shown. But again, were we not given to understand – am I too presumptuous? [...] To me at least it was indicated that we are members one of another. Each is part of the whole [...] We act different parts; but are the same. (*BTA* 114)

Streatfield's interpretation, with its emphasis on unity and 'sameness', aims to erase difference and appears to be part of a similar project of class conciliation. It also, interestingly, overlooks the dramatisation of class conflict we actually find in the pageant, for instance Flavinda's observation during the raucous Restoration comedy: '*La! the red in their cheeks! They never got* that *in the fields, I warrant!*' (*BTA* 82). This act of contemporary interpretation within the novel, while often dismissed as an example of the community's failure to engage with the radical design of Miss La Trobe's pageant, may also be read as Woolf's gesture to the very urgent contemporary debates surrounding the project and aspirations of village drama. Against the critical assumption that Woolf was antagonistic to the pageant form, Jed Esty has argued that Woolf found potential in its rites and 'ritual occasion': 'While she may doubt the value of the pageant's conventionalized content, Woolf has a genuine interest in the power of the pageant's form'.[93] Contemporary efforts to reinvigorate the pageant are a significant context for this interest and in *Between the Acts* we arguably find Woolf responding to the theorisation of village drama in late 1930s and early 1940s by its key proponents Mary Kelly and Nora Ratcliff.[94] To conclude this discussion of *Between the Acts*, I chart some of the ways in which Miss La Trobe's pageant represents Woolf weighing into these debates.

* * *

Mary Kelly's 1936 book *How to Make a Pageant* is a distinctive combination of advice manual and theoretical treatise on the form. While its opening seems to reiterate the assumptions about the pageant and village drama that we encountered earlier in this chapter, 'that they are great levellers of class, that they bring out talents in people who would never appear on an indoor stage',[95] as we move deeper into her argument, Kelly's dissatisfaction with the pageant form as it currently exists becomes clear. The phrasing of a complaint early in the text is telling:

> Such is now the conventional idea of a 'Pageant' and such it will remain until some original and constructive minds, both dramatists and producers, realize its possibilities as drama, and lift it into a fine and potent form of artistic expression.[96]

Kelly's aspirations for the pageant and her lofty use of 'artistic expression' and the notion of it being lifted seem initially to indicate some snobbery towards the form. However, her reference to 'the conventional idea of a "pageant"' reveals a significant understanding of the pageant's constructedness, while her belief that it could be converted into a more 'potent' form hints at Kelly's interest in the political and social possibilities of the pageant. Kelly goes on to critique the pageant's romantic preoccupation with 'continuity' and its tendency 'to praise famous men, and our forefathers that begat us'.[97] In a rather radical move, she suggests that practitioners of the pageant look East for inspiration: 'The experiments of the Russian Soviet Theatre, in bringing the mass action outside the limits of the stage, and uniting players and audience, has been extremely interesting.'[98]

Kelly's desire to move away from the pageant's conventional male-centred narrative arguably anticipates Miss La Trobe's matrilineal pageant, while her interest in ways in which the audience can be drawn into the performance of the pageant are mirrored in La Trobe's final reflective flourish. Equally striking is Kelly's interest in alternative source material for the pageant:

> Besides these biased histories, there are numbers of books on social life and customs, letters, diaries, memoirs, and so on, all of which supply detail and throw light on personality. The plays, stories, and novels of any period will give 'the very age and body of the time his form and pressure.[99]

Kelly appears to share Woolf's abiding interest in obscure lives and the alternative histories that the traditionally low-status forms of memoirs, diaries and letters provide. Similarly her suggestion that the literature of a period can provide the pageant maker with the most inspiring and faithful insight into the life of an age compellingly foreshadows Woolf's staging of literary history in *Between the Acts*.

Nora Ratcliff's 1939 text *Rude Mechanicals: A Review of Village Drama*, although not exclusively concerned with the pageant form, is similarly preoccupied with the current, staid condition of village drama. Ratcliff is, however, more blunt in identifying the factors hampering experimentation in village drama. Her description of local censorship is particularly interesting and chimes with Woolf's presentation of the reception of Miss La Trobe's pageant:

> the experimental play – which sometimes has some slight inclination to the Left, or is suspected of some such deviation since it isn't the type of play they're used to – is definitely taboo. It is unwise that the villager should be encouraged to think – he might 'get above himself'.

The mischief of it is that these dictators have too often very effective means of enforcing this censorship. Only recently plays produced by a village group met with the disapproval of the local influentials, who were the trustees of the hall. These plays were modern, of no political bias, but admittedly 'unusual.' A demand was made that, in future, all proposed plays should be submitted for approval before being put into production. Now since this censoring body happens to be composed of the employers of the majority of the players, they have little choice but to comply. The alternative and obvious argument that people who dislike a play need not go to see it does not seem to have occurred to these guardians of morals.[100]

I quote from Ratcliff at length not only because this passage reveals her shared belief in the need for developments in village theatre but also because in this wonderfully forthright anecdote she is clear about both the political imperatives of experimental village theatre and the kinds of politically motivated censorship practitioners faced. Ratcliff's story of local censorship and the way in which she presents it as typical provide another context in which to read Woolf's wariness about her own involvement with the Rodmell WI's plays. Just as Woolf resented being associated with the gentrifying forces at work in Rodmell, she would have wanted to resist at all costs any association with this kind of censorship. The audience's reactions to Miss La Trobe's pageant reveal Woolf's awareness of this disciplinary, conservative instinct that Ratcliff believed stifled experimentation in village drama. This is most clear in Etty Springett's bitter response to the pageant's satire on Victorian mores: ' "Cheap and nasty, I call it," snapped Etty Springett, referring to the play, and shot a vicious glance at Dodge's green trousers, yellow spotted tie, and unbuttoned waistcoat' (*BTA* 103). The way in which the play's 'nastiness' is imaginatively connected for Etty Springett to William Dodge's unconventional dress and his homosexuality, indicates quite how frightening and 'vicious', but also unthinking her response is.

Nora Ratcliff concludes her survey of village theatre by reflecting on its distinctive character as an inter-war movement:

We live to-day in a world whose sky is heavy with the threat of storms; storms that have already burst horridly over countries in Europe, Africa, and the Far East. The village drama movement came into conscious being with the readjustment and new awareness that followed the last great upheaval [...] Unless it really has meaning and has become part and parcel of the life of the village, it will fall into the background and disappear, dismissed as an idle frivolity and waste of time when greater issues are waiting. If it is the real thing it will gain an added strength from the increasingly urgent necessity of those whose mouthpiece it should be.[101]

Not only does Ratcliff's conclusion intimately connect the village drama movement with a nation's experience of war – 'the last great upheaval' – she lends her argument for a new, experimental village drama powerful urgency by placing it in the context of the coming world war. Miss La Trobe's pageant performed as fighter planes fly overhead surely responds to Ratcliff's demand for a new kind of rural community drama and echoes her awareness that the second great upheaval will necessitate even greater change that must be reflected in this drama.

* * *

And the village keeps tugging & jogging. The WI. party tomorrow. My old dislike of the village bites at me. I envy houses alone in the fields. So petty so teasing are the claims of Gardners & Chavasses. I dont like – but here I stop. Italy is being crushed. (*D5* 344)

Written less than a month after Woolf's reflections on her growing acceptance of life in Rodmell and her admission that it was 'familiar & even friendly', this diary entry from December 1940 once again emphasises the synonymity of village and WI for Woolf, but also her profound difficulty in reconciling herself to her last instance of social participation. Woolf's talk of the 'tugging and jogging' of the village and the 'petty and teasing claims' of her fellow WI members sound like the beginnings of private tantrum akin to the one I began this chapter with. Woolf's self-censorship in the truncated sentence 'I dont like – but here I stop', and the self-admonishment implied by her reference to Italy 'being crushed', while distinguishing this later diary entry, once again foregrounds Woolf's volatile relationship with Rodmell and with the WI.

Notes

1. Maroula Joannou's reading of *Between the Acts* offers Woolf's activity with the WI (pp. 18–19) as a context for her 'ambivalent patriotism' (p. 16) in that text and represents an important exception. *Women's Writing, Englishness and National and Cultural Identity: The Mobile Woman and the Migrant Voice, 1938–62* (Basingstoke: Palgrave, 2012).
2. See David Bradshaw, 'British Writers and Anti-Fascism in the 1930s. Part One: The Bray and Drone of Tortured Voices', 3–27, and 'British Writers and Anti-Fascism in the 1930s. Part Two: Under the Hawk's Wings', 41–66. See also Snaith, ' "Stray Guineas": Virginia Woolf and the Fawcett Library', 16–35; Merry M. Pawlowski (ed.), *Virginia Woolf and Fascism: Resisting the Dictators' Seduction* (Basingstoke: Palgrave, 2001) and Alice Wood, *Virginia Woolf's Late Cultural Criticism*.
3. 'I dont like any of the feelings war breeds: patriotism; communal &c, all sentimental & emotional parodies of our real feelings' (*D5* 302).
4. *Virginia Woolf, the Intellectual, and the Public Sphere*, p. 100.
5. *Virginia Woolf Manuscripts*, Reel 3, Diaries D30 1935–D36 1941 (Woodbridge, CT: Research Publications International, 1994).
6. 'What depresses me is that the workers seem to have taken on all the middle class respectabilities which we – at any rate if we are any good at writing or painting – have faced down and thrown out [...] One has to be "sympathetic" and polite and therefore one is uneasy and insincere' (*L4* 229).
7. *Virginia Woolf*, p. 431.
8. Falmer, University of Sussex Special Collections at The Keep, Monks House Papers, General Correspondence of Virginia Woolf, E. Bowen to V. Woolf, February 1941, SxMs18/1/D/20/1.
9. J. W. Robertson Scott, *The Story of the Women's Institute Movement in England & Wales & Scotland* (Idbury, Oxon: Village Press, 1925), pp. 49–50.
10. Inez Jenkins, *The History of the Women's Institute Movement of England and Wales* (Oxford: Oxford University Press, 1953), p. 9.
11. For a full account of the early history of the WI, see Jenkins, *The History of the Women's Institute Movement*, pp. 1–20.
12. *The Acceptable Face of Feminism: The Women's Institute as a Social Movement* (London: Lawrence & Wishart, 1997), p. 113.
13. This chimes with many other inter-war groups and organisations that championed rural values. See Burchardt, 'Rethinking the Rural Idyll:

The English Rural Community Movement, 1913–26', *Cultural & Social History*, 8 (2011), 73–94. Mark Hussey has written interestingly on the ways in which Woolf's own attitudes towards the Sussex countryside and those of her characters in *Between the Acts*, in particular her horror of villas and bungalows emerging around the Downs, reproduce the discourses of various rural preservation societies during the 1920s and 1930s. *'I'd Make It Penal', The Rural Preservation Movement in Virginia Woolf's Between the Acts* (London: Cecil Woolf Publishers, 2011).

14. Andrews, *The Acceptable Face of Feminism*, p. 20.
15. Jenkins, *The History of the Women's Institute Movement*, pp. 13–14; Robertson, *The Story of the Women's Institute Movement*, p. 34–5.
16. 'Citizens not Feminists: The Boundary Negotiated Between Citizenship and Feminism by Mainstream Women's Organizations in England, 1928–1939', *Women's History Review*, 9 (2009), 411–29 (p. 417).
17. See Ross McKibbin, *Classes and Cultures: England, 1918–1951* (Oxford: Oxford University Press, 1998), p. 88 and A. J. P. Taylor, *English History, 1914–1945* (Oxford: Oxford University Press, 2001), p. 264. In her recent reassessment of inter-war voluntary associations, including the WI, Helen McCarthy challenges the assumption that these groups were simply proponents of 'middle-class anti-socialism'. Opposing the argument that through their attempts to ameliorate class conflict groups such as the WI undermined the 'political aspirations of organized labour', McCarthy argues that non-party organisations 'played an important role in anchoring British politics ideologically in the centre-ground, therefore providing important insulation against the currents of political extremism which convulsed other European societies in the period'. 'Parties, Voluntary Associations, and Democratic Politics in Interwar Britain', *The Historical Journal*, 50 (2007), 891–912 (p. 893).
18. *The Rodmell Papers: Reminiscences of Virginia and Leonard Woolf by a Sussex Neighbour* (London: Cecil Woolf Publishers: 2008).
19. *The Rodmell Papers*, p. 22.
20. *The Rodmell Papers*, p. 22.
21. *The Rodmell Papers*, p. 22.
22. *The Rodmell Papers*, p. 22.
23. *The Rodmell Papers*, p. 22.
24. *The Rodmell Papers*, p. 23.
25. *Virginia Woolf*, p. 745.
26. The *East Sussex News* for 24 January 1941 reveals an interesting overlap between the subject of Angelica's talk and Woolf's research for her late essay 'Ellen Terry': 'Miss Angelica Bell (niece of Virginia

Woolf) was speaker, her subject being "Modern Drama". She described changes which have taken place during the last 50 years in stagecraft and production, stressing the point that in the '90s great actors like Sarah Bernhardt and Ellen Terry were outstanding in any play, but today the whole cast stands in a greater measure the honours of the production.'

27. *East Sussex News*, 20 December 1940, p. 4.
28. Woolf's 1940 engagement diary includes several interesting references to the WI. For instance, Woolf has recorded her talk in the 23 June section of her diary as 'W.I. 7.'. However, if we flick forward to 20 August we can see that the organisation of Woolf's talk seems to have been rather complicated. Beneath this date Woolf has quite violently crossed out an entry that reads 'W. Institute "Books" 6.30' and written instead 'Ly Reading W.I.'. These entries confirm that Woolf's initial talk was to have been on 'Books', something I will discuss at greater length later in this chapter, but also perhaps suggest that her decision to give a racier talk on the Dreadnought Hoax may have been in response to having to give up her original slot to Lady Reading and the WI plays. Falmer, University of Sussex Special Collections at The Keep, Monks House Papers, Virginia Woolf's Engagement Diaries, 1940, SxMs18/4/41.
29. *The Rodmell Papers*, p. 23.
30. *East Sussex News*, 29 November 1940, p. 4.
31. *East Sussex News*, 24 January 1941, p. 4.
32. See John Carey, *The Intellectuals and the Masses: Pride and Prejudice Among the Literary Intelligentsia, 1880–1939* (London: Faber and Faber, 1992), p. 210.
33. Jean E. Kennard, 'Power and Sexual Ambiguity: The *Dreadnought* Hoax, *The Voyage Out*, *Mrs Dalloway* and *Orlando*', *Journal of Modern Literature*, 20 (1996), 149–64 (p. 164); Kathy Phillips, *Virginia Woolf Against Empire*, p. 248; Panthea Reid, 'Virginia Woolf, Leslie Stephen, Julia Margaret Cameron, and the Prince of Abyssinia: Inquiry into Certain Colonialist Representations', *Biography*, 22 (1999), 322–56.
34. 'Virginia Woolf's Talk on the Dreadnought Hoax', *Woolf Studies Annual*, 15 (2009), 1–45. Subsequent references in the text are to the version of this talk published as an appendix in volume 6 of Woolf's essays (*E6* 560–80).
35. 'Virginia Woolf's Talk on the Dreadnought Hoax', 1.
36. Andrews, *The Acceptable Face of Feminism*, p. 26.
37. For more on Woolf's relationship to the wireless see Leila Brosnan, *Reading Woolf's Essays and Journalism*, pp. 163–71; Cuddy-Keane,

Virginia Woolf, the Intellectual, and the Public Sphere, pp. 37–9. For a history of the wireless and women's experience of domesticity, see Maggie Andrews, *Domesticating the Airwaves: Broadcasting, Femininity and Domesticity* (London: Continuum, 2012). In her history of village drama, Mary Kelly identifies the WI and radio as the two most significant developments in the lives of rural women in the inter-war period. *Village Theatre* (London: Thomas Nelson, 1939), p. 167.

38. *The Rodmell Papers*, pp. 23–4.
39. A 1955 letter from Miss Mundy to Dame Frances reads: 'Thank you so much for letting me see this; it was grand fun to read – but somewhat too long a story to consider for Home and Country.' London, The Women's Library (LSE), Records of the National Federation of Women's Institutes, The Dreadnought Hoax, 5FWI/H/45.
40. 'Sapphistry: Narration as Lesbian Seduction in *A Room of One's Own*', in *Virginia Woolf and the Languages of Patriarchy*, pp. 163–88 (p. 166). It is, however, important to recognise the crucial differences between these audiences. In contrast to the gathering of Cambridge undergraduates, the majority of the audience of her Dreadnought talk were working-class women, several of whom, it should be noted, were the Woolfs' employees.
41. Records of the National Federation of Women's Institutes, The Dreadnought Hoax, 5FWI/H/45.
42. *East Sussex News*, 24 July 1940, p. 8.
43. Gesturing to Woolf's involvement with the WI, Marina MacKay notes Woolf's use of a quotation from William Blake's poem in her essay 'Thoughts on Peace in an Air Raid' (1940) reminding us that for English audiences these words would be most familiar as lines from the hymn 'Jerusalem'. *Modernism and World War II* (Cambridge: Cambridge University Press, 2007), p. 92.
44. See Steven D. Putzel, *Virginia Woolf and the Theatre* (Madison, NJ: Fairleigh Dickinson University Press, 2011); Penny Farfan, *Women, Modernism and Performance* (Cambridge University Press, 2004); Elizabeth Wright, 'Bloomsbury at Play', *Woolf Studies Annual*, 17 (2011), 77–107; Penny Farfan, 'Freshwater Revisited: Virginia Woolf on Ellen Terry and the Art of Acting', *Woolf Studies Annual*, 4 (1998), 3–17.
45. *Virginia Woolf and the Theatre*, p. xiv.
46. *Virginia Woolf and the Theatre*, p. 42 and pp. 59–64.
47. 'Introduction', in Paul Brassley, Jeremy Burchardt and Lynne Thompson (eds), *The English Countryside Between the Wars: Regeneration or Decline?* (Woodbridge, Suffolk: Boydell, 2006), pp. 1–9 (p. 7).
48. 'Unlocking the Secret Soul: Mary Kelly, Pioneer of Village Theatre', *New Theatre Quarterly*, 16 (2000), 347–58.

49. *Village Theatre*, p. 142.
50. 'Unlocking the Secret Soul', 348.
51. 'Unlocking the Secret Soul', 349.
52. *Village Theatre*, p. 145.
53. 'Unlocking the Secret Soul', 349.
54. *Village Theatre*, p. 145.
55. Jenkins, *The History of the Women's Institute Movement*, p. 121.
56. *Village Theatre*, p. 143.
57. *Village Theatre*, p. 146.
58. *Village Theatre*, p. 148.
59. *Village Theatre*, p. 148.
60. Caitlin Adams, 'The Idea of the Village in Interwar England' (unpublished PhD thesis, University of Michigan, 2001), p. 105.
61. 'The Idea of the Village in Interwar England', p. 127.
62. 'The Idea of the Village in Interwar England', p. 159.
63. 'The Idea of the Village in Interwar England', p. 159. See also Kelly, *Village Theatre*, p. 184 and Nora Ratcliff, *Rude Mechanicals: A Short Review of Village Drama* (London: Thomas Nelson, 1938), p. 70.
64. 'The Idea of the Village in Interwar England', p. 124.
65. 'The Idea of the Village in Interwar England', p. 125.
66. Monthly letters to members from the executive committee of the East Sussex Federation reveal that the drama sub-division produced a 'list of suggested one-act plays' and that a 'non-competitive Drama festival of one-act plays' was held in the Lewes Corn Exchange in 1935. Falmer, The Keep, East Sussex Record Office, Records of the East Sussex Federation of Women's Institutes, Monthly Letters to Members from the East Sussex Federation of Women's Institutes, WI53/33/1.
67. 'The Idea of the Village in Interwar England', p. 126.
68. 'The Idea of the Village in Interwar England', p. 127.
69. Falmer, The Keep, East Sussex Record Office, Records of the East Sussex Federation of Women's Institutes, Press Cuttings January 1925–March 1963, *Sussex Express*, 23 March 1934, WI53/36/1/1.
70. Records of the East Sussex Federation of Women's Institutes, Press Cuttings January 1925–March 1963, *Sussex Express*, 23 March 1934, WI53/36/1/1.
71. Records of the East Sussex Federation of Women's Institutes, Press Cuttings January 1925–March 1963, *Sussex Express*, 23 March 1934, WI53/36/1/1.
72. Records of the East Sussex Federation of Women's Institutes, Monthly Letters to Members from the East Sussex Federation of Women's Institutes, WI53/33/1.

73. Records of the East Sussex Federation of Women's Institutes, Monthly Letters to Members from the East Sussex Federation of Women's Institutes, WI53/33/1.
74. Falmer, University of Sussex Special Collections at The Keep, Leonard Woolf Papers, Diary 1940, SxMs13/2/R/A/34.
75. *East Sussex News*, 23 August 1940, p. 8.
76. Adams, 'The Idea of the Village in Interwar England', p. 124.
77. Out of respect for its Quaker members, the WI 'felt obliged, both before and after the start of war, to impose close restrictions upon the participation of Institutes in war work'. Jenkins, *The History of the Women's Institute Movement*, p. 73.
78. *Sussex Express*, 23 August 1940. There is another mention of Ida Smith's and Alice Carter's plays in the 13 December 1940 edition of the *Sussex Express*, this time under the heading 'Southover Women's Institute': 'There was a large attendance of members and friends at the monthly meeting of the Southover Women's Institute, held at the Parish Hall on Tuesday. Members from Rodmell Institute gave two amusing and original plays. "Fond Relations," by Alice Carter, and "False Alarm," by Mrs. Ida Smith.' That these WI-authored plays toured to a neighbouring branch arguably supports my theory that the Rodmell WI drama society was part of a larger village drama movement of the period and that, as such, Woolf's participation with it ought to be read in the context of this movement.
79. 'A gritting day. As a sample of my present mood, I reflect: capitulation will mean all Jews to be given up. Concentration camps. So to our garage. Thats behind correcting Roger, playing bowls' (*D5* 292).
80. Leonard Woolf Papers, Diary 1940, SxMs13/2/R/A/34.
81. *East Sussex News*, 20 December 1940, p. 4.
82. Constanduros, *Shreds and Patches* (London: Lawson & Dunn, 1946) p. 130.
83. Howard Agg and Mabel Contanduros, 'Goose Chase, A Comedy in One Act' (London: Samuel French, 1940), p. 14.
84. Light, p. 260.
85. See Beer, *Virginia Woolf: The Common Ground*, p. 146, Marcus, 'Some Sources for *Between the Acts*', 1–3 and Joannou, *Women's Writing*, p. 19.
86. 'After *To The Lighthouse*', *Scrutiny*, 10 (January 1941), 295–7 (p. 297).
87. See Sallie Sears, 'Theatre of War: Virginia Woolf's *Between the Acts*', in Jane Marcus (ed.), *Virginia Woolf: A Feminist Slant*, pp. 212–35 and Patricia Klindienst Joplin, 'The Authority of Illusion: Feminism and Fascism in Virginia Woolf's *Between the Acts*', *South Central Review*, 6 (1989), 88–104 for readings of Woolf's feminism in *Between*

the Acts. For readings of *Between the Acts* as historically and political engaged, see Zwerdling, *Virginia Woolf and the Real World*, pp. 302–23 and Briggs, *An Inner Life*, pp. 370–92. For discussions of Woolf's engagement with questions of Englishness and community, see Jed Esty's *A Shrinking Island: Modernism and National Culture in England* (Princeton: Princeton University Press, 2004), pp. 85–107 and Marina MacKay, *Modernism and World War II*, pp. 22–44. Brenda Silver considers Woolf's concern with the role of the artist in society in her last novel, suggesting that in *Between the Acts* Woolf explores the 'possibility of community and its ability to survive' in the face of a world war. 'Virginia Woolf and the Concept of Community: The Elizabethan Playhouse', *Women's Studies*, 4 (1977), 291–8 (p. 296).

88. 'Introduction', in *Between the Acts* (Cambridge: Cambridge University Press, 2011), pp. xli–ii.
89. *Virginia Woolf's Late Cultural Criticism*, p. 126.
90. Esty, *A Shrinking Island*, p. 91. See also Marlowe A. Miller, 'Unveiling "The Dialectic of Culture and Barbarism" in British Pageantry: Virginia Woolf's *Between the Acts*', *Papers on Language and Literature*, 34 (1998), 134–66 and David McWhirter, 'The Novel, the Play, and the Book: *Between the Acts* and the Tragicomedy of History', *ELH*, 60 (1993), 787–810.
91. See Cuddy-Keane, 'The Politics of Comic Modes in Virginia Woolf's *Between the Acts*', *PMLA*, 105 (1990), 273–85; Silver, 'Virginia Woolf and the Concept of Community', 291–8; Ben Harker, ' "On Different Levels Ourselves Went Forward": Pageantry, Class Politics and Narrative Form in Virginia Woolf's Late Writing', *ELH*, 78 (2011), 433–56; Esty, *A Shrinking Island*, pp. 85–107.
92. Harker, 'On Different Levels Ourselves Went Forward', 433.
93. Esty, *A Shrinking Island*, p. 92.
94. A number of scholars have read Miss La Trobe's pageant in the context of pageant making by groups and individuals, including Edwardian pageant master Louis Napoleon Parker, Edith Craig and popular front dramatists. See Ayako Yoshino, '*Between the Acts* and Louis Napoleon Parker – the Creator of the Modern English Pageant', *Critical Survey*, 15 (2003), 49–60; Esty, *A Shrinking Island*, pp. 56–61, Marcus, 'Some Sources for *Between the Acts*', 1–3; Snaith, *Public and Private Negotiations*, pp. 150–3 and Joannou, *Women's Writing*, p. 21. Furthermore, in a recent study of Virginia Woolf and music, Emma Sutton has read Miss La Trobe's pageant as constructed in a critical dialogue with the English Musical Renaissance and the contemporary folk music revival. *Virginia Woolf and Classical Music: Politics, Aesthetics, Form* (Edinburgh: Edinburgh University Press, 2013), pp. 120–2.

95. *How to Make a Pageant* (London: Sir Isaac Pitman, 1936), p. 4.
96. *How to Make a Pageant*, p. 6.
97. *How to Make a Pageant*, p. 8.
98. *How to Make a Pageant*, p. 34.
99. *How to Make a Pageant*, p. 41.
100. Ratcliff, *Rude Mechanicals*, pp. 124–5.
101. *Rude Mechanicals*, p. 159.

Conclusion

> My puzzle is, ought artists now to become politicians? My instinct says no; but I'm not sure that I can justify my instinct. I take refuge in the fact that I've received so little from society that I owe it very little. But thats not altogether satisfactory; and anyhow it doesn't apply to you. I suppose I'm obtuse, but I cant find your answer in your letter, how it is that you are going to change the attitude of the mass of people by remaining an art critic. (*L6* 420–10)

This extract from Woolf's 1940 correspondence with Ben Nicolson on the subject of Bloomsbury's social commitments and their legacy initially sounds very like a restatement of her theory of women's outsidership in *Three Guineas*. This is clear in the rationale of her statement: 'I've received so little from society that I owe it very little'. Yet further probing of this tricky, heavily licensed passage suggests this reading does not ring true. This passage unravels the logic of its tentative central thesis and, rather than being an endorsement of operating outside the mainstream and a rejection of social participation, it is in fact a key statement of Woolf's ambivalence, full of equivocation and loaded with self-critique. This is most clear in Woolf's ambiguous admission: 'thats not altogether satisfactory'. It is unclear whether Woolf is suggesting that the rationale of receiving from and in turn owing society is itself faulty or if she is revealing a more specific uneasiness, as a privileged woman who admitted to being 'hampered by the psychological hindrance of owning capital' (*D1* 101), about her self-deceiving fantasy of having 'received so little' from society. This passage with its defensive and arch tone may seem a bathetic place to close this book on Woolf's activism, however it demonstrates acutely the ways in which questions of participation and social responsibility preyed on Woolf's mind and so seems appropriate.

It is tempting to read this extract as engaging specifically with the question of the political role of art and the artist. However, it seems clear that her final impatient question to Ben Nicolson – 'how it is that you are going to change the attitude of the mass of people by remaining an art critic' – is prompted by an understanding of the need for the artist and critic to engage in practical forms of political activism beyond their art or writing. Woolf's awareness of the need for action is where this book opened, interestingly, with another diffident question: 'Would it be any use if I spent an afternoon or two weekly in addressing envelopes for the Adult Suffragists?' (*L1* 421). Woolf's questions, to others and herself, punctuate the engagements this book charts. In the 'Morley Sketch' Virginia Stephen asks, 'So thin is the present to them; {how can I} <must not the> past remain a spectre always?', revealing not only her appreciation of contemporary debates about history, but also her alertness to institutional debates about the function of adult education. Her question of Nelly Cecil in 1910, 'By the way, are you an Adult Suffragist? This is a real question' (*L1* 426), has been recast as motivated by partisan commitment to adult suffragism, again revealing Virginia Stephen's sensitivity to the internal politics of the groups she worked with. The ambiguous questions that open the 'Introductory Letter' – 'What old arguments and memories does it rouse in me?' (*IL* xvii) – offer a new biographical context in which to read this essay, challenging prevailing readings of this text that neglect its writerly qualities. And perhaps most poignant are Woolf's anxious questions to herself in her diary, which speak of her vexed commitment to the Rodmell WI but also her continued self-reflection about her own participation right up until the end of her life: 'arent I on the Cttee of the WI – dont I go to a meeting on Monday?' (*D5* 341).

Each one of these questions reveals Woolf's awareness of the specific debates and arguments that animated the groups and organisations with which she was involved. These questions also frequently register unease and self-criticism; they reveal the ambivalence that characterised Woolf's life-long activism. The very preponderance of these questions testify to Virginia Woolf's curiosity and the seriousness with which she took this work, and also the significant ways in which she sought to understand the value and limits, the efficacy of the work she undertook with these groups. This self-reflexive, self-questioning quality accompanied all of Woolf's political activism and social participation and is characteristic of the rich, sometimes contradictory, but sustained way in which Woolf wrote this activity into her fiction and non-fiction texts throughout her career.

Appendix 1 The 'Morley Sketch'

Transcription: 'Report on Teaching at Morley College', 1905, Monks House Papers, University of Sussex Special Collections at The Keep, Falmer, SxMs18/2/A/22.

Symbols used in transcription:

<word> interlinear or marginal revision
{word} cancelled word or passage
[word] questionable transcription
{[word]} questionable transcription of a cancellation
[?] illegible word
{?} illegible cancellation

   July 1905

This is the season for another report upon that class of working women {which I led there} <whom I> have already {once before this} mentioned.
   It was to be a class of history this time; in spite of the fact that those in authority looked rather coldly on it; history they told me, was the least popular subject in the college; at the same time they could not confute me when I asserted that it was also one of the most important. My {numbers} <class> it is true dropped instantly to half {their} <its> previous size; I had four instead of a possible eight; but then those four were regular attendants, & they came with one serious desire in common. The change then, was {by} to my liking.

I have already described those four working women; so that my remarks this time are merely {in} a development of that tentative sketch. {But} <Only> in one instance did I find that {my} I must reconsider my judgment. That Miss Williams whom I described as the 'least interesting of my class' 'rather handsome & well dressed – with wits sharpened in the streets {rather} inattentive & critical' came to the first history class, & to my surprise {was} hardly missed {one} <a Wednesday> throughout the term. One night, too, I so far cornered her as to make her reveal herself; she then told me that she was a reporter on the staff of a Religious paper – reported {?} sermons in shorthand – {&} did typewriting, & also wrote reviews of books; {A journalist in a humble way in short!} the germ of a literary lady in short! <& a curious one>. {So we made much of this [having] we found we had a good deal in common; & I explored some of the more rather subterranean passages of my own profession: found out how {?} a certain <a rather sordid type of much that we> Literature regarded frankly as a} Hers was literature stripped of the least glamour of art; words were {produced cut into shape} <handled> by this woman as that other one {finished off} <manipulated> the bottles of a patent mouth wash. {If she were given a A review for instance, was <concocted on {cart}> merely a matter of business to her She could turn out a review as with the precision of a machine} <She was a writing machine to be> set in motion by the editor. For some reason <unconnected with the author> the notice was to be favourable or unfavourable; {neither} but to record this notice it was not necessary by any means to read the book; that indeed would be impossible, considering the number of reviews {that must} <to> be turned out; but with a little practise it was easy to get sufficient {idea of the truth} <material to support your statements> by a rapid turning of the pages with a keen eye; {most often it was only} quotations picked up at random need only be linked together by a <connecting> word, {or two of} & the column was filled out of someone else's pocket. {You might even make some vague There were also a many useful phrases which can be apply to any book, & therefore can be used save one the trouble of reading a word of it} But at the same time, {she made no so as she claimed she was} as she made no pretence that her <work was> {was other other than this} of any higher nature than this so there seemed to be no reason to condemn it; indeed she was certainly of a higher {level} level of intelligence than the other women.

The three other girls {were the} <have been> described already: the two friends & one of the two sisters, <who came last term> {who [one], as find, called Burke}. This sister, Burke was her name, had been as I found, writing that account of her own life which I had suggested before. It {was} <did> not take up many pages & only described certain {?} memories of childhood; it was a curious little production, {as it} <floundering> among long words, {&} involved {sentences} <periods,> with {an [?] tendency sprinkling of sententious remarks <through> like} <sudden ponderous> {reflections thrown} moral sentiments thrown into the {middle} <midst>. But she could write grammatical sentences, which followed each other {logical} logically enough; and she had evidently some facility of expression; in other circumstances I suppose, she would have been a writer!

The faithful pair of friends sat receptive & open mouthed as usual. Meanwhile, I had to administer each week some semblance of English history. Each week I read through a {certain} reign or two {of} in Freeman or Green; noting as I went. Each time I tried to include one good 'scene' {?} <upon> which I hoped to concentrate their interest. I talked from notes, with as little actual reading as possible. I found it not difficult to skim along fluently – though superficially: & I tried to make the {?} real interest of history – as it appears to me – visible to them. Often they were provided with {slips of paper on} <a> sheet of hard dates to take home with them; so that they might have something solid to cling to {out of} <in> the {rather} vagueness of my speech. So we {tramped through} made our way through Early British, & Roman, & Angles Saxons & Danes, & Normans, till we {had} were on the more substantial ground of the Plantagenet Kings. {By all the phantoms that I tried for the moment to} I do not know how many of the phantoms that passed through that dreary school room left any image of themselves upon the {four listening} women; I used to ask myself how is it possible {that these remote stories should have one meaning} to make them feel the {?} flesh & blood in these shadows? {Such a} So thin {?} is the present to them; {how can I} <must not the> past remain a spectre always? Of course it was not possible in the way I took to make them know <anything> accurately; my task, as I conceived it, was rather to prepare the soil for future sowers. Pictures I showed them, & I lent them books; sometimes they seemed to gape not in {sheer} <mere impotent> wonder {to be} but to be trying to piece together what they heard; to seek reasons; to connect ideas. {In spite of warning, I found them of a higher standard on the whole} On the whole they were possessed of more intelligence than I expected; though that intelligence was almost wholly uncultivated. But of this I am convinced; that it would not be hard to educate them sufficiently to give them a new interest in life; {whether it were history, language music, – or} They have {[as it]} tentacles languidly stretching forth from their minds, feeling vaguely for substance, & easily applied by a guiding hand to something that {would} <could> really <grasp> {nourish them}.

But like all other educational establishments, Morley College has to effect compromises {between the best & the worst} <& to prefer the safeness of mediocrity> to a {risky} <the possible> dangers of a high ideal. That is one way of saying that they {prefer} <would rather> {to dispense with my} <that> a {larger & [?]} <great> {class wl} number should learn a less valuable subject, like English Composition, than that a few should be encouraged to the study of English History. Accordingly I am to stop at {H} <King> John: & turn my mind next term to essay writing & the expression of ideas. Meanwhile, my four women, {are to be} <can> hear eight lectures on the French Revolution if they wish to continue their historical learning: {& then? Which from a knowledge of the state of their minds I conceive will be wholly useless to them. It will be another temptation to them to.} And what, I ask, will be the use of that? Eight lectures dropped into their minds, {without any <which are wholly unable to>} like meteors from another sphere infringing on this planet, {& which [has has] merely time to gape for a moment & ask what are you to whence? before they} <dissolving into dust again>. {So fragmentary and disconnected will these eight} Such disconnected fragments will these eight lectures be: to people who{se mind} <have> absolutely no power of receiving them as part of a whole, & {applying the} applying them {in} to their proper ends.

Figure 1 'Report on Teaching at Morley College', 1905, Monks House Papers, University of Sussex Special Collections at The Keep, Falmer, SxMs18/2/A/22. Photographic credit: University of Sussex Special Collections.

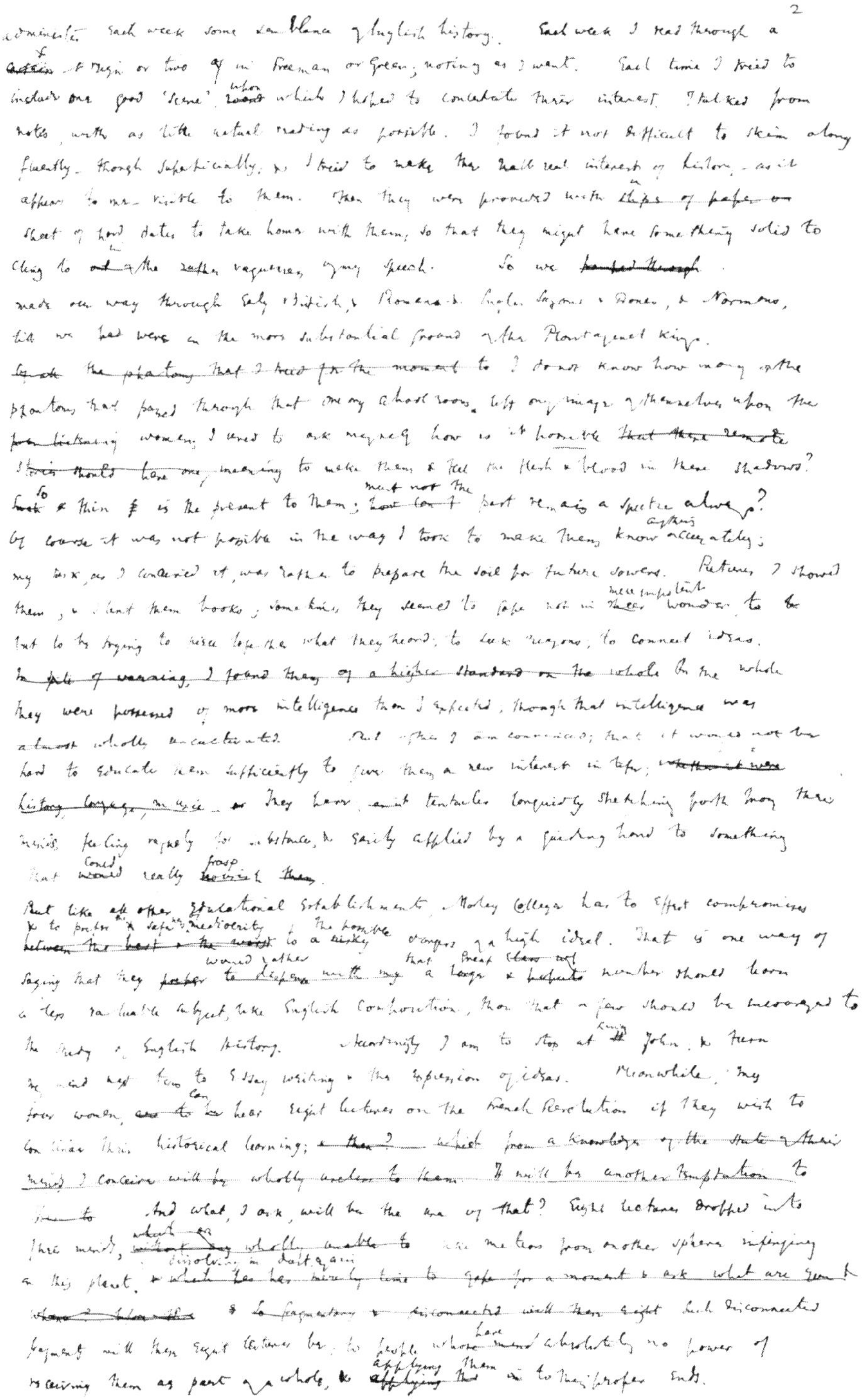

2

administer each week some semblance of English history. Each week I read through a ~~chapter~~ reign or two of Freeman or Green, noting as I went. Each time I tried to include one good 'scene', ~~[illegible]~~ upon which I hoped to concentrate their interest. I talked from notes, with as little actual reading as possible. I found it not difficult to skim along fluently, though superficially; & I tried to make the real interest of history, as it appears to me, visible to them. Then they were provided with ~~slips of paper or~~ a sheet of hard dates to take home with them; so that they might have something solid to cling to ~~out~~ in the rather vagueness of my speech. So we ~~[illegible]~~ made our way through Early British, & Romans & Anglo Saxons & Danes, & Normans, till we ~~had were~~ on the more substantial ground of the Plantagenet Kings.

~~[illegible] the phantoms that I tried for the moment~~ to I do not know how many of the phantoms that passed through that one my ghostly room, left any image of themselves upon the ~~[illegible] listening~~ women; I used to ask myself how is it possible ~~that these remote stories should have any meaning~~ to make them feel the flesh & blood in these shadows? So ~~[illegible]~~ thin is the present to them; must not the ~~[illegible]~~ past remain a spectre always?

Of course it was not possible in the way I took to make them know anything accurately; my task, as I conceived it, was rather to prepare the soil for future sowers. Pictures I showed them, & I lent them books; sometimes they seemed to grasp not in ~~these~~ more important wonder, to be led to be trying to piece together what they heard; to seek reasons; to connect ideas.

~~In spite of warning, I found them of a higher standard on the whole~~ On the whole they were possessed of more intelligence than I expected, though that intelligence was almost wholly uncultivated. But of this I am convinced; that it would not be hard to educate them sufficiently to give them a new interest in life; ~~whether it were history, language, music~~ or They have, ~~as it~~ tentacles languidly stretching forth from their minds, feeling vaguely for substance, & easily applied by a guiding hand to something that could really grasp ~~[illegible] them~~.

But like all other Educational establishments, Morley College has to effect compromises & to prefer a safe mediocrity ~~between the best & the worst~~ to a risky the horrible dangers of a high ideal. That is one way of saying that they ~~prefer~~ would rather ~~to deepen with my~~ that a ~~large~~ great ~~[illegible]~~ number should learn a less valuable subject, like English Composition, than that a few should be encouraged to the study of English history. Accordingly I am to stop at King John, & turn my mind next term to Essay writing & the expression of ideas. Meanwhile, my four women, ~~are to~~ can hear eight lectures on the French Revolution if they wish to continue their historical learning; ~~& then? — which from a knowledge of the state of their minds I conceive will be wholly useless to them~~. It will be another temptation to ~~them to~~ And what, I ask, will be the use of that? Eight lectures dropped into their minds, ~~without any~~ which are wholly ~~unable to~~ like meteors from another sphere impinging on this planet, ~~& which leaves them merely time to gape for a moment & ask what are [illegible] [illegible]~~ dissolving in dust again & so fragmentary & disconnected will these eight such disconnected fragments will these eight lectures be, to people who have ~~[illegible]~~ absolutely no power of receiving them as part of a whole, & ~~applying them~~ applying them to their proper ends.

Figure 2 'Report on Teaching at Morley College', 1905, Monks House Papers, University of Sussex Special Collections at The Keep, Falmer, SxMs18/2/A/22.
Photographic credit: University of Sussex Special Collections.

Appendix 2 The 'Cook Sketch'

Transcription: Letter to a Young Poet: Autograph Manuscript, 1931 Sept. 24, The Pierpont Morgan Library, New York, MA3333, ff. 44–6.

For symbols used in transcription please see page 210.

Oh yes, oh yes, oh yes, certainly we will have mutton for dinner. {And} But what is the price of mutton in this neighbourhood, I said to my cook. And she said, I think you ought to go [yourself] & speak to Mr Livestock – {Why} He has been palming us off with second rate joints ever so often lately. You can tell New Zealand by its pink [vein] They send them over by [haunches]. They arent what we're accustomed to. They arent what the best families have. Its said Princess Mary wont have an ounce of Mr L. meat in her kitchen. Think of her little princes growing up on fully [grown] meat. They do say {her} the Pss goes into the kitchen every morning. And the tricks they play, if ones not watching: the innards & the neck cant weigh all that: not two pounds 3 {oz} ounces which is what they charge us for: & then the backs come so high – its wicked in these days of want; when every penny counts; & the girls in the shops say "Prices wont stay down after this [quarter]. Of course they've the old stock on hand now. They're not making a penny change different at the moment. But if the Budget rises, [they'll] rise too. Prices follow suit. {My} Thats daylight: [reason]; though what the government is for if its not to protect us working classes I dont know I saw Mr Macdonald once myself – a disappointment

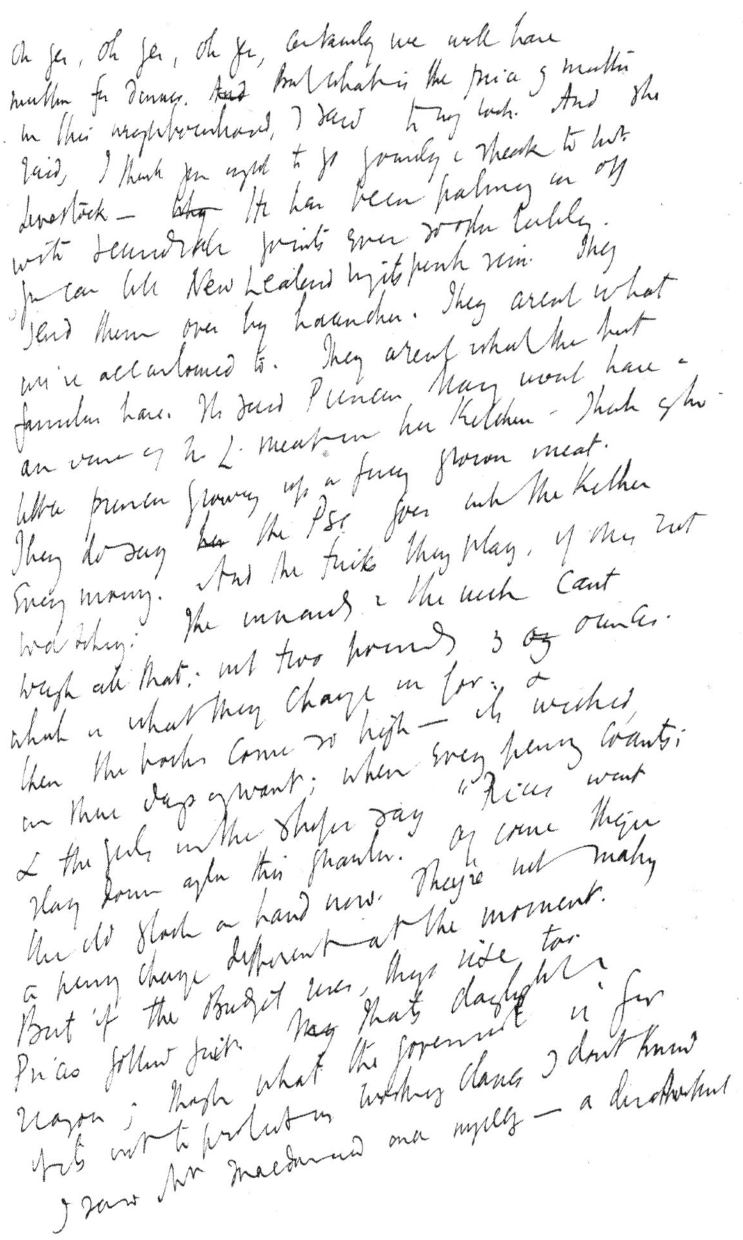

Figure 3 Letter to a Young Poet: Autograph Manuscript, 1931 Sept. 24, The Pierpont Morgan Library, New York, MA 3333, f. 44. Purchased on the Fellows Fund with the special assistance of Miss Anne S. Dayton, Mrs. Enid A. Haupt, Mrs. James H. Ripley, Mr. and Mrs. August H. Schilling, and Mr. John S. Thacher, 1979.

Photographic credit: The Pierpont Morgan Library, New York.

he was too. Neither one thing nor the other. But then the cares that man's been through – waking at 5 they say with a [shower bath] thrown at him by one of the young ladies they keep for that very purpose. Wake she says. And thats true of the king too. {They wake him:} He has a parrot. George it says: Come along: time to get up – thats the bird that pulled him through his illness that the Queen wdnt let them take away but when they bought him past all [convalescence]. A white parrot with a yellow tuft, like my {son's} <dads> parrot that he bought back from the Indies when he went to fight the Zulus, we had it hanging in our kitchen – never a drop drunk in our house but the parrot had its share. And [green stuff; sugar,] {&} [sometimes] a {a} bullocks liver – when it was killing day {th} we begged a bit off the butcher, whose son's now in hospital with a bad leg. They dont tell him, but what I'm thinking is they know for certain he wont stand again. And his hands no good to him – what use is hands to a man trained {to a} in a bacon factory where its hauling hauling hauling by day, by night, corpses of pigs,

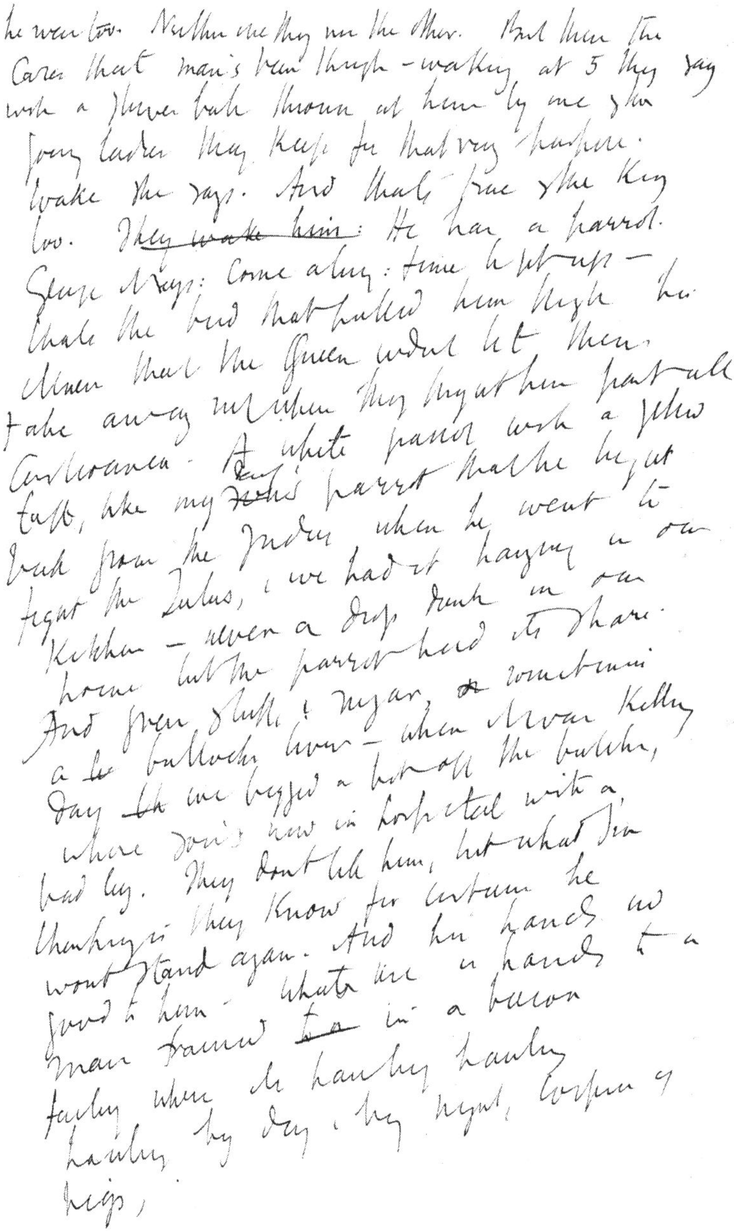

Figure 4 Letter to a Young Poet: Autograph Manuscript, 1931 Sept. 24, The Pierpont Morgan Library, New York, MA 3333, f. 45. Purchased on the Fellows Fund with the special assistance of Miss Anne S. Dayton, Mrs. Enid A. Haupt, Mrs. James H. Ripley, Mr. and Mrs. August H. Schilling, and Mr. John S. Thacher, 1979.

Photographic credit: The Pierpont Morgan Library, New York.

& off to Smithfield – his mother had to {?} stand his socks in vinegar to get out the brine which she showed me [herself]. And now lying in hospital, day in day out, George I says, aren't you [lost] here, [watching this prayer]? {And} For they have such a view – up the river, down the river: & some days the nurse says you see Hampstead Steeple, or Harrow it might be; or one of those places I've been to when I was a girl with my first baby: Tommy Atkins, the [bakers] son at Aldershot. His parents was real good to me. It was them gave me the brooch shaped like a lyre when I had to leave, because they cdnt pay me what they said, being very finest of their kind, a girl like me [?] could get, if she went out regularly into the houses of the gentry: so then I went with the Howls at Peckham; after them, with Mrs Bryce: & she was a lady after your own heart, buying in the [market herself]: sometimes a pair of Guinea Fowl: [again] a wild bird; {a ?} for that's the beauty of going early: anything [m]

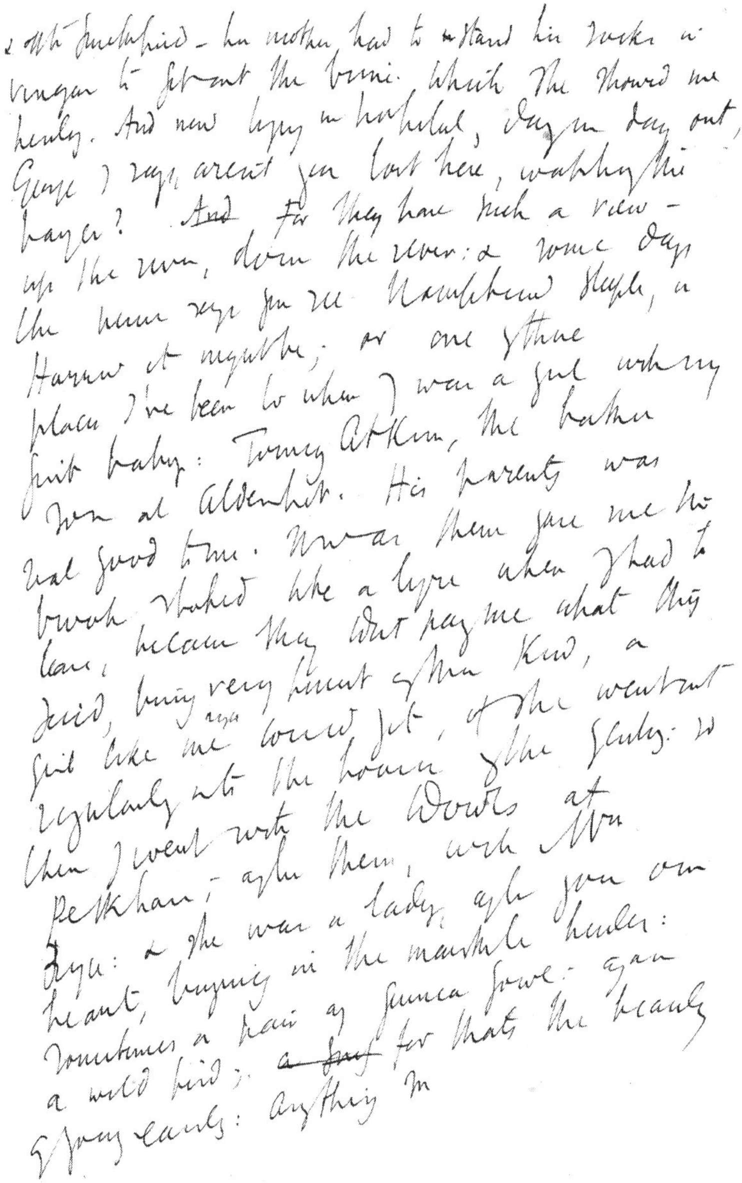

Figure 5 Letter to a Young Poet: Autograph Manuscript, 1931 Sept. 24, The Pierpont Morgan Library, New York, MA 3333, f. 46. Purchased on the Fellows Fund with the special assistance of Miss Anne S. Dayton, Mrs. Enid A. Haupt, Mrs. James H. Ripley, Mr. and Mrs. August H. Schilling, and Mr. John S. Thacher, 1979.

Photographic credit: The Pierpont Morgan Library, New York.

Bibliography

Archival and unpublished material

Adams, Caitlin, 'The Idea of the Village in Interwar England' (unpublished PhD thesis, University of Michigan, 2001).

Falmer, The Keep, University of Sussex Special Collections, Leonard Woolf Papers, Diary 1940, SxMs13/2/R/A/34.

Falmer, The Keep, University of Sussex Special Collections, Monks House Papers, General Correspondence of Virginia Woolf, Rosalind Nash to Virginia Stephen, 19 January 1910, SxMs18/1/D/101/1.

——, General Correspondence of Virginia Woolf, E. Bowen to V. Woolf, February 1941, SxMs18/1/D/20/1.

——, Manuscripts, Biographical, 'Report on Teaching at Morley College', 1905, SxMs18/2/A/22.

——, Unpublished Complete Stories and Sketches by Virginia Woolf, Incongruous/inaccurate Memories (Sir Henry Taylor), 1930, SxMs18/2/B/B.9/K.

——, Virginia Woolf's Engagement Diaries, 1940, SxMs18/4/41.

Falmer, The Keep, East Sussex Record Office, Records of the East Sussex Federation of Women's Institutes, Press Cuttings January 1925–March 1963, *Sussex Express*, 23 March 1934, WI53/36/1/1.

——, Monthly Letters to Members from the East Sussex Federation of Women's Institutes, WI53/33/1.

Hull, Hull History Centre, Papers of the Women's Co-operative Guild, *How to Start and Work a Branch, with Model Branch Rules*, 1895, U DCW/4/20.

——, Minutes of the Executive Committee of the Worker's National Committee, 1 March 1917, U DCW/7/10.

——, *Women's Co-operative Guild Congress Handbook, 1894*, U DCW/3/1.

Linchmere, Shulbrede Priory, Papers of Dorothea and Arthur Ponsonby, Diary of Dorothea Ponsonby, DPD1911.

——, Margaret Llewelyn Davies to Dorothea Ponsonby, 2 January [n.y.].

——, Margaret Llewelyn Davies to Dorothea Ponsonby, 2 March [n.y.].

London, British Library, Lady Ottoline Morrell Papers, Transcription of Add MS 88886/4/6, Journal for September 1909–April 1910, Add MS 88886/6/7.

London, King's College London Archives, *King's College Ladies' Department Syllabus of Lectures 1899–1900*, KW/SYL 8.

London, Lambeth Archives, Minet Library, Morley College Executive Committee Minutes, Vol. 3, 1901–12.

London, London School of Economics Library Collections, *Women's Cooperative Guild Thirty-first Annual Report, May, 1913–May, 1914*, COLL MISC 0657.

London, London School of Economics Library Collections, The Women's Library, Papers of Mary Sheepshanks, *The Long Day Ended*, 1952–3, 7MSH.

——, Records of the Fawcett Society and its Predecessors, Correspondence with Other Societies, National Council for Adult Suffrage, 1917–18, 2LSW/E/13/16.

——, Records of the National Federation of Women's Institutes, The Dreadnought Hoax, 5FWI/H/45.

——, Suffrage Pamphlets, *Adult Suffrage: An Address to Democrats* [1911], PC/06/396–11/20.

——, Suffrage Pamphlets, Appeal for Funds, 4 March 1910, 324.6230941 PEO.

——, Suffrage Pamphlets, *The First Annual Report of the People's Suffrage Federation. October 1909–1910*, PC/06/396–11/11.

London, Morley College Library, *Morley College Magazine*, September–October 1905.

——, *Morley College Magazine*, March 1906.

——, *Morley College Magazine*, May 1907.

——, *Morley College Report for 1904–1905*.

London, Trades Union Congress Library, Gertrude Tuckwell Papers, *Anti-Suffragist Anxieties*, 1910, 604 II/ 152, Box 25, Reel 12.

——, *Facts about the Franchise*, Leaflet No. 1 [n.d.], 604/64, Box 25, Reel 12.

——, Papers relating to the Adult Suffrage Society, 604/55 and 604/56, Box 25, Reel 12.

——, People's Suffrage Federation [October 1909], 604/64, Box 25, Reel 12.

——, Press Cuttings, *The Yorkshire Post*, 16 August 1916, 604 II/106, Box 25, Reel 12.

——, Press Cuttings, *The Christian Commonwealth*, 11 February 1917, 681/4, Box 37, Reel 17.

New York, The Pierpont Morgan Library, Letter to a Young Poet: Autograph Manuscript, 1931 Sept. 24, MA 3333.

Published material

'activism, n.', *OED Online*, June 2013, Oxford University Press, http://0-www.oed.com.catalogue.ulrls.lon.ac.uk/view/Entry/1957?redirectedFrom=activism [accessed 8 April 2015; requires membership].

Agg, Howard and Mabel Constanduros, *Goose Chase, A Comedy in One Act* (London: Samuel French, 1940).

Alberti, Johanna, *Beyond Suffrage: Feminists in War and Peace, 1914–1928* (Basingstoke: Macmillan, 1989).

Andrews, Maggie, *The Acceptable Face of Feminism: The Women's Institute as a Social Movement* (London: Lawrence & Wishart, 1997).

——, *Domesticating the Airwaves: Broadcasting, Femininity and Domesticity* (London: Continuum, 2012).

Barrett, Michèle, 'Towards a Sociology of Virginia Woolf Criticism', in Diana Laurenson (ed.), *The Sociology of Literature: Applied Studies* (Keele: University of Keele, 1978).

——, 'Virginia Woolf's Research for *Empire and Commerce in Africa* (Leonard Woolf, 1920)' *Woolf Studies Annual*, 19 (2013), 83–122.

—— (ed.), *Virginia Woolf: Women & Writing* (London: The Women's Press, 1979).

Beaumont, Catriona, 'Citizens not Feminists: The Boundary Negotiated Between Citizenship and Feminism by Mainstream Women's Organizations in England, 1928–1939', *Women's History Review*, 9 (2009), 411–29.

Beer, Gillian, *Virginia Woolf: The Common Ground* (Edinburgh: Edinburgh University Press, 1996).

Bell, Quentin, 'A "Radiant" Friendship' *Critical Inquiry*, 10 (1984), 557–66.

——, 'Bloomsbury and "The Vulgar Passions"', *Critical Inquiry*, 6 (1979), 239–59.

——, *Virginia Woolf: A Biography*, 2 vols (London: Hogarth Press, 1972).

——, 'Virginia Woolf, Her Politics', *Virginia Woolf Miscellany*, 20 (1983), 2.

Bennett, Arnold, *Journalism for Women: A Practical Guide* (London & New York: John Lane The Bodley Head, 1898).

Bentley, Michael, *Modernizing England's Past: English Historiography in the Age of Modernism, 1870–1970* (Cambridge: Cambridge University Press, 2005).

Berman, Jessica, *Modernist Fiction, Cosmopolitanism and the Politics of Community* (Cambridge: Cambridge University Press, 2001).

Bernd, Engler, 'Imagining Her-Story: Virginia Woolf's "The Journal of Mistress Joan Martyn" as Historiographical Metafiction', *The Journal of the Short Story in English*, 20 (1993), 9–26.

Black, Clementina, 'The Year's Progress in the Women's Suffrage Movement', *The Englishwoman*, January 1910, 255–60.

Black, Naomi, 'Virginia Woolf and the Women's Movement', in Jane Marcus (ed.), *Virginia Woolf: A Feminist Slant* (Lincoln: University of Nebraska Press, 1983), pp. 180–97.

——, *Virginia Woolf as Feminist* (Ithaca, NY: Cornell University Press, 2004).

Blain, Virginia, 'Narrative Voice and the Female Perspective in Virginia Woolf's Early Novels', in Patricia Clements and Isobel Grundy (eds), *Virginia Woolf: New Critical Essays* (London: Vision, 1983), pp. 115–36.

Bondfield, Margaret, *A Life's Work* (London: Hutchinson, 1948).

Bowlby, Rachel, *Feminist Destinations and Further Essays on Virginia Woolf* (Edinburgh: Edinburgh University Press, 1997).

——, 'Meet Me in St Louis: Virginia Woolf and Community', in Jeanette McVicker and Laura Davis (eds), *Virginia Woolf & Communities: Selected Papers from the Eighth Annual Conference on Virginia Woolf* (New York: Pace University Press, 1999), pp. 147–60.

Bradshaw, David, 'British Writers and Anti-Fascism in the 1930s. Part One: The Bray and Drone of Tortured Voices', *Woolf Studies Annual*, 3 (1997), 3–27.

——, 'British Writers and Anti-Fascism in the 1930s. Part Two: Under the Hawk's Wings', *Woolf Studies Annual*, 4 (1998), 41–66.

——, ' "Great Avenues of Civilization": The Victoria Embankment and Piccadilly Circus in the Novels of Virginia Woolf and Chelsea Embankment in *Howards End*', in Giovanni Cianci, Caroline Patey and Sara Sullam (eds), *Transits: The Nomadic Geographies of Anglo-American Modernism* (Oxford: Peter Lang, 2010), pp. 189–210.

——, 'Vicious Circles: Hegel, Bosanquet and *The Voyage Out*', in Diane F. Gillespie and Leslie K. Hankins (eds), *Virginia Woolf and the Arts: Selected Papers from the Sixth Annual Conference on Virginia Woolf* (New York: Pace University Press, 1997), pp. 183–90.

Brassley, Paul, Jeremy Burchardt and Lynne Thompson (eds), *The English Countryside Between the Wars: Regeneration or Decline?* (Woodbridge, Suffolk: Boydell, 2006).

Briggs, Julia, *Virginia Woolf: An Inner Life* (Penguin: London, 2006).

British Weekly, The, 6 July 1905, p. 315.

Brosnan, Leila, *Reading Virginia Woolf's Essays and Journalism: Breaking the Surface of Silence* (Edinburgh: Edinburgh University Press, 1997).

Brundage, Anthony, *The People's Historian: John Richard Green and the Writing of History in Victorian England* (Westport, CT: Greenwood Press, 1994).

Burchardt, Jeremy, *Paradise Lost: Rural Idyll and Social Change Since 1800* (London: I. B. Tauris, 2002).

——, 'Rethinking the Rural Idyll: The English Rural Community Movement, 1913–26', *Cultural & Social History,* 8 (2011), 73–94.

Caramagno, Thomas C., *The Flight of the Mind: Virginia Woolf's Art and Manic-Depressive Illness* (Berkeley: University of California Press, 1992).

Carey, John, *The Intellectuals and the Masses: Pride and Prejudice Among the Literary Intelligentsia, 1880–1939* (London: Faber and Faber, 1992).

Carroll, Berenice A., ' "To Crush Him in Our Own Country": The Political Thought of Virginia Woolf', *Feminist Studies,* 4 (1978), 99–132.

Childers, Mary M., 'Virginia Woolf from the Outside Looking Down: Reflections on the Class of Women', *Modern Fiction Studies,* 38 (1992), 61–79.

Church Family Newspaper, The, 13 January 1905, p. 818.

Clarke, Ben, ' "But the Barrier is Impassable": Virginia Woolf and Class', in Anna Burrells, Steve Ellis, Deborah Parsons and Kathryn Simpson (eds), *Woolfian Boundaries: Selected Papers from the Sixteenth Annual International Conference on Virginia Woolf* (Clemson, SC: Clemson University Digital Press, 2007), pp. 36–42.

Cole, G. D. H., *A Century of Co-operation* (Manchester: Co-operative Union, 1945).

Common Cause, The, 11 November 1909 and 9 December 1909.

Constanduros, Mabel, *Shreds and Patches* (London: Lawson & Dunn, 1946).

Cramer, Patricia Morgne, 'Virginia Woolf and Sexuality', in Susan Sellers (ed.), *The Cambridge Companion to Virginia Woolf,* 2nd edn (Cambridge: Cambridge University Press, 2000), pp. 180–96.

Crawford, Elizabeth, *The Women's Suffrage Movement: A Reference Guide 1866–1928* (London: University College London Press, 1999).

Cuddy-Keane, Melba, 'The Politics of Comic Modes in Virginia Woolf's *Between the Acts*', *PMLA,* 105 (1990), 273–85.

—, *Virginia Woolf, the Intellectual, and the Public Sphere* (Cambridge: Cambridge University Press, 2003).

Dangerfield, George, *The Strange Death of Liberal England* (London: Serif, 1997).

Daugherty, Beth Rigel, 'Taking a Leaf from Virginia Woolf's Book: Empowering the Student', in Mark Hussey and Vara Neverow-Turk (eds), *Virginia Woolf Miscellanies: Proceedings of the First Annual Conference on Virginia Woolf* (New York: Pace University Press, 1992), pp. 31–9.

—, 'Taking Notes, and Writing: Virginia Stephen's Reviewing Practice', in Jeanne Dubino (ed.), *Virginia Woolf and the Literary Marketplace* (Basingstoke: Macmillan, 2011), pp. 27–42.

—, 'Virginia Woolf Teaching/Virginia Woolf Learning: Morley College and the Common Reader', in Helen Wussow (ed.), *New Essays on Virginia Woolf* (Dallas: Contemporary Research Press, 1995), pp. 61–78.

Davies, Margaret Llewelyn (ed.), *Life As We Have Known It* (1931) (London: Virago, 1977).

—, *The Women's Co-operative Guild, 1883–1904* (Kirkby, Cumbria: Women's Co-operative Guild, 1904).

Deiman, Werner J., 'History, Pattern, and Continuity in Virginia Woolf', *Contemporary Literature*, 15 (1974), 49–66.

DeKoven, Marianne, *Rich and Strange* (Princeton: Princeton University Press, 1991).

DeSalvo, Louise, 'Shakespeare's *Other* Sister', in Jane Marcus (ed.), *New Feminist Essays on Virginia Woolf* (Lincoln: University of Nebraska Press, 1981), pp. 61–81.

—, *Virginia Woolf: The Impact of Childhood Sexual Abuse on Her Life and Work* (London: The Women's Press, 1989).

Dubino, Jeanne, 'From Book Reviewer to Literary Critic, 1904–1918', in Beth Carole Rosenberg and Jeanne Dubino (eds), *Virginia Woolf and the Essay* (New York: St Martin's Press, 1997), pp. 25–40.

Edmonds, Michael and Leila Leudeking (eds), *Leonard Woolf: A Bibliography* (Winchester: St Paul's Bibliographies, 1992).

East Sussex News, 24 July 1940, 23 August 1940, 29 November 1940, 20 December 1940 and 24 January 1941.

Ellis, Steve, *Virginia Woolf and the Victorians* (Cambridge: Cambridge University Press, 2007).

Esty, Jed, *A Shrinking Island: Modernism and National Culture in England* (Princeton: Princeton University Press, 2004).

—, *Unseasonable Youth: Modernism, Colonialism, and the Fiction of Development* (Oxford: Oxford University Press, 2012).

Eustance, Claire and Angela V. John (eds), *The Men's Share?: Masculinities, Male Support and Women's Suffrage in Britain, 1890–1920* (London: Routledge, 1997).

Farfan, Penny, 'Freshwater Revisited: Virginia Woolf on Ellen Terry and the Art of Acting', *Woolf Studies Annual*, 4 (1998), 3–17.

——, *Women, Modernism and Performance* (Cambridge: Cambridge University Press, 2004).

Fieldhouse, Roger, *A History of Modern British Adult Education* (Leicester: National Institute of Adult Continuing Education, 1996).

Flint, Kate, 'Reading Uncommonly: Virginia Woolf and the Practice of Reading', *The Yearbook of English Studies*, 26 (1996), 187–98.

Fordham, Finn, *I do, I undo, I redo: The Textual Genesis of Modernist Selves in Hopkins, Yeats, Conrad, Forster, Joyce and Woolf* (Oxford: Oxford University Press, 2010).

Forman-Barzilai, Fonna, *Adam Smith and the Circles of Sympathy: Cosmopolitanism and Moral Theory* (Cambridge: Cambridge University Press, 2010).

Forsythe, Bill and Joseph Melling, *The Politics of Madness: The State, Insanity and Society in England, 1845–1914* (London: Routledge, 2006).

Freeman, E. A., *The History of the Norman Conquest, Its Causes and Its Results*, vol. 1 (Oxford: Clarendon, 1870).

Fulford, Roger, *Votes for Women: The Story of a Struggle* (London: Faber and Faber, 1957).

Gardner, Diana, *The Rodmell Papers: Reminiscences of Virginia and Leonard Woolf by a Sussex Neighbour* (London: Cecil Woolf: 2008).

Goldman, Jane, *The Feminist Aesthetics of Virginia Woolf: Modernism, Post-Impressionism and the Politics of the Visual* (Cambridge: Cambridge University Press, 1998).

Gooch, G. P., *Under Six Reigns* (London: Longmans, 1958).

Gottlieb, Laura Moss, 'The War Between the Woolfs', in Jane Marcus (ed.), *Virginia Woolf and Bloomsbury: A Centenary Celebration* (Basingstoke: Macmillan, 1987), pp. 242–52.

Green, Barbara, *Spectacular Confessions: Autobiography, Performative Activism, and the Sites of Suffrage, 1905–1938* (Basingstoke: Macmillan, 1997).

Gualtieri, Elena, *Sketching the Past: Virginia Woolf's Essays* (Basingstoke: Macmillan, 2000).

——, 'Woolf, Economics, and Class Politics: Learning to Count', in Bryony Randall and Jane Goldman (ed.), *Virginia Woolf in Context* (Cambridge: Cambridge University Press, 2012), pp. 183–92.

Hall, Lesley A., *Sex, Gender and Social Change in Britain Since 1880* (Basingstoke: Macmillan, 2000).

Harker, Ben, ' "On Different Levels Ourselves Went Forward": Pageantry, Class Politics and Narrative Form in Virginia Woolf's Late Writing', *ELH*, 78 (2011), 433–56.

Hatton, Joseph, *Journalistic London* (1882) (London: Routledge, 1998).

Heady, Chene, 'Accidents of Political life: Satire and Edwardian Anti-Colonial Politics in *The Voyage Out*', in Jessica Berman and Jane Goldman (eds), *Virginia Woolf Out of Bounds: Selected Papers for the Tenth Annual Conference on Virginia Woolf* (New York: Pace University Press, 2001), pp. 97–104.

Henke, Suzette, 'De/Colonizing the Subject in Virginia Woolf's *The Voyage Out*: Rachel Vinrace as *La Mysterique*', in Mark Hussey and Vara Neverow-Turk (eds), *Virginia Woolf: Emerging Perspectives: Selected Papers from the Third Annual Conference on Virginia Woolf* (New York: Pace University Press, 1994), pp. 103–8.

Hill, Katherine C., 'Virginia Woolf and Leslie Stephen: History and Literary Revolution', *PMLA*, 96 (1981), 351–62.

Holtby, Winifred, *Virginia Woolf* (London: Wishart, 1932).

Holton, Sandra Stanley, *Feminism and Democracy: Women's Suffrage and Reform Politics in Britain, 1900–1918* (Cambridge: Cambridge University Press, 1986).

——, *Suffrage Days: Stories from the Women's Suffrage Movement* (London: Routledge, 1996).

Hotho-Jackson, Sabine, 'Virginia Woolf on History: Between Tradition and Modernity', *Forum for Modern Language Studies*, 27 (1991), 293–313.

Humphrey, Robert, *Poor Relief and Charity 1869–1945: The London Charity Organization Society* (Basingstoke: Macmillan, 2001).

Hussey, Mark, *'I'd Make it Penal': The Rural Preservation Movement in Between the Acts* (London: Cecil Woolf, 2011).

——, 'Introduction', in *Between the Acts* (Cambridge: Cambridge University Press, 2011), pp. xxxix–lxxiii.

——, 'Mrs Thatcher and Mrs Woolf', *Modern Fiction Studies*, 50 (2004), 8–30.

Jaffe, Audrey, *Scenes of Sympathy: Identity and Representation in Victorian Fiction* (Ithaca, NY: Cornell University Press, 2000).

Jenkins, Inez, *The History of the Women's Institute Movement of England and Wales* (Oxford: Oxford University Press, 1953).

Joannou, Maroula, *Women's Writing, Englishness and National and Cultural Identity: The Mobile Woman and the Migrant Voice, 1938–62* (Basingstoke: Palgrave, 2012).

Joannou, Maroula and June Purvis (eds), *The Women's Suffrage Movement: New Feminist Perspectives* (Manchester: Manchester University Press, 1988).

Johnston, Georgia, 'Virginia Woolf's Talk on the Dreadnought Hoax', *Woolf Studies Annual*, 15 (2009), 1–45.

Jones, Clara, 'Virginia Woolf's 1931 "Cook Sketch"', *Woolf Studies Annual*, 20 (2014), 1–25.

Joplin, Patricia Klindienst, 'The Authority of Illusion: Feminism and Fascism in Virginia Woolf's *Between the Acts*', *South Central Review*, 6 (1989), 88–104.

Keen, Suzanne, *Empathy and the Novel* (Oxford: Oxford University Press, 2007).

Kelly, Mary, *How to Make a Pageant* (London: Sir Isaac Pitman, 1936).

——, *Village Theatre* (London: Thomas Nelson, 1939).

Kennard, Jean E., 'Power and Sexual Ambiguity: The *Dreadnought Hoax*, *The Voyage Out*, *Mrs Dalloway* and *Orlando*', *Journal of Modern Literature*, 20 (1996), 149–64.

Kenyon-Jones, Christine and Anna Snaith, '"Tilting at Universities": Woolf at King's College London', *Woolf Studies Annual*, 16 (2010), 1–44.

Kirkpatrick, B. J. and Stuart N. Clarke, *The Bibliography of Virginia Woolf* (Oxford: Oxford University Press, 4th edn, 1997).

Lake, Marilyn, 'Essentially Teutonic: E. A. Freeman, Liberal Race Historian: A Transnational Perspective', in Catherine Hall and Keith McClelland (eds), *Race, Nation and Empire: Making Histories, 1750 to the Present* (Manchester: Manchester University Press, 2010), pp. 56–73.

Lambert, Andrew, *The Foundations of Naval History: John Knox Laughton, the Royal Navy and the Historical Profession* (London: Chatham, 1998).

Leavis, F. R., 'After *To The Lighthouse*', *Scrutiny*, 10 (January 1941), 295–7.

Lee, Hermione, *The Novels of Virginia Woolf* (London: Methuen, 1977).

——, *Virginia Woolf: A Biography* (London: Chatto and Windus, 1996).

Lee, Vernon, *The Beautiful: An Introduction to Psychological Aesthetics* (Cambridge: Cambridge University Press, 1913).

Lewis, Andrea, 'The Visual Politics of Empire and Gender in Virginia Woolf's *The Voyage Out*', *Woolf Studies Annual*, 1 (1995), 106–19.

Lewis, Pericles, *Religious Experience and the Modernist Novel* (Cambridge: Cambridge University Press, 2010).

Liddington, Jill and Jill Norris, *One Hand Tied Behind Us: The Rise of the Women's Suffrage Movement* (London: Virago, 1978).

Light, Alison, *Mrs Woolf and the Servants* (London: Penguin, 2007).

Low, Frances H., *Press Work for Women* (London: L. Upcott Gill, 1904).

Low, Lisa, 'Refusing to Hit Back: Virginia Woolf and the Impersonality Question', in Beth Carole Rosenberg and Jeanne Dubino (eds), *Virginia Woolf and the Essay* (New York: St Martin's Press, 1997), pp. 257–73.

Lowe, Brigid, *Victorian Fiction and the Insights of Sympathy* (New York: Anthem Press, 2007).

McCarthy, Helen, 'Parties, Voluntary Associations, and Democratic Politics in Interwar Britain', *The Historical Journal*, 50 (2007), 891–912.

MacKay, Marina, *Modernism and World War II* (Cambridge: Cambridge University Press, 2007).

MacKenzie, Charlotte, *Psychiatry for the Rich: A History of Ticehurst Private Asylum, 1792–1917* (London: Routledge, 1992).

McKibbin, Ross, *Classes and Cultures: England, 1918–1951* (Oxford: Oxford University Press, 1998).

McWhirter, David, 'The Novel, the Play, and the Book: *Between the Acts* and the Tragicomedy of History', *ELH*, 60 (1993), 787–810.

Malamud, Randy, 'Splitting the Husks: Woolf's Modernist Language in *Night and Day*', *South Central Review*, 6 (1989), 32–45.

Mansbridge, Albert, *An Adventure in Working-Class Education Being the Story of the Workers' Educational Association* (London: Longmans, 1920).

Marcus, Jane, 'Art and Anger', *Feminist Studies*, 4 (1978), 68–98.

——, 'The Niece of a Nun: Virginia Woolf, Caroline Stephen and the Cloistered Imagination', in Jane Marcus (ed.), *Virginia Woolf: A Feminist Slant* (Lincoln: Nebraska University Press, 1983), pp. 7–36.

——, 'No More Horses: Virginia Woolf on Art and Propaganda', *Women's Studies*, 4 (1977), 265–89.

——, 'Some Sources for *Between the Acts*', *Virginia Woolf Miscellany*, 6 (1977), 1–3.

——, 'A Tale of Two Cultures, *The Women's Review of Books*, 11 (1994), 11–13.

——, 'Thinking Back through Our Mothers', in Jane Marcus (ed.), *New Feminist Essays on Virginia Woolf* (Lincoln: University of Nebraska Press, 1981), pp. 1–30.

——, 'Tintinnabulations', in *Art and Anger: Reading Like a Woman* (Columbus: Ohio State University Press, 1988), pp. 157–81 (first publ. in *Marxist Perspectives*, 2 (1979), 145–67).

——, *Virginia Woolf and the Languages of Patriarchy* (Bloomington: Indiana University Press, 1987).

——, 'Wrapped in the Stars and Stripes: Virginia Woolf in the U.S.A', *The South Carolina Review*, 29 (1996), 17–23.

—— (ed.), *Virginia Woolf and Bloomsbury: A Centenary Celebration* (Basingstoke: Macmillan, 1987).

Marcus, Laura, 'Woolf's feminism and feminism's Woolf', in Susan Sellers (ed.), *The Cambridge Companion to Virginia Woolf*, 2nd edn (Cambridge: Cambridge University Press, 2010), pp. 142–79.

Marler, Regina, *Bloomsbury Pie: The Making of the Bloomsbury Boom* (New York: Henry Holt, 1997).

Middleton, Lucy (ed.), *Women in the Labour Movement* (London: Croom Helm, 1977).

Miller, Marlowe A., 'Unveiling "The Dialectic of Culture and Barbarism" in British Pageantry: Virginia Woolf's *Between the Acts*', *Papers on Language and Literature*, 34 (1998), 134–61.

Morgan, David, *Suffragists and Liberals: The Politics of Woman Suffrage in England* (Oxford: Blackwell, 1975).

Neverow, Vara, ' "Tak[ing] Our Stand Openly Under the Lamps of Piccadilly Circus": Footnoting the Influence of Josephine Butler on *Three Guineas*', in Diane F. Gillespie and Leslie K. Hankins (eds), *Virginia Woolf and the Arts: Selected Papers from the Sixth Annual Conference on Virginia Woolf* (New York: Pace University Press, 1997), pp. 13–24.

Noble, Joan Russell (ed.), *Recollections of Virginia Woolf by Her Contemporaries* (London: Peter Owen, 1972).

Nolan, Peter, 'Mental Health Nursing in Great Britain', in Hugh Freeman and German E. Berrios (eds), *150 Years of British Psychiatry, Volume II: The Aftermath* (London: Athlone Press, 1996), pp. 171–92.

Norton, B., *Freeman's Life: Highlights, Chronology, Letters and Works* (Farnborough: Norton, 1993).

Oldfield, Sybil, 'From Rachel's Aunts to Miss La Trobe: Spinsters in the Fiction of Virginia Woolf', in Laura L. Doan (ed.), *Old Maids to Radical Spinsters: Unmarried Women in the Twentieth-Century Novel* (Urbana: University of Illinois Press, 1991), pp. 85–104.

——, 'Margaret Llewelyn Davies and Leonard Woolf', in Wayne K. Chapman and Janet M. Manson (eds), *Women in the Milieu of Leonard and Virginia Woolf* (New York: Pace University Press, 1998), pp. 3–32.

——, *Spinsters of this Parish: The Life and Times of F. M. Mayor and Mary Sheepshanks* (London: Virago, 1984).

Owen, David, *English Philanthropy, 1660–1960* (Cambridge: Belknap Press of Harvard, 1965).

Park, Sowon K., 'Suffrage and Virginia Woolf: "The Mass Behind the Single Voice" ', *Review of English Studies*, 56 (2005), 119–34.

Paul, Janis M., *The Victorian Heritage of Virginia Woolf: The External World of Her Novels* (Norman, OK: Pilgrim Books, 1987).

Pawlowski, Merry M. (ed.), *Virginia Woolf and Fascism: Resisting the Dictators' Seduction* (Basingstoke: Macmillan, 2001).

Pecora, Vincent P., *Secularization and Cultural Criticism: Religion, Nation and Modernity* (Chicago: University of Chicago Press, 2006).

Pember Reeves, Amber, *Round About a Pound a Week* (London: Persephone Books, 2008).

Phillips, Kathy J., *Virginia Woolf Against Empire* (Knoxville: The University of Tennessee Press, 1994).

Poole, Roger, *The Unknown Virginia Woolf* (Cambridge: Cambridge University Press, 1978).

Putzel, Steven D., *Virginia Woolf and the Theatre* (Madison, NJ: Fairleigh Dickinson University Press, 2012).

Radeva, Milena, 'Re-Visioning Philanthropy and Women's Roles: Virginia Woolf, Professionalization, and the Philanthropy Debates', in Eleanor McNees and Sara Veglahn (eds), *Woolf Editing/Editing Woolf: Selected Papers from the Eighteenth Annual Conference on Virginia Woolf* (Clemson, SC: Clemson University Digital, 2009), pp. 206–14.

Raitt, Suzanne, 'Virginia Woolf's Early Novels: Finding a Voice', in Susan Sellers (ed.), *The Cambridge Companion to Virginia Woolf*, 2nd edn (Cambridge: Cambridge University Press, 2010), pp. 29–48.

Ratcliff, Nora, *Rude Mechanicals: A Review of Village Drama* (London: Thomas Nelson, 1938).

Ratcliffe, Sophie, *On Sympathy* (Oxford: Oxford University Press, 2008).

Reid, Panthea, 'Virginia Woolf, Leslie Stephen, Julia Margaret Cameron, and the Prince of Abyssinia: Inquiry into Certain Colonialist Representations', *Biography*, 22 (1999), 322–56.

Richards, Denis, *Offspring of the Vic* (London: Routledge & Kegan Paul, 1958).

Richmond Herald, 10 March 1917, 17 March 1917, 21 April 1917.

Rogat, Ellen Hawkes, 'The Virgin in the Bell Biography', *Twentieth Century Literature*, 20 (1974), 96–113.

Ronchetti, Ann, *The Artist, Society & Sexuality in Virginia Woolf's Novels* (New York: Routledge, 2004).

Rose, Jonathan, *The Intellectual Life of the British Working Classes* (New Haven, CT: Yale University Press, 2001).

Rosenbaum, S. P., *Edwardian Bloomsbury: The Early Literary History of the Bloomsbury Group, Volume Two* (Basingstoke: Macmillan, 1994).

Rosenberg, Beth Carole, 'Virginia Woolf's Postmodern Literary History', *MLN*, 115 (2000), 1112–30.

Rover, Constance, *Women's Suffrage and Party Politics in Britain, 1866–1914* (London: Routledge & Kegan Paul, 1967).

Schlack, Beverly Ann, 'Fathers in General: The Patriarchy in Virginia Woolf's Fiction', in Jane Marcus (ed.), *Virginia Woolf: A Feminist Slant* (Lincoln: University of Nebraska Press, 1983), pp. 52–77.

Schröder, Leena Kore, 'Who's Afraid of Rosamond Merridew?: Reading Medieval History in "The Journal of Mistress Joan Martyn"', *Journal of the Short Story*, 50 (2008), 1–12.

Schwarz, Bill, 'Englishry: G. M. Trevelyan's Histories', in Catherine Hall and Keith McClelland (eds), *Race, Nation and Empire: Making Histories, 1750 to the Present* (Manchester: Manchester University Press, 2010), pp. 117–32.

Scott, Gillian, *Feminism and the Politics of Working Women: The Women's Co-operative Guild, 1880s to the Second World War* (London: University College London Press, 1998).

——, 'Working-Class Feminism? The Women's Co-operative Guild, 1880s–1914', in Eileen Janes Yeo (ed.), *Mary Wollstonecraft and 200 Years of Feminism* (London: Rivers Oram, 1997), pp. 134–44.

Scott, J. W. Robertson, *The Story of the Women's Institute Movement in England & Wales & Scotland* (Idbury, Oxon: Village Press, 1925).

Sears, Sallie, 'Theatre of War: Virginia Woolf's *Between the Acts*', in Jane Marcus (ed.), *Virginia Woolf: A Feminist Slant* (Lincoln: University of Nebraska Press, 1983), pp. 212–35.

Showalter, Elaine, *A Literature of Their Own: British Women Novelists from Brontë to Lessing* (London: Virago, 1978).

——, *The Female Malady: Madness and English Culture* (London: Virago, 1987).

Silver, Brenda R., 'The Authority of Anger: *Three Guineas* as Case Study', *Signs*, 16 (1991), 340–70.

——, 'Virginia Woolf and the Concept of Community: The Elizabethan Playhouse', *Women's Studies*, 4 (1977), 291–8.

——, *Virginia Woolf Icon* (Chicago: University of Chicago Press, 1999).

Smith, Harold, *The British Women's Suffrage Campaign, 1866–1928* (London: Longman, 1998).

Snaith, Anna, 'Leonard and Virginia Woolf: Writing Against Empire', *The Journal of Commonwealth Literature*, 50 (2015), 19–32.

——, '"Stray Guineas": Virginia Woolf and the Fawcett Library', *Literature and History*, 12 (2003), 16–35.

——, *Virginia Woolf: Public and Private Negotiations* (Basingstoke: Macmillan, 2000).

——, '"Wide Circles": The *Three Guineas* Letters', *Woolf Studies Annual*, 6 (2000), 1–168.

—— (ed.), *The Years* (Cambridge, Cambridge University Press: 2012).

—— and Michael H. Whitworth (eds), *Locating Woolf: The Politics of Space and Place* (Basingstoke: Palgrave Macmillan, 2007).

'solidarity, n.', *OED Online*, June 2013, Oxford University Press, http://0-www.oed.com.catalogue.ulrls.lon.ac.uk/view/Entry/184237?redirected Fro=solidarity [accessed 8 April 2015; requires membership].

Squier, Susan M. and Louise A. DeSalvo, 'Virginia Woolf's *The Journal of Mistress Joan Martyn*', *Twentieth Century Literature*, 25 (1979), 237–69.

Squier, Susan M., 'A Track of Our Own: Typescript Drafts of *The Years*', in Jane Marcus (ed.), *Virginia Woolf: A Feminist Slant*, pp. 198–211.

——, 'Tradition and Revision: The Classic City Novel and Virginia Woolf's *Night and Day*', in Susan M. Squier (ed.), *Women Writers and the City: Essays in Feminist Literary Criticism* (Knoxville: University of Tennessee Press, 1984), pp. 114–33.

Stansky, Peter, 'To the Readers: An Editorial Comment on Woolfians and Lupines', *Virginia Woolf Miscellany*, 20 (1983), 1.

Stoddart, Jane T., *My Years of the Harvest* (London: Hodder and Stoughton, 1938).

Sussex Express, 23 August 1940 and 20 December 1940.

Sutton, Emma, *Virginia Woolf and Classical Music: Politics, Aesthetics, Form* (Edinburgh: Edinburgh University Press, 2013).

Swanson, Diana, L., '"My Boldness Terrifies Me": Sexual Abuse and Female Subjectivity in *The Voyage Out*', *Twentieth Century Literature*, 41 (1995), 284–309.

Sypher, Eileen, *Wisps of Violence: Producing Public and Private Politics in the Turn-of-the-Century British Novel* (London: Verso, 1993).

Szasz, Thomas, *'My Madness Saved Me': The Madness and Marriage of Virginia Woolf* (London: Transaction, 2006).

Taylor, A. J. P., *English History, 1914–1945* (Oxford: Oxford University Press, 2001).

Thane, Patricia, 'What Difference Did the Vote Make?: Women in Public and Private Life in Britain Since 1918', *Historical Research*, 76 (2003), 268–85.

Transue, Pamela, *Virginia Woolf and the Politics of Style* (New York: State University of New York Press, 1986).

Trevelyan, G. M., *An Autobiography and Other Essays* (London: Longmans, 1949).

Trombley, Stephen, *'All That Summer She Was Mad': Virginia Woolf and Her Doctors* (London: Junction Books, 1981).

Tyler, Lisa, '"Nameless Atrocities" and the Name of the Father: Literary Allusion and Incest in Virginia Woolf's *The Voyage Out*', *Woolf Studies Annual*, 1 (1995), 26–46.

Ugolini, Laura, ' "It Is Only Justice to Grant Women's Suffrage": Independent Labour Party Men and Women's Suffrage, 1893–1905', in Claire Eustance, Joan Ryan and Laura Ugolini (eds), *A Suffrage Reader: Charting Directions in British Suffrage History* (London: Leicester University Press, 2000), pp. 126–44.

Vellacott, Jo, *Pacifists, Patriots and the Vote: The Erosion of Democratic Suffragism in Britain During the First World War* (Basingstoke: Palgrave Macmillan, 2007).

Wallis, Mick, 'Unlocking the Secret Soul: Mary Kelly, Pioneer of Village Theatre', *New Theatre Quaterly,* 16 (2000), 347–58.

Webb, Catherine (ed.), *The Woman with the Basket: The History of The Women's Co-operative Guild 1883–1927* (Manchester: Co-operative Wholesale Society's Printing Works, 1927).

Westman, Karin E., 'The First *Orlando*: The Laugh of the Comic Spirit in Virginia Woolf's "Friendships Gallery" ', *Twentieth Century Literature*, 47 (2001), 38–71.

Wheare, Jane, *Virginia Woolf: Dramatic Novelist* (Basingstoke: Macmillan, 1989).

Whelan, Robert (ed.), *Octavia Hill's Letters to Fellow Workers, 1872–191* (London: Kyrle Books, 2005).

Wilson, Duncan, *Leonard Woolf: A Political Biography* (London: Hogarth Press, 1978).

Wittman, Emily O., 'The Decline and Fall of Rachel Vinrace: Reading Gibbon in Virginia Woolf's *The Voyage Out*', in Helen Southworth and Elisa Kay Sparks (eds), *Woolf and the Art of Exploration: Selected Papers from the Fifteenth International Conference on Virginia Woolf* (Clemson, SC: Clemson University Digital Press: 2005), pp. 160–8.

Woman Worker, The, 27 October 1909 and 10 November 1910.

Wood, Alice, *Virginia Woolf's Late Cultural Criticism: The Genesis of The Years, Three Guineas and Between the Acts* (London: Bloomsbury, 2013).

——, 'Facing *Life as We Have Known It*: Virginia Woolf and the Women's Co-operative Guild', *Literature and History*, 23 (2014), 18–34.

Woolf, Leonard, *Beginning Again: An Autobiography of the Years 1911–1918* (London: Hogarth Press, 1964).

——, *Downhill All the Way: An Autobiography of the Years 1919–1939* (London: Hogarth Press, 1967).

——, *The Hotel* (London: Hogarth Press, 1939).

Wright, Elizabeth, 'Bloomsbury at Play', *Woolf Studies Annual*, 17 (2011), 77–107.

Writers' Year-Book 1904, The (London: Writers' Year-Book Company, 1904).

Yoshino, Ayako, '*Between the Acts* and Louis Napoleon Parker – the Creator of the Modern English Pageant', *Critical Survey*, 15 (2003), 49–60.

Zorn, Christa, *Vernon Lee: Aesthetics, History, and the Victorian Female Intellectual* (Athens, OH: Ohio University Press, 2003).

Zwerdling, Alex, *Virginia Woolf and the Real World* (Berkeley: University of California Press, 1986).

Index

Acland, Alice, 110–11
Acland, F. D., 70
Adams, Caitlin, 179, 183
adult education, 19–20, 22, 44, 57n, 109; *see also* Morley College; 'Morley Sketch'
Adult Suffrage: An Address to Democrats (F. D. Acland), 7
Adult Suffrage in Other Countries (Ward), 70
Adult Suffrage Society, 99–100n
adult suffragism, 1, 65, 66–7, 78–9, 87–8, 98n, 100n, 106n; *see also* People's Suffrage Federation (PSF); Women's Co-operative Guild (WCG)
Advanced History of England, An (Ransome), 31
Agg, Howard, 186
Agricultural Organisation Society, 158
amateur dramatics *see* village drama movement
Ambrose, Helen (in *The Voyage Out*), 44, 45, 46
American vs. English views of VW, 8–9, 10, 12
Andrews, Maggie, 158, 159, 180
anti-fascism, 6, 14n, 154
anti-imperialism, 63n, 169, 176
anti-nationalism, 158; *see also* patriotism
Anti-Suffragist Anxieties (Russell), 70
Arnold, Thomas, 30, 31
Asheham, 114, 124, 133, 134
Asquith, Herbert Henry, 93
Auden, W. H., 177
autobiographical parallels in VW's fiction, 102n

autobiographies
  as history, 36, 37, 38, 43, 60n, 196
  WCGuildswomen's, 116–17, 118, 131, 132

Barrett, Michèle, 6, 10, 149n
Beaumont, Catriona, 159
Beer, Gillian, 6, 10, 188, 189
Bell, Angelica, 163, 167, 177, 185, 200–1n
Bell, Clive, 9, 92, 176
Bell, Quentin, 8–13, 23, 29, 58n, 123, 125, 146n
Bell, Vanessa, 114, 167
Benjamin, Walter, 12, 15n
Bennett, Arnold, 26
Bentley, Michael, 59n
Berman, Jessica, 4, 104n, 147n, 151n
Bernd, Engler, 40
Between the Acts, 187–98
  class dynamics, 191–4
  communal art, 188, 190–1
  the pageant, 188, 194–5, 196, 205n
  village life, 189–90
Bildungsroman, *The Voyage Out* as, 61n, 63n
biographical writing, 3, 37, 187
Black, Clementina, 74
Black, Naomi, 14n, 68, 71, 104n, 117, 146n
Bloomsbury group, 6, 9, 11–12, 33, 167, 176, 207
Bondfield, Margaret, 70, 93, 99n
book reviewing, 21, 24, 25, 26–7, 58n
Bowen, Elizabeth, 157–8, 161
Bowlby, Rachel, 7, 147n
Bradshaw, David, 14n, 52
bread shop, WCG, 4, 112–13, 114
Briggs, Julia, 10, 105n

British Weekly, The, 26
Brosnan, Leila, 26
Bucknill, John Charles, 134, 135
Burke, Miss (Morley student), 36, 37, 38
Burley Park nursing home, 124, 126, 134, 135
Buxton, Anthony, 169
Buxton, Charles Roden, 19, 20, 21, 23–4

Cambridge University, 60n, 109, 172, 173, 202n
Carlyle, Thomas, 30, 31, 32, 59n
Carroll, Berenice, 1, 2, 86
Carter, Alice, 182, 183, 184, 204n
Case, Janet, 1, 4, 5, 9, 12, 109
  and PSF, 71, 72, 73, 75, 87, 92
Cecil, Lady Eleanor (Nelly), 65, 66–7, 71, 194
Cecil, Lord Robert, 66
Charity Organisation Society (COS), 80–1, 109
Charleston, 176
Chavasse, Alice Greayer, 159–60, 162, 163, 164, 165, 175, 182
Childers, Mary M., 15n, 141, 142, 153n
Christian Commonwealth, The (journal), 93
Christian Socialism, 109
Church newspapers, 25–6
circumscription *see* passage motif in *The Voyage Out*
Clacton, Mr (in *Night and Day*), 78, 84–5, 88
Clarke, Ben, 147n
class, 136, 172, 199n
  cross-class identification, 118, 138, 164
  dynamics in the PSF and WCG, 73, 115, 133
  dynamics in *The Voyage Out*, 48, 51, 54, 55
  and gender, 45, 52, 55, 63n, 147n, 157, 180
  in history, 42–4
  and limited suffrage, 76
  and literature, 184–5
  and narrative voice, 125, 138–9, 140, 142, 144
  rural dynamics, 191–4, 196–7
  snobbery, 27–8, 41, 42–3, 66, 84, 137, 156
  VW and Morley student, 25, 27–8, 45
  and WI, 159–61, 200n
  see also middle-class women; working-class education; working-class women
Co-operative Movement, 4, 110, 111; *see also* Women's Co-operative Guild (WCG)
Co-operative Society Theatre, 177
Co-operative Union, 121
Coffee Palace Association, 18
Cole, G. D. H., 110
Cole, Horace, 169, 172
  collaborations with Leonard, 148–9n
Collingwood, R. G., 29
colonialism *see* imperialism
Common Cause, The (newspaper), 69, 73–4
communal art, 188, 190–1
communal kitchens *see* municipal kitchens
communism *see* Marxism
Conciliation Bills (1910, 1911, 1912), 75, 98n, 102n
Cons, Emma, 18–19, 57n
Constanduros, Mabel, 185–6
'Cook Sketch', 136–8, 139–40, 141, 142, 144, 193
  text and facsimile, 216–21
Cox, Katherine, 123
Cramer, Patricia Morgne, 64n
Criterion, The (journal), 127; *see also* *New Criterion, The* (journal)
Critical Inquiry, 8, 9, 12
Crum, Ella, 21, 24, 57n
Cuddy-Keane, Melba, 2, 22, 24–5, 29, 38
cults of personality, 81–2
culture, 91, 157
  high, 26, 84
  masculine, 47, 85
  political, 8, 12, 171

Daily Mirror, 169
Dalingridge Place, 124, 134
Dangerfield, George, 68
Datchet, Mary (in *Night and Day*), 77, 94–5
  suffrage work, 78, 79–80, 82, 105n
  writing, 86–7, 88–92
Daugherty, Beth Rigel, 21–2, 32, 36–7
Davies, Margaret Llewelyn *see* Llewelyn Davies, Margaret
Davies, (Sarah) Emily, 109
Deiman, Werner J., 28
DeKoven, Marianne, 47, 61n

democracy, 2, 3, 192, 193–4
  WI principle, 157, 159, 167, 187, 191
Denham, Ralph (in *Night and Day*), 77, 89, 91, 92
Denman, Gertrude, Baroness, 185, 186
DeSalvo, Louise, 38, 43, 46–7, 62n
Dickinson, Violet
  and the *Guardian*, 25
  letters to, 12, 17, 20–1, 23, 35, 57n, 60n, 76, 123, 133
divorce law reform, 110
drama, 176–7; *see also* Rodmell WI: plays; village drama movement
Dreadnought Hoax talk, 6, 163, 164, 165, 169–76, 201n
  complicity with audience, 172–4
  controversial elements, 170–1
  humour, 169–70, 174, 175
  Mrs Decur remembers, 174–5
  pacifism, 173–4
  the prank, 169
  satirising WI, 171
  social criticism, 172
dreams, 47–8, 49, 54, 62n
Duckworth, George, 124
Duckworth, Stella, 18, 55n, 80, 164
duty, 51, 52, 55, 135
  public, 5, 105n, 165

East Sussex Federation of Women's Institutes (ESFWI), 180, 181–2, 203n
East Sussex News, 165–6, 175, 182–3, 185–6, 200–1n
education
  VW's, 30–2
  wealthy men, 172
  women, 20, 22, 30, 45–6, 57n, 60n, 109, 173
  working-class, 19–20, 22, 28, 156
Eliot, T. S., 127, 177
Ellis, Steve, 102n
empathy, 131, 132
Empire and Commerce in Africa (Leonard Woolf), 149n
'England at the time of the French Revolution' (G. M. Trevelyan lecture), 35
English vs. American views of VW, 8–9, 10, 12
Englishwoman, The (journal), 74
equality of the sexes *see* adult suffragism
Esty, Jed, 63n, 188, 195

Fabian Society, 11, 122, 123
Fabian Women's Group, 114
Facts about the Franchise (PSF), 82
Family Reunion, The (Eliot), 177
feminism, 6, 7–9, 68, 83, 84, 110, 187
feminist criticism on VW, 10, 12, 13, 15n, 29
feminist history, 36, 38, 43, 60n
feminist-labour alliance, 67, 73, 77
feudalism, 39–40, 41, 159, 194
Fieldhouse, Roger, 19, 57n
First World War, 9, 83, 98n, 113, 173
food, 4, 112–14, 113, 124, 125, 137
force-feeding of suffragettes, 98n
Forman-Barzilai, Fonna, 129–30
Forster, E. M. (Morgan), 112, 167, 177
Freeman, E. A., 30, 31, 34–5, 59n
French Revolution, 33–4
French Revolution: A History, The (Carlyle), 30
Freshwater, 176
Freudian psychology, 5, 9, 47–8
'Friendships Gallery', 60n
Froude, J. A., 30, 31, 59n
Fry, Roger, 92, 146n, 187

Gardiner, Samuel Rawson, 31
Gardner, Diana, 5, 159–60, 165, 166, 171, 173, 175
gender, 8, 48
  and class, 45, 52, 55, 63n, 147n, 157, 180
  roles, 46, 47, 110, 134
General Strike, 11
George, David Lloyd *see* Lloyd George, David
Girton College, Cambridge, 60n, 109, 173
Goldman, Jane, 2, 98n
Gooch, G. P., 31–2
'Goose Chase' (Constanduros and Agg), 185–6
Gottlieb, Laura Moss, 94
Grant, Duncan, 169, 171, 173
Green, J. R., 30, 34, 59n
Group Theatre, 177
Grub Street, 45, 58n
Gualtieri, Elena, 147n, 151n
Guardian (newspaper), 21, 25–7, 58n

Hardie, Keir, 76
Hare, Augustus, 132
Harker, Ben, 194
Hatton, Joseph, 25–6

Henderson, Arthur, 70
Hilbery, Katharine (in *Night and Day*), 77, 88, 91, 92
Hill, Octavia, 18–19
historiography, 40, 43
history, 28–37
   feminist, 36, 38, 43, 60n
   literary, 188
   as progress, 'Whiggish history', 30, 31, 32, 34, 35, 59n
   VW studying, 30–2
   VW teaching, 30, 32, 33–4, 35–7
   VW writing, 28–9, 35
   see also 'Journal of Mistress Joan Martyn, The'
History of England from the Fall of Wolsey to the Defeat of the Spanish Armada (Froude), 30
History of Rome, The (Arnold), 30
History of the Norman Conquest of England, The (Freeman), 34
Hogarth House, 111, 146n
Hogarth Press, 117, 127, 128
Holtby, Winifred, 3
Holton, Sandra Stanley, 67, 68–9, 73, 76, 100n, 101n, 102n
Home and Country (WI magazine), 158, 171, 174, 178, 202n
'Hotel, The' (Leonard Woolf), 177
Hotho-Jackson, Sabine, 29, 38
How to Make a Pageant (Kelly), 195
Howard, Geoffrey, 74
Hume, David, theory of sympathy, 131
Hussey, Mark, 141, 187, 200n

imperialism, 63n, 103n, 169, 176
'Inaccurate Memories', 122–3
Independent Labour Party (ILP), 70, 102n
inequality, 3, 147–8n; *see also* class
inter-war England, 159, 177, 199n, 200n, 202n; *see also* village drama movement
International Suffrage Movement, 120
'Introductory Letter to Margaret Llewelyn Davies', 112, 115–23
   and class, 133, 136, 138–9, 140
   and mental illness, 124, 126–7, 127–8
   narrative voice, 116–17, 118–19, 120, 121–2, 125, 132, 140–5
   recreated memory, 122–3
   scholarly assessments of, 147–8n
   sympathy, 128–30, 131, 132–3

WCG 1913 Newcastle congress, 116–17, 119–20, 121–2, 164
   working-class women, 126–7
   see also 'Cook Sketch'
irony, use of, 88–9, 142, 153n
Isham, Virginia, 181
Isherwood, Christopher, 177

jargon, VW's dislike of, 84, 85, 171, 183, 184
Johnston, Georgia, 169
Jones, Christine Kenyon *see* Kenyon-Jones, Christine
'Journal of Mistress Joan Martyn, The', 37–44
   class in history, 42–4
   exploitation of historical sources, 39–42
journalism, 21, 24–7, 45, 58n
Journalism for Women: A Practical Guide (Bennett), 26
Journalistic London (Hatton), 26
Jus Suffragii (International Suffrage Movement), 120, 148–9n

Keen, Suzanne, 131
Kelly, Mary, 178–9, 195–7
Kelly Players, 178
Kenyon-Jones, Christine, 2, 31, 32
Keynes, John Maynard, 9, 71–2
King's College London, 2, 30–2

Labour Government defeat 1924, 6
Labour Movement, 5, 69, 70, 76, 102n
Labour Party, 3, 4, 11, 70, 76, 93, 99n, 100n
   hosting meetings of, 161–2
   and NUWSS, 102n
Lansbury, George, 70
Laughton, J. K., 30, 31–2
League of Nations Society, 92
'Leaning Tower, The', 11, 56n, 155, 172, 184, 185
Leaska, Mitchell, 11
Leavis, F. R., 10, 187
Lee, Hermione, 2, 6, 55n, 62n, 98n, 145n, 150n, 151n
   on VW in Rodmell, 156, 162
Lee, Vernon (pseud. Violet Paget), 131, 132
'Letter to a Young Poet, A' *see* 'Cook Sketch'
Lewis, Andrea, 48, 63n
Lewis, Pericles, 58n

Liberal Association, 70
Liberal Party, 69, 75
Life As We Have Known It (writings of WCG members), 116, 136, 138, 147n
Life of Carlyle (Froude), 30
Life of Cromwell (Carlyle), 30
Life's Work, A (Bondfield), 99n
limited suffrage *see* property qualification for suffrage
literary history, 188
Llewelyn Davies, John, 109
Llewelyn Davies, Margaret, 5, 9, 12, 65, 72, 93, 106n
  and 'Introductory Letter', 116–17, 121, 122, 143, 144–5
  and Leonard Woolf, 146n, 148–9n
  and PSF, 69–70, 74, 75
  and suffragism, 67, 79, 100n, 101n
  and VW, 108–9, 115–16, 118, 125, 156, 161
  and Women's Co-operative Guild (WCG), 110, 111–12, 113, 145n
Llewelyn Davies, Theodore, 57n, 109
Lloyd George, David, 70, 72
Local Defence Volunteers, 183
London and National Society for Women's Suffrage, 97n
London County Council, 44
London life, 44, 46, 55n, 79, 107n
London Studio Theatre, 177
London Village Players, 177
London Women's Service Library, 97n
Long Day Ended, The (Sheepshanks), 57n
love, problematic, 5, 77, 94
Low, Frances H., 26
Lowe, Brigid, 131
Lyttelton, Mrs Arthur, 21, 25
Lytton, Lady Constance, 98n
Lytton, Lord (Bulwer-Lytton, Neville, 3rd Earl of Lytton), 98n

Macarthur, Mary R., 70
Macaulay, Thomas Babington, 30, 32, 35, 59n
MacCarthy, Desmond, 72
MacCarthy, Mary (Molly), 72
MacDonald, Ramsay, 137, 139
McNeillie, Andrew, 25
male aggression *see* masculine domination
male prerogatives, 172; *see also* masculine domination

male suffragists, 99n, 102n
manic depression *see* mental illness
Mansbridge, Albert, 19, 20, 56n
Marcus, Jane, 8, 9–13, 15n, 88, 98n, 104n, 117–18, 172–3
Marcus, Laura, 7–8
Markham, Miss (in *Night and Day*), 81–2
Markham, Violet, 83
marriage, 41–2, 52–3, 89
  VW's own *see* Woolf, Leonard
Marxism, 8, 9, 11–13, 15n
masculine domination, 47, 62–3n, 84–5, 89, 91
Maurice, F. D., 57n
Mayer, Louie, 152n
Mechanics' Institutes, 19
Melymbrosia, 46–7, 48, 49, 51, 62n
'Memoirs of a Novelist', 80
memory, subjectivity of, 119, 122–3
mental illness, 57n, 105n, 123–9, 146n
  care of sufferers, 133–6, 150n, 151–2n, 152n
  scholarly assessments, 149–50n
Merridew, Rosamond (in 'The Journal of Mistress Joan Martyn'), 37–44
middle-class patronising, 18, 19, 104n, 114, 121, 165
middle-class women, 119–20
  circumscription of, 49–50, 52–3
  place in WCG, 145n
  place in WI, 159–60, 166
  and servants, 47–9, 50–1, 53
Middleton, James Smith, 93
misogyny *see* masculine domination
Mitchell, Silas Weir, 124
modernism, 77, 177
Monk's House, 161, 168
Morley College, 3, 5, 6, 17, 18–19, 20–4, 32
  annual report 1904–5, 25
  college magazine, 19, 25
  involvement of family and friends, 167
  teaching, 44–5, 56–7n, 57n, 66, 108; *see also* history: teaching
  University Tutorial Class (WEA), 56n
'Morley Sketch'
  deletions, 45
  Miss Williams, 24–5, 25–6, 26–7, 28, 48, 50
  narrative voice, 22–3, 24, 35
  'subterranean passages', 47, 55
  text and facsimile, 210–15
  value of history, 29, 33–6, 37, 38, 43–4

Morrell, Lady Ottoline, 71–2
municipal kitchens, 113–15

narrative voice, 105n, 106n
  On Being Ill, 131–2
  and class, 138–9
  'Cook Sketch', 136–8, 139–40, 142, 144
  'Introductory Letter', 116–17, 118–19, 120, 121–2, 125, 126–7, 132, 140–5
  'Journal of Mistress Joan Martyn, The', 38–40
  'Morley Sketch', 22–3, 24, 35
  Night and Day, 105n
Nash, Rosalind, 70, 72–3
National Council for Adult Suffrage (NCAS), 92, 93, 106n
National Federation of Women's Institutes (NFWI), 159, 178–80; *see also* Women's Institute Movement
National Men's Guild, 121
National Union of Women's Suffrage Societies (NUWSS), 67, 69, 73–4, 75, 76–7, 102n
nationalism *see* patriotism
New Criterion, The (journal), 150n; *see also* *Criterion, The* (journal)
Newnham College, Cambridge, 60n, 173
Nicolson, Ben, 207, 208
Night and Day, 77–83, 84–5, 86, 87, 88–92, 94–5
  criticism of, 115
  narrative voice, 105n
  see also Clacton, Mr (in *Night and Day*); Datchet, Mary (in *Night and Day*); Markham, Miss (in *Night and Day*); Seal, Mrs (in *Night and Day*)
night schools, 44
Nolan, Peter, 134
NUWSS *see* National Union of Women's Suffrage Societies (NUWSS)

Old Vic theatre, 18–19
On Being Ill, 127–8, 130–1, 131–2
Orlando, 29

pacifism, 9, 84, 98–9n, 111, 172, 173–4, 187
pageants, 195–7, 205n
Pankhurst, Christabel, 20, 82, 83
Pankhurst, Emmeline, 82, 83, 85–6, 102n

Pargiters (in *The Years*), 83, 95–7, 104n, 106n
Pargiters, The, 11
Park, Sowon K., 83, 91, 106n
passage motif in *The Voyage Out*, 45, 46–50, 51, 52, 53–5, 61n
paternalism, 19, 81, 193
patriarchy, 47, 55, 63n, 169, 173
  and class, 51–2, 53, 151n
patriotism, 83, 199n
  of English history, 36, 59n, 188
  WI, 155, 158–9, 168, 169, 171, 187
Paul, Janis M., 102n
Pecora, Vincent P., 27, 62n
People's Suffrage Federation (PSF), 4–5, 68–77, 78, 80, 84
  constitution, 69–70
  hostility to, 73–5, 76–7, 99n
  legacy in *Night and Day* and *Three Guineas*, 85–7
  membership, 70, 71–2
  and National Council for Adult Suffrage, 93
  opposition to limited franchise campaigns, 81, 82, 83
  VW's involvement, 71–3, 75–6, 77, 87, 92
personality cults, 81–2
philanthropy, 18, 19, 23–4, 55n, 80–1, 109, 164
Play Reading Society, 176
political poetry, 184
politics, 4–5, 72, 84, 87, 117–18, 145
  activism and ambivalence, 5–7, 88, 95, 97, 104–5n, 155, 167
  of class and gender, 15n, 45, 48, 62n, 137–8, 140–1, 147n, 156
  colonial, 63n
  gestural, 96–7
  scholarly assessments, 1–2, 3, 7–13, 15n
  sexual, 49
  writing vs. activism, 91, 108
  see also adult suffragism; Dreadnought Hoax talk; People's Suffrage Federation (PSF); Women's Co-operative Guild (WCG); women's suffragism
Ponsonby, Arthur, 75
Ponsonby, Dorothea, 69, 75, 118
poor, deserving and undeserving, 81
Press Work for Women (Low), 26
private and public, concepts of *see* public and private, concepts of

private house, shadow of, 50
private members' bills on women's
    suffrage, 100n; see also Conciliation
    Bills (1910, 1911, 1912)
'Professions for Women', 171
property qualifications for suffrage, 69,
    70, 76, 81, 93, 99n, 101n
prostitutes, 53, 64n
PSF see People's Suffrage Federation
public and private, concepts of, 2, 3, 85,
    105n, 145
public show, mistrust of, 85–6, 96
public spirit, 17, 109, 145n; see also
    philanthropy

questions, VW's, 208–9

radio, 170, 201–2n
Ransome, Cyril, 31
Ratcliff, Nora, 195, 196–8
rationing see food
Reading, Stella Isaacs, Marchioness of,
    182, 183, 201n
Reeves, Amber, 20
Reeves, Maud Pember, 114
religious snobbery, 27–8, 58n
Reminiscences (Carlyle), 30
'Report on Teaching at Morley College'
    see 'Morley Sketch'
Representation of the People Act (1918),
    78
residential qualifications for suffrage, 69
Richards, Denis, 18, 56n
Richmond Herald (newspaper), 113–14
Ridley, (Cecil) Guy, 169
Rodmell WI, 3, 5, 6, 7
    class make-up, 159–61, 173–4
    plays, 154, 155, 157, 162–3, 176,
        177, 182–6; see also village drama
        movement
    VW's feelings about, 154–7, 160–1,
        162–3, 163–4, 167–8, 198
    VW's roles within, 165–7, 168, 174–5
    see also *Between the Acts*;
        Dreadnought Hoax talk
Rogat, Ellen Hawkes, 8–9
Room of One's Own, A, 60n, 90, 119,
    140, 144, 172–3
Rose, Frank, 70
Rose, Jonathan, 20
Rosenberg, Beth Carole, 29
Rover, Constance, 75, 99n
*Rude Mechanicals: A Review of Village
    Drama* (Ratcliff), 196–8

ruralism, 157, 158, 159, 177, 199–200n
Russell, Bertrand, 57n, 69, 70
Russian Revolution, 13
Russian Soviet Theatre, 196

Sackville-West, Vita, 162, 166–7, 177,
    181
satire, 40, 137, 171
    'Introductory Letter', 140, 141–2, 161
    on suffrage campaigners, 78, 82, 83, 84
    in *The Voyage Out*, 44, 62n, 63n
Savage, George, 20, 123
Schröder, Leena Kore, 38
Scott, Gillian, 110
Seal, Mrs (in *Night and Day*), 78, 79,
    80–2, 83, 84, 88
Second World War, 162, 171, 183, 197–8
    VW's anxiety, 155, 184
servants, 47–9, 50, 53, 191–3, 202n
    life without, 115
    mental health workers, 133–4, 135–6,
        151–2n
    see also 'Cook Sketch'
sexual abuse, 62–3n
Sheepshanks, Mary, 5, 17, 18, 20, 57n,
    72, 109, 145n
Silver, Brenda R., 7, 12
Simon, Shena, Lady, 156
Smith, Adam, theory of sympathy,
    129–30, 131, 132
Smith, Agnes, 60n, 104n
Smith, Ida, 182, 183, 184, 185–6, 204n
Smyth, Ethel, 128, 162, 164, 166
Snaith, Anna, 2, 3, 60n, 97n, 106n, 141
    on *Night and Day*, 78, 88, 105n
    VW's education, 31, 32
snobbery see class: snobbery
social class see class
social participation see Morley College;
    Rodmell WI
socialism, 9, 10, 11, 66, 67, 69, 81, 101n
Speaker's Conference 1917, 93
Spender, Stephen, 177
Stansky, Peter, 8, 10
Stephen, Adrian, 167, 169
Stephen, Barbara, 116
Stephen, Caroline, 12
Stephen, Judith, 162, 182
Stephen, Julia, 18, 55n
Stephen, (Julian) Thoby, 109
Stephen, Leslie, 109
Stoddart, Jane T., 26
Strachey, Lytton, 126
Strachey, Rachel (Ray), 111

Student's History of England, A (Gardiner), 31
Suffragette, The (journal), 98n
suffragism *see* adult suffragism; women's suffragism
suicide, 152n
Sussex Express, 181, 183
Sussex Rural Community Council, 181–2
Swanson, Diana L., 62n
Swanwick, Helena, 93
Sydney-Turner, Saxon, 177
sympathy, 128–31, 132

temperance movement, 18, 19
theatre *see* drama
Thomas, Miss Jean, 124, 135–6
Thompsett, Annie, 165
Three Guineas, 4, 50, 117, 155, 158–9, 161, 172, 173–4, 207
    Diana Gardner and, 160, 171
    influence of *Life As We Have Known It*, 147n
    links with *Night and Day* and *The Years*, 78, 87, 88
    public show, mistrust of, 85–6, 96
    reception of, 2, 7–8, 60n, 104n
Ticehurst private asylum, 135–6
Times, The (newspaper), 98n
To The Lighthouse, 105n
Trade Union Movement, 5, 70
Transue, Pamela, 2, 61–2n, 80
Trevelyan, G. M., 32–5, 56–7n, 60n
Trevelyan, Robert, 112, 167
Trial of a Judge (Spender), 177
Tyler, Lisa, 62n

Unity Theatre, 177
universal suffrage *see* adult suffrage
University Tutorial Class (WEA), 56n

Vaughan, Emma, 23, 25, 81
Vaughan, Marny, 81, 109
village drama movement, 178–80, 185, 195–8, 204n; *see also* East Sussex Federation of Women's Institutes (ESFWI); National Federation of Women's Institutes (NFWI)
Village Drama Society (VDS), 178, 179
village life, 188, 189–90
    Rodmell, 156–7, 161, 162–3, 165, 168
Vinrace, Rachel (in *The Voyage Out*), 45–52, 53, 54, 62n
Virginia Woolf Miscellany, 8, 10–11

voluntarism *see* Morley College: teaching
Votes for All group, 93
votes for women *see* adult suffragism; women's suffragism
Voyage Out, The, 27–8, 44–55, 61–2n, 138
    passage motif, 45, 46, 50, 51, 52, 53–5, 61n

Waifs and Strays' Society, 80
Wallis, Mick, 178
Ward, Maud M. A., 70, 99n
Ward, Mrs Humphry, 33, 80, 83
Waterlow, Sydney, 72
Watt, Mrs Alfred, 158
Waves, The, 137, 138
WCG *see* Women's Co-operative Guild (WCG)
WEA *see* Workers' Educational Association (WEA)
Webb, Beatrice and Sidney, 122
Webb, Catherine, 148n
weight, preoccupation with, 125–6
Westman, Karin E., 60n
Wheare, Jane, 49, 52, 80, 88
Whitworth, Michael H., 78
WI *see* National Federation of Women's Institutes (NFWI); Rodmell WI; Women's Institute Movement
Williams, Miss (Annie?) (Morley student), 24–5, 45, 48, 50, 58n
wireless, 170, 201–2n
Wise Virgins, The (Leonard Woolf), 122
Woman with the Basket: The History of the Women's Co-operative Guild 1883–1927 (Catherine Webb), 148n
Woman Worker, The (journal), 99n
women in history *see* feminist history
women, middle-class *see* middle-class women
women, working-class *see* working-class women
Women's Co-operative Guild, The (Margaret Llewelyn Davies), 145n
Women's Co-operative Guild (WCG), 3, 4–5, 7, 12, 65, 69, 70, 100n
    1913 Newcastle congress, 111, 137, 148–9n
    1916 congress, 120–1
    foundation, 110–11
    VW and Richmond branch, 111–15, 137, 146n, 166, 167
    VW's relationship with, 108
    see also 'Introductory Letter to Margaret Llewelyn Davies'

women's education, 20, 22, 30, 45–6, 57n, 60n, 109, 173
Women's Institute Movement, 157–9, 164; see also National Federation of Women's Institutes (NFWI); Rodmell WI
Women's Labour League, 70, 100n, 121
Women's Local Government Association, 113–14
Women's National Anti-Suffrage League, 83
Women's Social and Political Union (WSPU), 82, 83, 85–6, 106n
women's suffragism
  and legislation, 75, 98n, 100n, 101n, 102n
  militancy, 104n, 106n
  and Morley College, 20
  in *Night and Day*, 77, 79, 80, 87, 89
  in *Three Guineas*, 104n
  VW's critical attitude to, 82, 83, 85–6
  see also adult suffragism
Women's Trade Union League, 70, 100n
Women's Voluntary Service (WVS), 183, 184
women's writing, 89–91, 116–17
Wood, Alice, 2, 141, 147–8n, 188
Woolf, Leonard, 5, 63n, 81, 91, 118, 122, 186
  adult suffragism, 92–3, 94, 106n
  and Margaret Llewelyn Davies, 146n
  play writing, 177
  and VW's mental illness, 123, 126, 133, 134
  on VW's political activism, 4
  and Women's Co-operative Guild (WCG), 111, 120–1, 148–9n
Woolf studies, 7–13
Workers' Educational Association (WEA), 19–20, 22, 56n, 155–6, 172, 184
working-class education, 19–20, 22, 28, 156
working-class women, 104n, 110, 120–1, 133–4, 151n
  VW on, 125, 126–7, 136
  see also 'Cook Sketch'
Working Men's Colleges, 19, 57n, 109
writing process, 44–5, 105n, 117–18, 187–8
WSPU see Women's Social and Political Union (WSPU)

Yale Review 1930, 117, 144
'Year's Progress in the Women's Suffrage Movement, The' (Clementina Black), 74
Years, The, 78, 80, 83–4, 87, 92, 94, 95, 106n; see also Pargiters (in *The Years*)
Yoxall, Elizabeth, Lady, 114

Zeldwyn, Cyril (Morley student), 66
Zwerdling, Alex, 1–2, 3, 67, 79